SOCIAL JUSTICE AND EMPOWERMENT

SOCIAL JUSTICE AND EMPOWERMENT

Editor
Praveen Yogi

KALPAZ PUBLICATIONS
Delhi-110052

SOCIAL JUSTICE AND EMPOWERMENT
(Sociology, Human Right,)

ISBN: 81-7835-009-2

Published in 2000 in India by
Kalpaz Publications
C-30, Satyawati Nagar
Ashok Vihar Phase-III
Delhi-110052
E-Mail: kalpaz@hotmail.com

Laser Typeset at A.S. Printers
Printed at Mehra Offset Printers, New Delhi

Contents

Preface

Social justice is one of the important function of the Government. Its main object is to help the poor, the destitutes, the minorities, the handicaps etc. In this direction it sets out several tasks and projects to alleviate the misery of the unfortunate, rehablitate, the dishonoured, and so on. This book is an elaborate study of this social justice aspects which the Government and Non- Governmental Organisations (NGOs); Agencies have undertaken to alleviate the suffering of the masses on a large scale.

Since Independence, India has been striving to alleviate the poverty and emphasising on the social problems of the weaker sections of the society. In order to reach the grassroot level to mitigate the sufferings of the handicap, the destitutes and the downtrodden, the Central Government has established Central Welfare Boards. This Board overlooks the policy, planning and implementation of the schemes through State Social Welfare Advisory Boards set up at state levels. Together they coordinate and reach out to a larger section of people

The Ministry of Social Justice and Empowerment undertakes a large number of Welfare activities and schemes for the social disadvantaged, weaker and marginalised sections of society which include Scheduled Castes, Scheduled Tribes, minorities, the Other Backward Classes, Handicapped, destitute children, the aged, Drug addicts, alcoholics, beggars, etc. Several National Programmes are directly run by the Ministry which can have a bearing in the reduction of mortality and morbidity and also have a salutary effect on efforts to improve the quality of life of the common man.

1

WELFARE OF THE MINORITIES

The Constitution of India protects the interest of minorities both religious and linguistic and recognises their rights to conserve their language, script or culture and establish and administer educational institutions of their choice vide Article 29 and 30 of the Constitution. The Constitution also provides right to freedom of religion and freedom to manage religions affairs Article 350-A provides for instructions in the mother tongue at the primary stage of education to children belonging to linguistic minorities. Article 350-B provides for a Special Officer to investigate all matters relating to the safeguards provided for linguistic minorities under the Constitution.

Government has notified 5 communities namely Muslims, Sikhs, Christians, Buddhists and Zoroastrians as Minorities for the purposes of National Commission of Minorities Act, 1992. As per 1991 Census population of minority groups constitute 17.17% of the total population of the country.

15-Point programme for welfare of minorities

15 Point Programme for welfare of minorities classifies

measures broadly under three categories namely, safety and protection of life and property, representation in the jobs under State and Central Governments and socio-educational development. The programme envisages special consideration for minorities in recruitment and fair and adequate share in development programmes. The programme is being implemented by States/UTs and the concerned Central Ministries/Departments.

Monitoring of the 15 point programme

The Ministry obtains reports in respect of Points 1 to 8 from the Ministry of Home Affairs. Half-yearly Reports in respect of Points 11 to 14 are obtained from the State. Governments/Departments. The information received from concerned agencies is compiled, analysed, reviewed and the deficiencies noticed in the implementation of the Programme are brought to the notice of the authorities concerned for remedial action. At the State level, the progress under the Programme is monitored at the level of Chief Minister/Chief Secretary. At the District level the Programme is monitored by Deputy Commissioner/District Magistrate.

Recasting and updating of 15 point programme

The 15 Point Programme for the welfare of Minorities drawn up in 1983 is being recast so as to make it an effective instrument for ensuring nondiscrimination against the minorities and to focus on the positive steps required of be taken to create a feeling of confidence amongst them. The recasting of the 15 Point Programme is under active consideration of the Government of India.

Concrete measures taken by the concerned ministries/departments

Ministry of Home Affairs has set up a Rapid Action Force charged with the special task of quelling communal riots. Guidelines have been issued to the State

Governments on the measures for prevention of riots, dealing with situation arising out of riots and providing relief and rehabilitation to the riot victims. The guidelines for promotion of communal harmony, issued to State Governments in October, 1997 by Ministry of Home Affairs, included enhancement of the amount of ex-gratia in case of death or permanent incapacitation. There is a provision for assistance to the children of families affected by communal violence under National Foundation for Communal Harmony set up under the Ministry of Home Affairs which includes educational and vocational training to these children. According to the information received by the Home Ministry from different States/UTs, 8 States and one Union territory have constituted Special Courts specifically for communal offences. The total number of such Courts constituted so far are 22.

All India Radio and Doordarshan have been playing a major role in restoring communal harmony and peace in areas affected by communal riots. A communal harmony programme entitled "Bhagwan Se Poochun Ya Khuda Se" has been telecast on Prime Time every Sunday by Doordarshan and two current affairs programme highlighting economic development and Government efforts to promote the economic conditions of the minority communities in the North-East are regularly telecast on National Network of Doordarshan. All India Radio broadcasts a number of programmes on national integration and communal harmony through various stations across the country.

The Department of Education, Ministry of Human Resource Development started programmes of educational development in 41 identified districts; in the country with minority concentration. An Area Intensive Programme is being implemented at the block level of these 41 identified districts to provide basic educational infrastructure and facilities under this scheme 100% assistance is given by the Central Government.

Department of Education has introduced a Scheme to provide financial assistance for modernisation of Madras Education and for teaching of Science, Mathematics, Social Studies and Languages in traditional educational institutions (Madrasas/Maktabs) on a voluntary basis. Under this Scheme 100% grant is given by the Central Government.

The 41 Minority concentration districts are also covered under the Scheme of Community Polytechnics to impart technical skills to eligible persons belonging to Minority communities. The enhancement of existing 41 minority concentration districts is under active consideration of Government.

According to the information available from the States, 2965 trainees belonging to Minorities were trained in the ITIs from the year 1982-83 to 1996-97. Director General, Employment & Training Ministry of Labour also issued instructions to State Governments to ensure that there is no discrimination in matters of registration and sponsoring of minority candidates for vocational training courses.

Ministry of Social Justice and Empowerment set up an apex financial Corporation namely, National Minorities Development and Finance Corporation (NMDFC) with an authorised capital of Rs. 500 crores for providing concessional finance to eligible beneficiaries belonging to minorities for setting up self-employment ventures. Government of India's contribution to the equity capital of NMDFC was restricted to 25% of the paid up share capital. The balance will be held by the State Governments/Corporations and individuals. During VIII Plan Rs. 125 crores have been released to the Corporation. The Government of India have raised the level of its contribution from Rs. 125.00 crores to Rs. 300.00 crores during the year 1998-99 subject to pro-rata contribution from the State Governments/UT Admns. towards the share capital of the Corporation. During the financial year 1998-99, (till February, 1999), the Corporation disbursed Rs. 30.92 crores as loan covering 6900 beneficiaries. The cumulative assistance provided by the Corporation since 199495 amounts to Rs. 134.85 crores for 36,899 beneficiaries.

National Minorities Development and Finance Corporation's share capital allocation and contribution by Government of India, year-wise sanctions/assistance and year-wise beneficiaries assisted may be seen at charts/ graphs. Department of Personnel and Training has issued instructions making it mandatory for all recruiting authorities of Central Government and PSUs to have one member belonging to minority community in the Selection Boards/Committees constituted for, making recruitment to 10 or more vacancies in Group 'C' and 'D' posts/services. Those sections of minorities which have been included in OBC list are eligible to take advantages of reservation provisions in the Civil Services and Posts under government of India at par with other OBC candidates.

Ministry of Social Justice and Empowerment has been operating a Scheme of Pre-Examination Coaching for Weaker Sections based on Economic Criteria among Minorities and other backward classes to enable them to compete on equal terms with other candidates in competitive examinations for various jobs. The Scheme is being implemented through institutions of repute. Rs. 3.65 crores have been released during VIIIth Five year Plan for this purpose. Since its inception in 1992-93 till 1997-98 the Scheme has covered 228 institutions while 10,840 candidates have been coached for various competitive examinations. During this financial year, i.e.,

1998-99 (till February, 1999) Rs. 1.22 crores have been released under this Scheme. A similar Scheme is being implemented by University Grants Commission in 21 Universities and 32 colleges.

In pursuance of the strategy of area based approach for tackling the problems of minorities, the scheme of multi-sectoral development plans has been launched during 1995-96 in 41 minorities concentration districts. Under this Scheme, the concerned States are required to undertake surveys and prepare project reports through an expert agency in respect of activities conspicuously pursued by the minorities in these districts with a view to identify the requirements of credit, marketing, training, technological support etc. for carrying out such activities in a viable way for development and welfare of minorities. An amount of Rs. 18.85 lakhs was disbursed during 1997-98 to the State Governments of Uttar Pradesh, Karnataka and Haryana. For 1998-99, an amount of Rs. 6.00 crores has been allocated for the Scheme. An amount of Rs. 23.00 lakhs has been released to the State Governments of Uttar Pradesh and Gujarat under the Scheme during 1998-99.

National commission for minorities

In May, 1992, the National Commission for Minorities Act, 1992, was enacted giving statutory status to the erstwhile Minorities Commission and thus making it a more effective body to safeguard the interests of minorities. The National Commission for Minorities has been reconstituted w.e.f. 26.11.1996.

That National Commission for Minorities has so far submitted its 1st, 2nd, 3rd, 4th and 5th Annual Reports for placing the same before both the Houses of Parliament. Their recommendations are being examined in consultation with other Ministries/Departments. The National Commission for Minorities have constituted a

High Powered Study Committee in June, 1997 to undertake a comprehensive study exclusively for the problems being faced by the major religious minorities in the country. The National Commission for Minorities have also constituted a Minority Education cell to exclusively look after the problems being faced by Minority educational institutions in regard to recognition, affiliation, grants-in-aid etc.

Special officer for linguistic minorities

The Office of the Special Officer for Linguistic Minorities (commonly known as the Commissioner for Linguistic Minorities) was created in July, 1957, in pursuance of the provision of Article 350-B of the Constitution, which came into existence as a result of the recommendations of the State Reorganisation Commission. Under the said Article, it shall be the duty of the Commissioner for Linguistic Minorities to investigate all matters relating to the safeguards provided for the Linguistic Minorities under the Constitution and report to the President upon these matters at such intervals as the President may direct.

The Commissioner for Linguistic Minorities submits Annual Reports to the President of India. The Commissioner has so far submitted 34 Annual Reports, out of which 33 Annual reports have been tabled in Parliament. The organisation of the Special officer for Linguistic Minorities has its headquarters at Allahabad with Regional offices at Calcutta, Belgaum and Madras. The Commissioner for Linguistic Minorities is assisted by a Deputy Commissioner, 4 Asstt Commissioners for Linguistic Minorities and other officers and staff.

2

SCHEDULED CASTES DEVELOPMENT

Approximately 13.82 crore people belong to the Scheduled Castes. To a large extent, members belonging to the Scheduled Castes mainly earn their livelihood by working on land belonging to land owners or in unclean occupations like scavenging flaying and tanning of leather. More than three quarters of the SC workers are engaged in primary occupations the population of those engaged in the tertiary sector is nearly half the national average. More than 50% of the SC workers are agricultural wage labourers; against the national average of 26%. Though with the spread of urbanisation and governmental measures such as protective legislation and positive discrimination improvements have taken place in the occupational mobility and living standards of the SCs, the majority of them still continue to be worse off than members of other communities. In the field of literacy, as against the national average of 52% the literacy rate of SCs is around 37%. These disparities are further compounded by higher drop out rates in formal education. As a result of all these disadvantages and disparities the proportion of SCs below the poverty line is substantially higher than the national average. Amongst the SCs community itself women are even at a greater disadvantage.

The vulnerability of the Scheduled Castes severely constrains their access to facilities and programmes of universal coverage. The concept of the Special Component Plan (SCP) was adopted from 1979-80 onwards in recognition of this fact so that there would be a focus on and enhancement of the flow of funds to the Scheduled Castes.

The National Commission for Scheduled Castes and Scheduled Tribes was constituted under Article 338 of the Constitution to provide a high level independent body to monitor the safeguards provided for scheduled castes and scheduled tribes and also review and report on issues concerning them. The Commission has wide powers and an extensive mandate. The Commission is required to be consulted on major policy matters which effect scheduled castes and scheduled tribes. Like-wise, the National Commission for Safai Karamcharis focuses on the community of safai karamcharis.

There are schemes for educational, economic and social development including protective measures under the Protection of Civil Rights Act 1955 and the Scheduled Castes and Scheduled Tribes (Prevention of Atrocities) Act 1989 alongwith the policy of reservation in public employment and education for upliftment of people belonging to scheduled castes. These schemes are implemented through State Governments/Union Territories as Centrally Sponsored Schemes. Most of the schemes have been revised in the 9th Plan. This has been done to enhance the impact of these schemes and make them more suitable to the needs of the scheduled castes in changing times. The report of the Working Group on Development and Welfare of Scheduled castes during the

9th Plan, submitted in May, 1996, has been taken into account while formulating the Action Plan for the 9th Plan.

The scheme of Post-Matric Scholarship for scheduled castes and scheduled tribes has played a major role in last 50 years in assisting SC/ST students to pursue higher education. Around 20 lakh students are provided Scholarship under this scheme each year. In the 9th Plan, changes such as enhancement of maintenance allowance, raising of income-eligibility ceiling and relaxation of restrictions on the number of male children in a family eligible for scholarship were affected. The scheme of Pre-Matric Scholarships is primarily targeted at the children of those scheduled castes who are engaged in unclean occupations such as scavenging. The scheme of National Overseas scholarship for SCs/STs which has been revised now provides financial assistance to those students who pursue higher studies in higher technical - fields abroad. 532 students have benefited under this scheme and have undergone studies in well known universities in Europe, Australia and U.S.A. The scheme for upgradation of Merit of SC/ST students was transferred to the Ministry of Social Justice and Empowerment from the Department of Education, Ministry of Human Resource Development in 1993-94 and was reviewed by all the State. Governments in 1996-97. Under the scheme for Construction of Hostels for SC girls and boys, it was decided to take into account actual costs while computing the central assistance. This scheme is very important as it helps to retain ~SC students in formal education by providing them with boarding and lodging facilities.

Economic development and employment generation

The National SC/ST Finance and Development Corporation (NSFDC) and the State level SCDCs, to whom the central government provides 49% contribution equity capital, play a major role in the promotion of self employment and income generating activities. The National Safai Karamcharis Finance and Development Corporation (NSKFDC) was also established in 1996-97.

The Protection of Civil Rights Act and the SC and (Prevention of Atrocities) Act and Rules are important Central Statutes which are administered a enforced. Central assistance is provided to State Govts. under a Centrally Sponsored Scheme. The scheme provides funding for evaluation a other research as well as training and awareness workshops. Since 1995-96, in addition to long term studies, several short term studies with a sharp focus on, key schematic issues have been commission through Universities and Governmental as well Non-Governmental institutions. NIRD, IIPA a several voluntary organisations have been funded conduct awareness and training programmes, decision makers, implementers and target groups

Dr. B.R. Ambedkar foundation

Under the aegis of the Ministry, Dr. Baba Saheb Ambedkar Foundation was established in the context of his centenary celebrations to pursue important projects relevant to Dr. Ambedkar's mission such the establishment of a National Library, the institution of University Chairs and award of fellowships advanced studies abroad. During 1998, the 30th Report of the erstwhile Commissioner for Scheduled Castes and Schedule Tribes and the First, Second and Special Report the National Commission for Scheduled Castes a Scheduled Tribes alongwith Action Taken Memorandum thereon were laid on the Table of Houses of Parliament in July, 1998. During 1996-97, an expenditure of Rs. 708.38 crore was incurred for development of scheduled caste During 1997-98, an amount of Rs. 610.24 crores was spent. Revised estimates for expenditure during 1998-99 is Rs. 735.70 crores.

Special component plan (SCP)

The State/UT wise distribution of the Scheduled Castes in the State/UT having significant population of the SCs is given below (1991 Census).

Sl. No.	*State/UT*	*% of SC Population to the Total Population of the State/UT*
1.	Andhra Pradesh	15.93
2.	Assam	7.40
3.	Bihar	14.55
4.	Gujarat	7.41
5.	Haryana	19.75
6.	Himachal Pradesh	25.34
7.	Jammu & Kashmir	8.30
8.	Karnataka	16.38
9.	Kerala	9.92
10.	Madhya Pradesh	14.55
11.	Maharashtra	11.09
12.	Manipur	2.02
13.	Orissa	16.20
14.	Punjab	28.31
15.	Rajasthan	17.29
16.	Sikkim	5.93
17.	Tamil Nadu	19.18
18.	Tripura	16.36
19.	Uttar Pradesh	21.05
20.	West Bengal	23.62
21.	Chandigarh	16.51
22.	Delhi	19.05
24.	Pondicherry	16.25

With the objective of overall development of SCs to bring them above the poverty line and into the mainstream of national life with equal social and economic status with other sections of the population, the strategy of Special Component Plan was evolved in the year 1979. Special Component Plan is designed to channelise the flow of outlays and benefits from the general sectors in the plans of State/UTs and the Central Ministries, at least in proportion to the Scheduled Castes population both in physical and financial terms. It is not a scheme by itself. It is an umbrella under which all schemes implemented by State and Central Governments are dovetailed for addressing different needs of the Scheduled Castes.

Objectives

(1) Direct flow of benefits through family and individual oriented programmes aimed at economic development of the Scheduled Castes, covering major occupational groups like agricultural labourers, small and marginal farmers, primary leather workers (flayers, tanners etc.) rural artisans, fishermen sweepers and scavengers, urban unorganized labourers etc. The objective is to provide income generating assets and skill to enable the SC families to earn sustained income and cross the poverty line.

(2) Provision of drinking water, health services, house sites and housing, drainage, link roads education, vocational guidance etc.

At present 24 State/UTs having sizeable SC population are formulating Special component Plan for the Scheduled Castes.

Flow of funds under SCP

Guidelines have been issued by the Government of India from time to time to the effect that earmarking of funds, for SCP out, of total state- plan outlays should be atleast in proportion to the SC population in the total population of the respective states. The SC population of the country as per 1981 Census was 15.75% of the total population of the country. It has increased to 16.48% in the 1991 census.

Coverage

The details of SC families economically assisted to cross the poverty line, which was monitored under Point 11-A of Twenty Point Programme, during the period 1994-95 to 1997-98 are as under:

Year	*No. of SSC families Economically assisted*
1994-95	26,96,412
1995-96	24,82,075
1996-97	22,98,900
1997-98	20,65,987

The target for 1998-99 is to assist 24.25 lakhs families.

Impact of special component plans on SC population

The percentage of SC population below the poverty line during the last two decades is given below:

Year	*Percentage of SC Population below the poverty line*	
	Rural	*Urban*
1977-78	64.60	54.30
1983-84	53.10	40.40
1993-94	48.11	49.48

It may be seen that the percentage of SC population below the poverty line in the rural areas has come down from 64.60% in 1977-78 to 48.11% in 199394. The same in case of urban areas had shown a dramatic fall from 54.3% in 1977-78 to 40.40% in 1983-84. But in the next decade this figure went up to 49.48 in 1993-94, this may be due to large-scale migration of SC population from the rural to the urban areas.

Action plan for special component plan

It has been observed that even though the State Govt./ UT Administration shave improved their SCP allocations over the years, it has not yet reached to the required minimum level. SCP expenditure in most of the States/ UTs has been quite low during VIII Plan. Since the problems being faced in the SC development continue to be social, economic and educational and the incidence of poverty among SC population is still high, the efforts for the development of SCs need to be accelerated vigorously. Besides increasing the allocation for SCP to the level of percentage of SCs in the States/UTs, strict monitoring to ensure full utilization of funds earmarked under SCP and effective implementation of schemes under SCP of various development departments has become quite essential. The following suggestions have been issued to the State Governments/UT Administrations in connection with the formulation and implementation of SCP:

(i) Earmarking of funds of SCP from Total State Plan outlay, at least, in proportion of SC population in the total population of the State/ LIT.

(ii) Making the Social Welfare Department/or the department concerned with the SC welfare and development of SCs as nodal department for formulation and implementation of SCP.

(iii) Placing the funds earmarked for SCP at the disposal of the nodal department concerned with the SC welfare and development, which in turn will re-allocate the funds to the sectional departments for implementing schemes directly relevant to SC development.

(iv) Placing the funds earmarked the SCP under separate budget head/sub-hear for each development department implementing SCP.

(v) To constitute State and District/Block level Monitoring Committees to monitor the implementation of various schemes under SCP of various development department. The District/ Block level Committees may review the progress of implementation of schemes and utilization of funds on monthly basis and the State level Committee may review the progress on quarterly basis.

(vi) Members of parliament, State Legislative Assembly in the concerned Zilla Parishad/ Block Panchayat area, prominent SC personnel/social worker who are well acquainted with the problems of SCs, representative of NGOs working for the welfare of SCs and SC members of village Panchayats may also be included in the State/ District/Block level Monitoring Committees.

(vii) The District/Block level Monitoring Committees may be made responsible for identifying the developmental needs of SCs living in various Panchayat areas falling under the jurisdiction of concerned District/Block and suggest suitable schemes for their developments. This process may be completed by the end of the third quarter of the financial year and reported to the nodal department concerned with SC welfare and development which will in consultation with concerned development departments may formulate suitable schemes with financial and physical targets for implementation during the next financial year.

(viii) The nodal department may ensure timely release of funds to the concerned development departments and the development departments may ensure immediate release of funds soon after the receipt of funds from nodal department, to their field level implementing agencies. Any lapse on the part of field level implementing agencies in timely utilisation of funds and proper implementation of the schemes may be viewed seriously.

(ix) Evaluation of assess the impact of economic development schemes implemented under SCP, on the socio-economic conditions of SCs may be got conducted by the nodal department on regular basis. Dissemination of information to SCs all over the State/UT about the schemes/programmes available for their development may be the responsibility of the nodal department. The nodal department may also ensure the follow up of the schemes implemented and maintenance of proper records on assets Districts/Blocks etc.

Special component plan of central ministries

The strategy of special component plan at the central Govt. level involve participation of central government ministries/departments in formulating specific plans for the scheduled castes under Annual Plans of respective Ministries/Departments. Many Central Ministries cater to the areas of vital importance to the SCs. The ministry of Social Justice and Empowerment has maintained close liaison with Central Ministries Departments and impressed upon them the need to the formulate and implement comprehensive Special Component Plan. The Ministries have also been requested to open separate Budget Head/Sub He, for Special Component Plan.

The main objective of the Special Central Assistance to Special Component Plan for Scheduled Castes to give a thrust to the development programmes for scheduled castes with reference to their occupation pattern and the need for increasing their productivity and income from their limited resources. It would help in bringing about occupational diversification in the labour surplus economy. Further the SCA is expected to fill the gaps which various central an state development programmes are not in a position to fill. It was realised that the programmes for which the SCA could be used by the State Governments would vary from state to state and region to region within the same sate depending on the local occupational patterns and the economic activities, available. Even within the same state and region they would vary from time to time.

As an additive to the state's plan and programmes, the Special Central Assistance is expected to be an effective instrument in catalysing and strengthening the Special Component Plans as a whole in each state. The quantum of Special Central Assistance is related to the special component plans of the States/ UTs especially in concrete terms such as number of scheduled castes families that will cross the poverty line by the programmes and outlays in each sector, and the optimality of the state special component plan in comparison with the scheduled caste population in the state. The performance of the states in implementation of the programmes for the scheduled castes is also taken into account.

The Central scheme of Special Central Assistance (SCA) to Special Component Plan of States/UTs is linked to Government of India's strategy for the socio-economic development of the scheduled castes. It is an additive to the Special Component Plan (SCP) of the states/UTs and is intended for augmenting the totality of States efforts for the economic development of SCs. The underlying objective of the SCA which is a central grant to the States/UTs is that it should be used to give an added thrust to the development programme for SCs with reference to their occupational needs for increasing the productivity of and income from their limited assets by taking up family oriented schemes for them. It is used to fill the critical gaps and provide the central government a leverage in directing flow of funds in areas critical -to the development needs of the SCs.

The scheme was started in 1979-80 with a token provision of Rs. 5.00 crores. It has evolved as an alternative instrument at the disposal of Government of India to bring about qualitative change in the living conditions of the SCs and among more vulnerable groups of SCs (such as scavengers, flayers and tanners). In order to provide greater scope for effectiveness of SCA in achieving government's objective, the existing guidelines on SCA have been amplified in the year 1993. The amplified guidelines stipulate that states/UTs can utilise the SCA for infrastructural development programmes in blocks having 50% or more of Scheduled Castes population subject to the condition that the SCA allocation should be made use of in a such a way as to encourage 'larger efforts on the development of SCs on the part of the States/UTs. The condition of blocks having 50% or more of SO population for use of SCA for infrastructural development programmes has been relaxed and villages having 50% or more of SO population can now be considered for infrastructural development programmes with the support of SCA funds. Only 10% of the total SCA released to the state government/UT Administration in a year should be utilised for infrastructural development programmes. According to the amplified guidelines, SCA to SOP can be used for various development sectors on specific viable schemes covering Scheduled Castes population individually and/or in clusters.

Utilisation of SCA

States/UTs have been given full flexibility in utilising SCA subject to the condition that it should be used in conjunction with SOP on family oriented income generating economic development programmes/ schemes and for infrastructural development programmes in the villages having 50% or more of SC population.

(1) 15% of the total SCA released to the States/UTs, on the basis of the criteria mentioned below will be utilised by the State Government/UT Administrations exclusively on viable income-generating economic development schemes/ programmes for SO Women.

(2) 5% of the total SCA released to the States/UTs will be utilised by them exclusively for the economic development of disabled persons among SCs.

(3) 3% of the total SCA released to the States/UTs will be utilised by the States/UTs for supervision, monitoring and evaluation of economic development schemes implemented with the support of SCA funds.

Criteria for the release of SCA

SCA is released to the States/UTs implementing SCP on the following criteria-

1.(a) on the basis of SO population of the State/UT 40%

(b) on the basis of relative backwardness of the State/ UT 10%

2.(a) on the basis of percentage of SO families in the State/UT covered by composite economic development programmes in the State/UT Plan to enable them to cross the poverty line 25%

(b) on the basis of percentage of SOP to the Annual Plan as compared to SO population percentage in the state/UTs. 25%

Second instalment of SCA should be released to the States/UTs after ensuring expenditure of cumulative opening balances of the previous year and 75% of the first instalment for the current year. 2% of the total budget allocation for the scheme will be earmarked for North Eastern States which implement SOP of SCs.

Disbursement of SCA

The amount of SCA released by the Government of India and utilised by the States/UTs for the period 1994-95 to 1998-99 is given below:

(Rs. in lakhs)

Period	*Released*	*Utilised*	*% Utilised*
Sixth Five Year Plan	60,000.00	56810.94	94.68
Seventh Five Year Plan	87,600.00	86191.58	98.39
Eighth Five Year Plan	134,476.96	135,058.20	100.43
1997-98	308,27.00	31096.57	100.87
1998-99	218,62,96.00	11308.96	51.72
		(upto Sept. 98)	

State/UT wise details of release and utilisation of SCA to SOP for the year 1994-95 to 1998-99 are given in the Annexure II.

During the financial year 1998-99, an amount of Rs. 361.00 crore has been allocated and out of which Rs. 218.63 crores have already been released to the States/UTs till now.

The utilisation of SCA is monitored through quarterly/annual progress report from the State Governments/UT Administrations. The details of utilisation of SCA during the VIII Plan period and during 1997-98 have been examined and it is observed that the utilisation has been satisfactory. In fact over the years, SCA has become a powerful instrument for the poverty alleviation programmes for SCs. However, in a few cases shortcomings were noticed. There is undue delay by the State/UTs in releasing funds to the implementing agencies which results in funds lying unspent at the end of financial year.

Late release of funds to the implementing agencies/ departments non-utilisation of funds sanctioned/released to the implementing agencies/departments to the implementing agencies/departments for the purpose for which it is sanctioned, accumulation of unspent balance of funds for considerable long period with the implementing agencies/department keeping funds in Civil Deposits, Fixed Deposits, Saving Bank Accounts, P.L.A. etc. for considerable long period, lack of proper action plan for implementation of schemes, sanction of funds for schemes without ascertaining their feasibility and viability, leakage of benefit of schemes meant for SCs to Non-SCs, etc. decelerate the process of economic development of the target group.

An effective device needs to be evolved to remove such shortcomings/loopholes so that the purpose of SCA could be served meaningfully. Amongst various measure for effective implementation of development schemes for SCs, the following points may be given more stress.

The Government of India have suggested the following points for effective implementation of the programmes:

i) Release of funds to the implementing agencies without loss of time after getting the SCA from the Government of India.

ii) Separate account of SCA released to the implementing agencies may be maintained and utilisation of SCA funds by the implementing agencies may be watched regularly through periodical progress reports from the implementing agencies.

iii) It may be ensured the Utilisation Certificates from

the concerned implementing agencies are obtained in time.

iv) Annual Audit of SCA Accounts of State and District/Block level implementing agencies may be ensured.

v) Keeping SCA funds in civil deposits, fixed deposits, saving Bank accounts, PLA etc. for long periods by implementing agencies or nodal department may be discouraged. Release of funds to the implementing agencies without ascertaining the utilisation of funds released to them earlier leads to accumulation of unspent balances and increase in the deposit in various accounts. Identification of viable schemes as per the developmental needs of SCs and identification of eligible beneficiaries to be considered assistance in a financial year should completed well before the commencement the financial year. Sanction of schemes, release of assistance can thus be ensured time soon after the receipt of SCA funds. This will help in avoiding last minute sanction schemes at the fag end of the financial year and in ensuring full utilisation of funds.

In march, 1979, the Centre initiated a Centra sponsored scheme of assistance to State Governments for participating in the share equity the Scheduled Castes Development Corporation (SCDCs) in the ratio of 49:51. At present, SCDCs are functioning in 25 States/UTs which includes SCDCs which are common to SCs and STs.

Functions of SCDCs

(i) Identification of eligible SC/ST families and motivating them to undertake economic development schemes.

(ii) Sponsoring the schemes to financial, institutions for credit support.

(iii) Providing financial assistance in the form c margin money at low rate of interest an subsidy in order to reduce the repayment liability.

(iv) Providing necessary tie up with other proverb alleviation programmes.

Implementation of the schemes

The SCDCs have been acting as guarantors and promoters for credit support and providing missing inputs by way of margin money loans and subsidy to the target group. They have a useful role in the mobilisation for fiances for economic development of scheduled castes living below the poverty line. The SCDCs mainly take up employment oriented schemes in the following areas-

(i) Agriculture and allied including minor Irrigation

(ii) Small Scale Industry.

(iii) Transport

(iv) Trade and Service Sector

Performance

Project assistance from banks is arranged by SCDCs besides providing margin Assistance out of share capital assistance and subsidy out of Special Central Assistance (SCA) funds. The SCDCs are experiencing difficulties in arranging bank finances. The share from banks is unduly delayed or highly inadequate. Besides, there are other structural, organisational and managerial factors which hamper the activities of the SCDCs. The beneficiaries covered so far under scheme are as under:

Year	*No. of beneficiaries (in lakh)*
1980-85	28.69
1985-90	29.22
1990-91	5.42

1991-92	4.52
1992-93	5.35
1993-94	5.32
1994-95	6.31
1995-96	4.20
1996-97	4.61
1997-98	3.71

Modification in the scheme

In order to streamline the criteria of release of Central Share Equity to SCDCs, following conditions have been laid for release of Central funds to them w.e.f. current year:

(i) Minimum recovery rate of the loans disbursed should be 60% in a financial year.

(ii) Minimum utilisation of Central Share should be 75% in a financial year.

(iii) Prior release of State Share to SCDC.

(iv) Ability of the SCDCs to raise additional resource from financial institutional including banks.

The National Scheduled Castes and Scheduled Tribes Finance and Development Corporation (NSFDC) was established on 8th February, 1989 as a Government Company not for profit under Section 25 of the Companies Act, 1956. The focus of NSFDC is on the special developmental and financing needs (loans only) of the SCs and STs over the above the credit available through priority sector lending of banks and other institutions. The authorised share capital of NSFDC has been enhanced from Rs. 300 crores to Rs. 1000 crores during the current financial year. The paid up capital of this Corporation is Rs. 342.43 crores.

NSFDC provides financial assistance at concessional rates for income generating activities and training in skill development to SCs and STs whose annual income is below double the poverty line criteria i.e. Rs. 22,000 per annum in rural areas and Rs. 23,700 per annum in urban areas. The assistance is provided through the various States Scheduled Castes Development Corporations (SCDCs) and other State Channelising Agencies (SCAs) for implementing technically feasible and financially viable schemes/projects besides providing grants for skill development programmes organised by SCAs and Non-Govern mental Organisations (NGOs).

Budgetary support

Plan outlay and expenditure details of Central share capital assistance to SCDCs are given below:

(Rs. in Crores)

Year	Plan Outlay	Expenditure
1992-93	20.00	22.07
1993-94	22.00	29.34
1994-95	22.00	22.00
1995-96	30.00	31.00
1996-97	30.00	31.99
1997-98	45.00	45.00
1998-99 (30.11.98)	60.00	35.85

Implementation of schemes

The Corporation provides term loans, seed capital, bridge loans etc. at concessional rates of interest. A maximum loan of 85% of the project cost is provided. With the revision of the financing pattern w.e.f. 1-10-95, projects upto Rs. 30 lakhs, can be, financed by the Corporation. NSFDC finances schemes in the following sectors:-

(i) Agriculture and Allied

(ii) Horticulture

(iii) Animal Husbandry and dairying

(iv) Minor Irrigation

(v) Small Industries

(vi) Trade Services and

(vii) Transport etc.

NSFDC's performance has gained momentum over the years. Disbursements have risen substantially from Rs. 35 lakhs in 1989-96 to Rs. 486.57 crores (cumulative) as on 30th November, 1998. The details of disbursements are as under:

Recovery

The recovery position of NSFDC from its channelising agencies is around 87.67%. However, recovery from the beneficiaries is reported to much lower.

National scheme of liberation and rehabilitation of scavengers and their dependants (NSLRS)

The National Scheme of Liberation and Rehabilitation of Scavengers and their dependants was launched by the Government of India in March, 1992, in pursuance of the commitment to eliminate 'the inhuman practice of manual handling of might soil and filth by the end of VIII Plan period, with the following three components:

(i) a period survey to identify scavengers and their dependants and their aptitude for alternative trades and professions,

(ii) training of scavengers and their dependents and

(iii) rehabilitation of scavengers through projects with a prescribed funding pattern.

(Rs. in Crores)

Year	Amount
1989-90	0.35
1990-91	6.22
1991-92	40.50
1992-93	43.93
1993-94	32.21
1994-95	77.59
1995-96	90.11
1996-97	71.47
1997-98	93.89
1998-99	30.26
(30th November, 1998)	

The Corporation has so far sanctioned 1490 projects, which on completion would benefit around 218497 beneficiaries.

The implementation of the Scheme at the grass level is looked after by the SCAs/SCDCs. National Safai Kara-mcharis Finance Development Corporation (NSKFDC) has entrusted with the responsibility of day-to-day implementation and monitoring of the scheme as well as coordination and collaboration with the SCDCs implementing the scheme. The 0 implementation of the scheme has been entrusted to the District Collectors/ Deputy Commissioners Training is imparted through existing institutes Central Govt., State Govts., Semi Government and Non-government-organisations.

Financial assistance

Training

The scavengers are imparted training in such trades of their aptitude which can successfully provide them alternative placement. The training cost is borne by the

Government of India and during the course of training, the trainee gets stipend upto Rs. 500/- per month, besides honorarium to trainer upto Rs. 300/- per month and tool kit allowance upto Rs. 800/ as per the TRYSEM norms.

The Government approved the setting up of the National Safai Karamcharis Finance and Development Corporation (NSKFDC) under Section 25 of the Companies Act, 1956 with its registered office at Delhi, with an authorised share capital Rs. 200 crores. The NSKFDC has been incorporated on 24-01-1997. The paid up share capital of the Corporation is Rs. 14.75 crores. The major objectives for setting up a separate Financial Corporation for Safai Karamcharis are to promote economic development/self employment for the economic rehabilitation of safai karmacharis besides providing training in technical and entrepreneurial skills and extending loans to students from safai karamchari community for pursuing higher education. The NSKFDC will function as an apex institution for channelising funds through the State Chennelising Agencies authorised by the State Governments/UT Administrations. The NSKFDC will also coordinated and monitor the scheme programmes implemented through authorised State Finance and Development Corporations/Boards/UT Administrations financed by the Corporation.

The Corporation had started its operations by the last quarter of 1997 and during 1997-98 the Corporation disbursed Rs. 384.39 lakhs for 14 schemes to its various channelising agencies benefiting 459 safai karamcharis. A budgetary provision of Rs. 10 crores was made for this Corporation during the current financial year which has since been released to them. Upto December 1998 the Corporation sanctioned 29 projects benefitting 2320 safai karamcharis.

There is a prescribed financial package for rehabilitation of scavengers in alternative trades through provision of financial assistance upto Rs. 50,000/- per beneficiary. This includes a subsidy of 50% of the capital cost subject to a ceiling of 10,000/- per project, margin money loan of 15% of the project cost at 4% rate of interest, and the remaining portion by way of loan finance to be provided by commercial banks. The Govt. of India have released Rs. 525.16 crores to the State during the period 1991-92 to 1997-998, for implementation of the Scheme. The year-wise details alongwith physical progress are indicated below:

Year	*Funds released to State Govts. (Rs. in crore)*	*No. of Scavengers*	
		Trained	*Rehabilitated*
(1)	*(2)*	*(3)*	*(4)*
1991-92	50.50	–	–
1992-93	60.73	16220	18411
1993-94	70.97	22241	41160
1994-95	73.00	25272	62269
1995-96	91.96	26493*	80016
1996-97	90.00	21779*	60565
1997-98	90.00	15359	27887

*Also include figures proposed by State Govts. and the actual achievements are awaited.

The Scheme was last modified w.e.f. 1.4.1996 to bring further improvements in its implementation. The important modifications done are mentioned below:–

(i) Release of Central Assistance to Scheduled Castes Development Corporations directly.

(ii) Adoption of TRYSEM norms for training.

(iii) Higher project cost of Rs. 50,000/- per beneficiary, for rehabilitation.

(iv) Cluster approach for training & rehabilitation.

Centrally sponsored scheme of post matric scholarship to students belonging to SCs and STs

The Scheme provides financial assistance to such students belonging to SCs and STs who pursue recognised post matriculation courses in recognised institutions, including correspondence courses, within the country. The financial assistance includes provision of maintenance allowance, reimbursement of compulsory non-refundable fees, thesis typing/printing charges, study tour charges, book allowance for students pursuing correspondence courses and special provisions for such students with disabilities who are covered under the scheme. The Scheme is implemented by the respective State Governments and Union Territory Administrations receive 100% central assistance from Government of India over and above their respective Committed Liability, which is borne by them.

The Scheme which was introduced in the year 1944 with a coverage of 114 students, has picked up very well over the years and is at present covering over 20 lakhs students. The Following table shows the performance of the scheme during Eighth Five-Year Plan period.

Year	*Budget allocation (Rs. in crores)*	*Central assistance released (Rs. in crores)*	*No. of beneficiaries*
1994-95	96.35	96.35	1,42,656
1995-96	145.00	144.86	17,90,355
1996-97	149.00	179.93	*17,12,420
1997-98	54.17 (R.E.)	54.17	**17,21,994
1998-99	100.00 (R.E.)	99.86	**20,99,159
		(Upto Dec '98)	(Anticipated)

*Excludes Kerala, Delhi and U.P. (ST), as information is not available.

** Excludes Kerala and Delhi, as information is not available.

Modifications done

It has been decided to continue the scheme during the Ninth Five Year Plan period also with following modifications

(1) Income ceilings

The following table shows the pre-revised and revised income ceiling w.e.f. 1.4.98-

Income ceiling limits of Parents Revised

Scholarship eligibility towards maintenance allowance

Pre-revised	Revised	
Rs. 33,400	Rs. 38,220	Full maintenance allowance, full fees.
Rs. 44,500	Rs. 50,920	(I) Full maintenance allowance and fees in Group A. (II) Half maintenance allowance and full fees for courses in Group B, C, D and E.

The revised income ceilings account-for consumer price index for industrial workers upto Oct, 1997.

(II) Removal of restrictive clause

Prior to modifications in the scheme, only two male children of the same parents/guardians were eligible to get the benefits under the scheme and there was no such restriction in case of female children. In the modified scheme, the restrictive clause has been totally removed w.e.f. 1.4.98 and now all children of the same parents/guardians are eligible to get the benefits of the scheme, if otherwise eligible.

(III) Dispensation of committed liability of north eastern states

The funding pattern of the scheme is such that 100%

central assistance is provided to State/UTs implementing the scheme, over and above their respective Committed Liability, which is equal to the expenditure reached during the terminal year of the last Five Year Plan period and this level of expenditure is required to be borne by them. The North Eastern States were not in a position to provide for the Committed Liability in their State resources, owing to their severe financial constraints arising out of substantial expenditure required to be incurred by them on maintenance of law and order for containing insurgency etc. As a consequence, the North Eastern States could not receive any central assistance during 1997-98 and resultantly a large number of students could not get benefits of the scheme. The Government is since committed towards accelerating the development of North Eastern States, therefore, it has been decided to dispense with the Committed Liability of the North Eastern States from the commencement of Ninth Five Year Plan period. This has eased the financial burden of North Eastern States to an extent of Rs. 20.83 crores per year, thus benefiting around 2 lakhs students, every year. As a consequence of the dispensation of Committed Liability, central assistance of Rs. 32.61 crores has already been released to the North Eastern States during 1998-99 (upto December, 1998).

(IV) Additional provisions for SC and ST students with disabilities

Keeping in view the provisions of the Persons with Disabilities (Equal Opportunities Protection of Rights and Full Participation) Act 1995, the following additional provisions for students with disabilities have been introduced in the Scheme w.e.f. 1.4.98. The disability as per the Act is defined as blindness, low vision, leprosy-cured, hearing impairment, locomotor disability, mental retardation and mental illness.

Timely sanction/disbursements

Sanction and disbursement of scholarship by States/UTs involves a large number of students and a multiplicity of levels. The Ministry in this regard have circulated to all States/UTs. on 4.4.95, the detailed guidelines for streamlining sanction and disbursement procedures under the Scheme.

Centrally sponsored scheme of pre matric scholarship to the children of those engaged in unclean occupations

Objectives

The Scheme financially assists the children of scavengers, sweepers having traditional link with scavenging, flayers and tanners, irrespective of their religion, to pursue education upto matriculation level.

Implementing agency and funding pattern

The Scheme is implemented by the State Governments and Union Territory Administration. Central assistance is provided to the State Government on 50:50 basis and 100% to Union Territory Administration over and above their Committed Liability.

Elements of scholarship

The Scheme covers day scholars from class I to X with scholarship rates from Rs. 25 per month for classes I to V, Rs. 40 per month for classes VI to X and Rs. 50 per month for classes IX and X. The scheme also covers hostellers from classes III to X. The scholarship rate for hostellers in classes III to VIII is Rs. 200 per month and is Rs. 250 per month-for classes IX and X The scholarship is provided for 10 months in a year. Besides scholarship, an adhoc grant of Rs. 500 per annum is also provided to day scholars as well as hostellers.

Performance

It has been decided to continue the scheme during the Ninth Five-year Plan period also. There is no income ceiling prescribed under the scheme. Upto two children of the same parents/guardians can get the benefits of the scheme, if pursuing classes IX and X. For pursuing classes upto class VIII, though there is no such restriction, however, if a 3rd or subsequent child is borne after 1.4.93, then only upto two children of the same parents can get benefits of the scheme.

The scheme was initially introduced in the year 1978 and over the year the scheme has picked up and the present likely coverage of beneficiaries is over 3 lakhs. The following table gives the performance of the scheme since 1994-95:

(Rs. in crores)

Year	*Budget Allocation Released*	*Central Assistance (in lakhs)*	*No. of Beneficiaries*
1994-95	10.00	6.25	1.76
1995-96	7.50	8.92	2.83
1996-97	7.50	14.04	3.00
1997-98	2.00	2.00	*3.62
1998-99	4.00	3.95 (upto* Dec '98)	*4.09 (Anticipated)

The State/UT wise coverage of beneficiaries and central assistance released since 1997-98.

National overseas scholarship scheme for SC, ST etc. students for higher studies abroad

The Scheme provides financial assistance to meritorious selected students for pursuing higher studies abroad in specified fields of Masters level courses, Ph.D and Post - Doctoral research programmes in Engineering, Technology and Science only. It has been decided to revive the Scheme w.e.f. 1998-99 to 2000-2001, with modifications. The regulations governing the scheme are accordingly being finalised. The modified scheme when finalised would provide enhanced maintenance allowance of US $77001- per annum or Pounds Sterling 5000/- per annum for candidates in U.K., for all levels of courses covered under the scheme. Prior to modifications, the maintenance allowance varied from US $59404 per annum to US $77004 per annum, depending upon the levels of the courses. The contingency allowance for books, essential apparatus, study tour charges, typing and binding of thesis etc., has also been raised from US $3854 to US $5004 per annum or Pound Sterling 325/- per annum, for candidates in U.K. The modified scheme would also provide reimbursement of actual visa fees in Indian rupees. The scheme also provides air passage by the shortest route and by economy class, by arrangements with the national carrier, poll tax, equipment allowance and incidental journey expenses, actual fees charged by the institution and the medical insurance premia. The awardees are also permitted to supplement their prescribed allowance by undertaking research/teaching assistantship upto US $2400/- per annum or Pounds Sterling 1560/- per annum, for candidates in U.K. and beyond these ceilings, the maintenance allowance will be proportionately reduced. The financial assistance under the scheme is available to the finally selected students sent abroad, for the maximum period of 4 years for Ph.D. research, for 3 years for Master's Programme and for 1 and 112 year for Post Doctoral research. The income of the awardees if employed, or of their parents/guardians, should not exceed Rs. 120O0/- per month. Not more than one child of the same parents/guardians is eligible to get benefits of the scheme and the awardee can get only one time benefit under the scheme. The prospective awardee should not be more than 35 years of the age as on the first day of the month of the advertisement of the scheme. The scheme provides for 30 awardees per year, out of which 17 are for SCs, 9 are for STs, 1 is for Denotified, Nomadic and Semi-nomadic Tribes, 2 are for SCs converts to other religion and 1 is for landless agricultural labourers and traditional artisans.

Performance

The scheme was introduced in 1954-55 and since then a total, of 732 awards have been offered, out of which 532 awards have been availed of budget allocations and the expenditure incurred under this non-plan Scheme since 1994-95 is given below:

(Rs. in lakhs)

Year	*Budget Allocation*	*Expenditure*
1994-95	562.00	562.00
1995-96	490.00	390.81
1996-97	490.00	180.00
1997-98	490.00	226.00
1998-99	390.00	80.60 (Upto Dec'98)

Nine passage grants in a year to Scheduled Castes (4 grants), Scheduled Tribes (4 grants) and Denotified, Nomadic and Semi-Nomadic Tribes (one grant) are also provided, which are open throughout the year. Only those candidates who are in receipt of a merit scholarship for Post Graduate- Studies, Research or Training abroad (excluding attending seminars, workshops, conferences), from a foreign government/organisation or under any other scheme, where the cost of passage is not provided, are eligible. The candidates should possess a Master's or an equivalent degree in Technical, Engineering and Science disciplines. The candidates who have already reached abroad, are not considered for passage grants. The eligibility conditions otherwise are same as under the Scheme of National Overseas Scholarship for SC, ST etc. candidates. The air passage is provided by economy class and by shortest route through arrangements with the national carrier.

Central sector scheme of special educational development programme for scheduled castes girls belonging to very low literacy level

The Scheme was introduced during 1996-97 on pilot basis with an objective to provide a package of educational inputs through residential schools for SC girls in areas of very low SC female literacy where traditions and environment are not conducive to their learning. The schools are intended to supplement the existing measures to impart and consolidate literacy and to promote quality education to such girls who are first generation learners in areas of low literacy.

The school premises consist of classrooms, hostels, kitchens and staff quarters. The schools function from the suitable hired premises. Grant-in-aid under the scheme comprises the package of Rs. 11,340/- per student in class I only, which includes direct facilities to the students as well as cost towards infrastructure, staff and other running cost. No fees, charges or contributions are charged from the students.

Implementing agency

The Scheme is implemented by the Zila Parishads (District Level Panchayats) of the concerned district. The Zila Parishads may run the schools themselves or through credible NGOs of proven integrity, competence and experience. The grant is given directly to concerned Zila Parishads, which are required to send their proposals to the Ministry through their State Governments.

Selection of districts

As per 1981 census, 48 districts situated in Bihar, Madhya Pradesh, Rajasthan and Uttar Pradesh have been identified where the literacy of SC girls is less than 2%. The scheme accordingly covers only such districts.

The Scheme was introduced on pilot basis in the year 1996-97. As against the target of 21 residential schools in the year 1996-97, 20 residential schools were sanctioned to Zila Parishads in Bihar, Madhya Pradesh, Rajasthan and Uttar Pradesh with grant-in-aid of Rs. 34 lakhs, out of the total budget provision of Rs. 60 lakhs for the year.

The performance of the scheme since 1996-97, is given below:

Year	*Budget*	*Grant-in-aid Allocation funded (Rs. in lakhs)*	*No. of schools released (Rs. in lakhs)*
1996-97	60.00	34.00	20
1997-98	15.00 (R.E.)	11.75	7
1998-99	150.00 (R.E.)	4.62 (upto Dec '98)	3

The main objective of the Scheme of Hostels for scheduled Castes is to provide hostel facilities to Scheduled Caste students studying in middle school, higher secondary school, colleges and universities. Under this scheme, financial assistance is provided to the State Governments on 50:50 matching share basis 11,00% to UTs) for the construction of boundary walls, two room set for hostel warden and one room set for chowkidar. A Sew rooms/blocks of the hostels should be constructed barrier free and facilities like ramps etc. should be incorporated in the design of their construction so as to enable the disabled SC student to reside in them conveniently. The expenditure on maintenance of these hostels is to be borne by the State Governments from their own funds. The cost of construction of hostels is worked out on the basis of State/CPWD schedule of rates.

The releases out of the allocated Central share and number of covered inmates is as follows:-

(Rs. in Crores)

Year	*Allocation (CA)*	*Release sanctioned*	*Hostels seats*	*No. of*
1994-95	6.20	6.20	73	7,208
1995-96	7.00	5.65	90	7,546
1996-97	7.00	6.48	37	1,441
1997-98	8.00	6.00	78	12,851
Total	28.20	18.33	278	29,046

During the year 1998-99 against the Budget allocation of Rs. 8.00 Crores an amount of Rs. 4.61 has been released upto Dec., 1998 to the States/UT's. The Scheme has been revised w.e.f. the financial year 1998-99. The salient feature of the revised scheme are:

1. Financial Assistance is given for construction of SC/ST hostels to the State Governments on 50:50 basis.
2. 100% grant to Union Territories.
3. 90% grant to Centrally Controlled Universities.
4. In case of other Universities the share of Central Government will be 45% that of concerned State Government will be 45% and the University will contribute 10% towards total cost. However in case the concerned State Government is not able to contribute its expected share of 45%, the University may bear the share of former also thereby bringing up its net contribution to 55%.
5. Land for construction of hostel has to be provided by the State Government, Union Territory and Universities.

6. NGOs are given Central Assistance for expansion of existing hostels on 45 Central share, 45% State share and 10% by the NGO themselves.
7. Universities are also funded on the same basis as NGOs.
8. A few rooms blocks of the hostels should be constructed barrier free to enable the disabled SC student to reside in them conveniently.
9. In order to integrate the SC students with the mainstream accommodation of 10% non-SC students in such hostels should be compulsory. However, if after accommodating all applicant SC candidates first, certain teats are left vacant, then accommodating to the non-SC students may be considered. The percentage of non-SC students in any case shall not exceed 25%. For general category student some charges may be levied for better maintenance of the hostels.

The Scheme started from the year 1989-90 is implemented on the same pattern as that of Girls Hostels described earlier. The outlay under is Scheme is as under:

(Rs. in Crores)

Year	*Allocation (CA)*	*Release sanctioned*	*Hostels seats*	*No. of*
1994-95	6.20	10.00	327	24,071
1995-96	10.00	14.83	134	11,297
1996-97	10.00	9.40	90	3,580
1997-98	11.00	9.05	27	282
Total	37.20	43.28	578	39,230

During the year 1998-99 against the allocation of Rs. 11.00 crores an amount of Rs. 5.75 crores has been released upto Dec., 1998 to State/UT's.

The Scheme is intended to provide SC/ST students access to the latest text books for Medical (including Indian systems of medicine and Homeopathy), veterinary, Engineering, Agriculture and Polytechnic courses, which require expensive books, through the establishment of book banks. The scheme also includes Law Courses, Chartered Accountancy, MBA and Bio-Sciences. Each set of books is shared by two students at various stages except in respect of Post-Graduate courses and Chartered Accountancy where it will be one set for each student and the scheme is open to all those in receipt of post-matric scholarships. The life period of one set of book has been fixed for 3 years. The scheme also provides upto Rs. 2,000/- for purchase of cup-boards. The ceiling cost per set of text books varies from Rs. 2,400/- to Rs-. 7,500/- depending on the course. Central Assistance is provided to the states on 50% basis (100% to UT's.)

A.	Degree Course (1 set for 2 students)	Cost of one set
1.	Medical	Rs. 7,500.00

(Contd..)

2.	Engineering	Rs. 7,500.00
3.	Veterinary	Rs. 5,000.00
4.	Agriculture	Rs. 4,500.00
5.	Polytechnics	Rs. 2,400.00
B.	Post-Graduate Course	
1.	Post Graduate courses in Medical Engg., Agriculture and Veterinary Courses and such other technical/ alike Courses as are approved by the Universities/Institutes of Higher Learning.	Rs. 5,000.00 (1 set per student)
2.	Law Courses L.L.B (3 years and 5 years L.L.B. (2 years)	Rs. 5,000.00 (1 set per student)
3.	Chartered Accountancy (Inter-mediate and Final)	Rs. 5,000.00 (1 set per student)

4.	M.B.A (2 years) and similar courses	Rs. 5,000.00 (1 set per student)
5.	Bio-Sciences	Rs. 5,000.00 (1 set per student)

Note: The said sets of books will also include Braille Books, talking Books/Cassettes for the Visually Handicapped Students.

The expenditure/re leases out of the Central share and number of SC/ST students benefited under the Scheme is as follows:

(Rs. in Crores)

Year	*Allocation*	*Releases students*	*No. of SC/ST*
1994-95	3.50	2.96	37,877
1995-96	3.60	2.64	26,567
1996-97	3.60	1.83	18,927
1997-98	3.60	1.50	16,482

During the year 1998-99 against the allocation of Rs. 3.60 crores an amount of Rs. 0.25 crores has been released upto Dec., 1998 to State/U.T's.

Centrally sponsored coaching & allied scheme for SC/ST students

Under this scheme free coaching facilities are provide to SC/ST, candidates through Pre Examination Training Centres to enable them to compete successfully in the competitive examination conducted by UPSC, SSC, Railway Board, from the financial year 1998-99. Under the revised scheme Post Graduate level courses including Law, Chartered Accountancy, MBA have been included.

Central assistance to States/UT's for setting up of Book Banks is limited to the following ceiling or actual cost of a set, whichever is less: Commissions, Public Undertakings and various other recruiting bodies with a view to improving the representation of SCs/STs in various services and posts under Central/State

Governments and Public Under-takings etc. This Scheme has been revised for imple-mentation during IXth Plan period. Under the revised scheme Central Assistance is provided on per unit cost basis. Universities and Private Institutes are funded 100% on contractual basis while State owned PETCs will be funded 50% of the contractual amount.

The Main feature of the revised Scheme is (i) payment of central assistance to PETCs on contractual basis on per student basis as per the rates provided for in the scheme. (ii) Universities and private institutes to funded on 100% of contractual basis while States owned PETCs will be funded 50% of contractual amount. (iii) The system of deducting committed liability of the State Government has been done away with. (iv) The income ceiling of candidates eligible for admissions has been raised from Rs. 24,000 per annum to Rs. 44,500 per annum. (v) While the Central Government will give financial assistance for coaching in respect of exams of all-India recruitment character, the. State Governments Civil Services Exams and other subordinate examinations limited to State Government jobs will- not be covered under the scheme. The expenditure/releases out of the Central share and number of SC/ST students benefited under the Scheme is as follows:-

(Rs. In Crores)

Year	*Allocation*	*Releases*	*No. of Beneficiaries*
1994-95	2.00	2.00	9449
1995-96	3.00	2.05	10323
1996-97	3.00	1.89	N.A.
1997-98	3.00	1.50	N.A.

During the year 1998-99 against the allocation of Rs. 3.00 crores an amount of Rs. 0.92 crores has been released upto Dec., 1998 to State/U.T's. The objective of the Scheme is to upgrade the merit of Scheduled Castes/ Scheduled Tribes students by providing them with facilities for alround development through education in residential schools.

The Scheme of Upgradation of Merit of SC/ST students provides for 100% Central Assistance to States/ UTs for arranging remedial and special coaching for Scheduled Castes and Scheduled Tribes students studying in class IX to XII. While remedial coaching aims at removing deficiencies in school subjects, special coaching is provided with a view to prepare students for competitive examinations for entry into professional courses like Engineering and Medical. Scheme of Upgradation of Merit of SC/ST students was started in 1987-88 in the Ministry of Human Resource Development (Department of Education). The scheme was transferred to Ministry of Welfare in the middle of 1993-94. Under this scheme coaching is provided in linguistic skills Science and Mathematics.

The expenditure/ releases out of the Central share and number of SC/ST student benefited under the Scheme is as follows-

(Rs. In Crores)

Year	*Allocation*	*Releases*	*Physical Target (No. of students per class)*	*Achievement (Students Benefited)*
1994-95	1.00	1.00	1000	2336
1995-96	1.00	0.22	1000	884
1996-97	1.00	0.16	1000	280
1997-98	1.00	0.76	1000	609

During the year 1998-99 against the allocation of Rs. 1.00

crores an amount of Rs. 0.85 crore has been released upto Dec., 1998 to States/U.Ts.

The Scheme has been modified w.e.f. 1998-99 and the main features of the revised Scheme is—

(i) State/U.T. may use their own discretion in deciding number and location of schools to be covered under the Scheme.

(ii) Number of awards in respect of each State/U.T. fixed as given under the Scheme, but each State/U.T. will have a minimum of 5 awards.

(iii) Package grant of Rs. 15,000/- per year per student will be given.

(iv) Besides (iii) above, student with disabilities will be eligible for additional grants as provided for in the Scheme.

The main purpose behind the Scheme of Aid to Voluntary Organisations for the Welfare of Scheduled Castes is to improve their educational and socio-economic conditions through voluntary efforts. Assistance is provided for establishing centres and developing services which could equip the SCs with skills to enable them to start income generating activities on their own or get gainfully employed. Grants in aid to voluntary organisations under the Scheme is given mainly for the following purposes:

(a) Opening of schools and hostels, ashram schools, training in Arts and Crafts and any other income generating skills.

(b) Running Balwaries and Bal Kendras i.e. creches to look after the deprived children of Scheduled Caste Communities.

(c) For providing medical facilities to Scheduled Castes through establishment of Hospitals or Mobile Dispensaries.

The Scheme has been modified and renamed as Grant in aid to Voluntary organisations working for Scheduled Castes. The main objective has been to simplify the procedure and also to expand the scope of the scheme. In the revised scheme, focus has been given for (i) Scheduled Castes persons with disability to receive special attention, (ii) Scheduled Castes beneficiaries living in North-Eastern Region to be given focused attention; (iii) Programmes for Scheduled Castes Women to receive priority; etc.

The revised scheme has been circulated to all the concerned.

Details of allocation vis a vis expenditure during last three years and till date-

(Rs. in Lakhs)

Year	*Budget Allocation*	*Expenditure*
1995-96	2033	1084
1996-97	1733	1000
1997-98	2000	1003
1998-99	1800	1420 (As on 31.12.98)

The section is working with the following staff:

i. Section Officer 1
ii. Assistants 3
iii. UDC 1
iv. LDC 2 (one post is vacant)

There are about 425 on going organisations who are running about 650 projects for SCs. The section is dealing with the cases of grant in aid for all these projects. In addition, 505 fresh proposals are, pending in the section which are awaiting consideration. These proposals could not be considered as the funds allocated for fresh proposals have exhausted. The work load in the section has tremendously increased and it is very difficult to cope up with the work of the Section.

The Voluntary organisations getting grant in aid under the scheme of Aid to- Voluntary, organisation during 1998-99. The Protection of Civil Rights Act, 1955 was enacted in furtherance of Article 17 of the Constitution by which untouchability was abolished and its practice in any from forbidden. Further in order to check and deter crimes against SCs AND STs by persons belonging to other communities, the Scheduled Castes and the Scheduled Tribes (Prevention of Atrocities) Act 1989 was brought into force from January, 1990. These enactments have extended the concept of positive discrimination in favour of SCs and STs to the field of criminal Law in as much as they generally prescribe penalties that are more stringent than for corresponding offences under the Indian Penal Code (IPC) And other laws. Comprehensive Rules were also notified under the POA Act in 1995 which lay down, in particular, enhanced scales for relief and rehabilitation. These statutes require the State Governments/UT Administrations to undertake various measures for preventing and penalising untouchability practices and atrocities and generally, for effective implementation of the Acts. The Central Government is required to coordinate measures taken by the State and UTs.

Under Centrally Sponsored Scheme, financial assistance is provided to the State Governments in the ratio of 50:50 (100% to UTs) over and above the committed liability to be borne by them for all measures they have undertaken or propose to undertake for the effective implementation of these Acts and the Rules. Such measures may include strengthening of the administrative, enforcement and judicial machinery, publicity, and relief and rehabilitation. The year-wise position of sanction of Central Assistance is as follows:

(Rs. in crores)

Year	*Central Assistance*
1994-95	9.75
1995-96	15.37
1996-97	12.50
1997-98	16.47
1998-99	14.28(As on 30.11.1998)

During 1998-99 a sum of Rs. 15.50 crores have been allocated for the scheme. This Ministry also made special efforts during the year to release adhoc central assistance to the State Governments for timely disbursement of relief to the victims of atrocities.

Implementation of protection of Civil Rights Act, 1955

Section 15-A of the PCR Act requires the State Govts. to take measures to ensure that the rights arising from the abolition of untouchability are made available to, and are availed of, by persons subjected to any disability arising out of untouchability. These measures may include:

(i) the provision of adequate facilities, including legal aid, to the persons subjected to any disability arising out of "untouchability" to enable them to avail themselves of such rights;

(ii) the appointment of officers for initiating or exercising supervision over prosecution for the contravention of the provisions of this Act;

(iii) the setting up of Special Courts for the trial of offences under this Act.

(iv) The setting up of Committees at such appropriate levels as the State Governments may think fit to assist the State Government in formulating or implementing such measures;

(v) Provision for a periodic survey of the working of the provisions of this Act with a view to suggesting measures for the better implementation of the provisions of this Act.

(vi) The identification of the areas where persons are under any disability arising out of "untouchability" and adoption of such measures as would ensure the removal of such disability from such areas.

In most States/UTs, Committees/Special Cells/ Squads and/or officers -have been constituted or appointed at different levels for supervising various aspects of the implementation of the Act. Most States/UTs also have legal aid schemes under which assistance is provided to SC/ST persons in various kind of cases indirectly related to untouchability offences and atrocities, such as land disputes, etc. although some States provide free legal aid irrespective of income, some others prescribed income ceilings for eligibility.

The establishment or even specification of Special Courts is not mandatory under the PCR Act, though the Act does stipulate that most categories of offences would be triable by Judicial Magistrates (First Class) or Metropolitan Magistrates. Some States have designated existing Courts as Special Courts. Exclusive Special Courts have also been set up to try offences under the Act in the States of Andhra Pradesh (22), Bihar (4), Karnataka (4), Madhya Pradesh (4) and Rajasthan (6).

Though the prevalence of untouchability is on the decline, yet its prevalance is still reported, in one form or "he other, in some parts of the country viz. Andhra Pradesh, Bihar, Goa, Gujarat, Haryana, Himachal Pradesh, Jammu & Kashmir, Karnataka, Kepla, Madhya Pradesh, Maharashtra, Orissa, Punjab, Rajasthan, Tamil

Nadu, Uttar Pradesh, Delhi and Pondicherry. Over the years, the registration of cases under the Protection of Civil Rights Act, 1955 has been declining as will be seen from the following:-

Year	*No. of cases registered under PCR Act*
1994	1794
1995	1599
1996	1489
1997	1304
1998	537 (provisional)

Source: National Crimes Records Bureau, Ministry of Home Affairs.

In order to check and deter crimes against SCs/STs by persons belonging to other communities, the SCs and STs Prevention of Atrocities (POA) Act, 1989 was brought into force from 30.1.90. The POA act defines certain categories of offences against SCs and the STs as 'atrocities' for the purposes of the Act, Comprehensive Rules were also notified under the POA Act in 1995 which lay down, among other things, norms for relief and rehabilitation. The POA Act prescribes punishments which are higher than for corresponding offences under the Indian Penal Code.

Under the POA Act, State Governments are required to undertake various measures which may include:

(i) provision of adequate facilities, including legal aid;
(ii) travelling and maintenance expenses to victims and witnesses;
(iii) appointment of officers for initiating and exercising supervision over prosecutions;
(iv) setting up of Committees at different levels for formulation or implementation of such measures;

(v) periodic surveys of the working of the Act with a view to suggesting measures for better implementation,

(vi) identification of atrocity-prone areas, and adoption of measures to ensure the safety of SCs/ STs in such areas.

(vii) relief and rehabilitation to victims/dependents of atrocities.

Provisions regarding special courts

For the purpose of speedy trial, Section .14 of the POA Act requires the State.Governments to specify, with the concurrence of the Chief Justice of the respective High Courts, a Court of Sessions for each district as a Special Court to try offences under the Act. All States/UTs (except for the predominantly tribal States of Arunachal Pradesh and Nagaland) have specified existing Sessions Courts for each district as Special Courts. In addition, although this is not mandatory under the Act, Six States namely, Andhra Pradesh (3), Gujarat (3), Karnataka (4), Madhya Pradesh (25), Rajasthan (16) and Tamil Nadu (4) have also set up separate Special Courts exclusively for trying cases under the SCs & STs (Prevention of Atrocities) Act, 1989.

The data on atrocity cases against the SCs and STs in the country during 1997 as maintained by National Crimes Record Bureau of Ministry of Home Affairs.

Monitoring of point 11(A) of twenty point programme

Performance of Point 11(A) of Twenty Point Programme related to "Justice of Scheduled Castes" is monitored, inter-alia, in terms of the number of Scheduled Castes families assisted through various income generation schemes. During VIII Plan 118.67 lakh Scheduled Caste families were assisted against a target of 127.6 lakhs Scheduled Caste families showing 93% achievements.

During IX Plan 124 lakh Scheduled Caste families have been targeted to be assisted. During 1997-98, 20.66 lakh Scheduled Caste families have been assisted against a target of 25.95 families.

The year-wise targets and achievements during the Eight and Ninth Plan period are as below:-

SC Families Assisted			
Period	*Target*	*Achievement*	*%*
1992-93	25,95,568	20,65,987	79.60
1993-94	25,24,800	23,23,722	92.60
1994-95	25,83,500	26,96,412	104.37
1995-96	25,62,000	24,82,075	96.88
1996-97	25,00,100	22,98,,900	91.95
IX Plan	124,00,000		
1997-98	25,95,568	20,65,987	79.60
1998-99	24,35,030	11,61,000	

Research and training scheme

Ministry of Social Justice and Empowerment invites research proposals from Government and non Governmental organisations and various research Institutes/Universities for conducting evaluation studies regarding various developmental programmes for Scheduled Castes. Details of research studies, seminars/ workshops sponsored under the scheme during 1997-98 and current financial year are as follow:-

Year	*Research Studies*	*Seminars Workshops*
1997-98	40	29
1998-99 (Upto Nov., 98)	22	Nil

Year-wise out-lay and expenditure under the scheme during 1997-98 and during current year is as shown below-

(Rs. in lakhs)

Year	*Outlay*	*Expenditure*
1997-98	50.00	33.00
1998-99	190.00	19.00
		(Upto Nov., 98)

The studies undertaken during VIII Plan under the scheme cover wide range of aspects of development of Scheduled castes including the performance of Scheduled Castes Finance and Development Corporations functioning in various States, implementation of Post-matric Scholarship, Prematric Scholarship for the children of those engaged in unclean occupations, hostels for Scheduled Caste boys and girls and Coaching and Allied Scheme. Effectiveness of Special Component Plans in States and its impact on the development of Scheduled Castes, liberation of scavengers scheme and, its effectiveness in achieving occupational mobility trend among Scheduled Caste people, aspirations of Scheduled Castes and various other subjects have also been taken up under the scheme.

The Research Studies are sponsored with an aim to improve the formulation and implementation of educational and economic development plans etc. for development of Scheduled Castes.

The scheme is implemented under the guidance of a Research Advisory Committee of the Ministry.

Dr. Ambedkar foundation

Dr. Ambedkar Foundation was established by the Government of India under the aegis of the Ministry of

Welfare on March 24, 1992 as a registered society under the Societies Registration Act, 1860.

The Foundation has been entrusted with the responsibility to manage, administer and carry on the important and long term Schemes and Programmes identified during the Centenary Celebrations of Bharat Ratna Baba Saheb Dr. B. R. Ambedkar.

The important Schemes and Programmes of the Foundation are:

(i) Dr. Ambedkar National Public Library in Delhi.
(ii) Dr. Ambedkar Chairs in Universities/ Institutions for research on the thoughts and ideals of Baba Saheb.
(iii) Dr. Ambedkar National Award for Social Understanding and Upliftment of Weaker Sections.
(iv) Dr. Ambedkar International Award for Social Change, Harmony, Equity, Justice and Human Dignity for- the exploited and the under-privileged.
(v) Publication of the Collected Works of Baba Saheb Dr. Ambedkar in Hindi and other Indian languages.
(vi) Putting up Memorial for Dr. Ambedkar at 26, Alipur Road, Delhi.
(vii) Various General Activities like organising seminars. Conferences, Workshops, Exhibitions and Melas on Dr. Ambedkar, his life and mission.

The present position of the above Schemes and Programmes is as follows:

Dr. Ambedkar national public library

Land for the Library has been allotted by the Ministry of Urban Affairs & Employment in the Institutional Areas between Raisina Road and Dr. Rajendra Prasad Road. Out of the five Bungalows in the allotted area, actual possession of one Bungalow has already been taken over and possession of the rest of the Bungalows are expected to be obtained shortly. Since the working Group which was constituted in 1994 could not prepare a proper design and plan for the Library, it has since been decided to appoint an Architect Designer for the purpose. An amount of Rs. 5.50 crores has already been provided to the Foundation for this project. The project is likely to cost about Rs. 100 crores.

As per the existing scheme and annual grant of Rs. 200 lakhs is being released to the Chairs for meeting their yearly expenditure. In addition, in the beginning a one-time grant of Rs. 50,000/- is also provided for meeting the initial equipment/ establishment expenditure. A proposal is under consideration to increase the amount of grant to be provided to the Chairs as well as to set up more Chairs.

Dr. Ambedkar overseas fellowship

Four Dr. Ambedkar Overseas Fellowships are being awarded every year for students since the year 1992-93, to pursue their studies abroad in the field of Law Economics, Sociology and International Relations. The Scholarships are awarded solely on the basis of merit and so far 12 scholars have been provided fellowships for the year 1992-93, 1993-94 and 1994-95. The Governing Body of the Foundation in their meeting held on 14.9.97 has reviewed this Scheme and decided to discontinue it. However, the Scholars who have already been sent abroad and are making good progress will be allowed to continue their course.

Dr. Ambedkar national award for social understanding and upliftment of weaker sections

Dr. Ambedkar National Award for the year 1993 has been presented to NISWASS of Orissa and the Award for the year 1994 has been given away to Rayat Shikshan

Sansthan of Satara, Maharashtra. Nominations received for the Award for the years 1995 and 1996 have been processed and are being put up for selection before the National Jury which has been reconstituted recently.

Dr. Ambedkar International award for social change

Dr. Ambedkar International Award for Social change has also been instituted. The award which carries a cash prize of Rs. 1.50 million and a citation, will be conferred every year on eminent Individual(s) Group(s)/Organisation(s)/Institution(s) who have contributed in the light against inequality and injustice to bring about social changes. The jury for the Award has been constituted, and necessary actions are underway for calling nominations.

The writings and speeches of Dr. Ambedkar published in English by the Govt. of Maharashtra have been taken up by the Foundation for Translation and Publication in Hindi, Bengali, Gujarati, Kannada, Malayalam, Oriya, Punjabi, Tamil, Telugu, Marathi, Asameese and Urdu. Eleven Volumes in Hindi, eight in Tamil, four in Punjabi, ten in Bengali, fifteen in Gujarati, five in Kannada, eight in Telugu, four in Malayalam and two in Oriya have been brought out the work in other languages is in progress. Small low priced booklets containing Dr. Ambedkar's Philosophy and thoughts are being brought out.

The Govt. had resolved to construct a Memorial for Dr. Ambedkar at 26, Alipur Road, Delhi where he had lived and attained Parinirvan, Pursuant to this, an amount of Rs. 10.00 crores was released to the Foundation during 1996-97 out of which Rs. 7.12 crores as 80% of the estimated cost of acquisition of Rs. 8.90 crores has been released to the Govt. of NCT Delhi as per their request. The Delhi Govt. have already issued Notifications under section (4) and subsequently under section 6 of the Land Acquisition Act, The actual possession of the land expected to be obtained shortly and the construction of the Memorial will be commenced immediately thereafter. Already a high-level Committee has been constituted to conceptualise the Memorial as well as to firm up its cost estimates.

In addition to these Schemes aims and objectives of Dr. Ambedkar Foundation also include other activities such as holding of National/Regional Seminars/ Conferences/Workshops, lectures and Symposia on socio-economic issues, holding of Annual Functions on 14th April and 6th December to commemorate Birth Anniversary and Mahaparinivaran Diwas of Baba Saheb and publication pamphlets/periodicals.

The Foundation is bringing out a quarterly, viz Dr. Ambedkar Foundation Patrika and the first issue has already been released. The work on the subsequent issues is in progress. It is observed that at present there is a lot of verification/mis-information campaign going on against Baba Saheb. To counter this and to bring out facts in the correct perspective, a Research Cell has been constituted in the Foundation which has already begun its work.

3

Information and Mass Education

The concept of Welfare State as enshrined in the constitution finds emphatic expression in its preamble and Directive Principles of State Policy. These envisage a positive role for the State in bringing about the Welfare and Development of disadvantaged and marginalised groups of society. Through successive plans socio-economic programmes have been aimed at improving and uplifting the economic conditions of the people. In order to bring the goals of economic and social development to the weaker sections of the society a number of programmes have been grown up by the Government and concerted efforts have been made for their upliftment.

The Ministry of Social Justice and Empowerment undertakes a large number of Welfare activities and schemes for the social disadvantaged, weaker and marginalised sections of society which include Scheduled Castes, Scheduled Tribes, minorities, the Other Backward Classes, Handicapped, destitute children, the aged, Drug addicts, alcoholics, beggars, Animal welfare etc. There is need to give wide publicity to the various schemes being implemented by this Ministry for awareness and education of the masses. The information and Mass Education Cell in the Ministry caters to this vital need. The above objective is sought to be achieved through multi media publicity campaign. The programmes in this regard are developed through mass media including radio, video spots/quickies films, advertisements, print material, plays, ballets, village folk dances etc.

Objectives

The specific objectives of the programme are:-

(i) To inform and educate the public regarding various welfare schemes sponsored by the Ministry of SJ&E for various sections of the society.

(ii) To promote positive social attitude which is condusive to better care growth and development.

(iii) To produce educative material and develop to appropriate aids for reaching out to the specific targets and risk groups.

In view of the large number of sensitive subjects being dealt by this Ministry, the need for an appropriate multi-media campaign for prohibition, Drug Abuse Prevention, Welfare of the SCs/STs. Backward Classes, Minorities, Handicapped, Animal Welfare etc. will have to be continued and intensified with the objective of following for these sections.

The Planning Commission in the plan document relating to the Social Defence sector has made a categorical mention about the need for enlargement of the role of the media with regard to the various programmes dealing with the socially vulnerable sections of the society. This would require a Manifold stepping up in the publicity activities of this Ministry.

The various schemes and achievements of this Ministry are publicised through a Multi-Media campaign consisting following media:

Radio

(1) 10 mts. Drama based radio sponsored Programme "Aao Haath Badhayen" entered the thirteenth year of its broadcast during 1998-99. 52 Programmes have been produced in Hindi and eleven regional languages on welfare of schemes for weaker and disadvantaged sections of the society. These are broadcast over 30 commercial channels (Vividh Bharati) of AIR throughout the year and 26 programmes have been produced and broadcast over 15 prime channels of North East in 8 NE region languages w.e.f. October, 1998.

(2) Coverage of Social Development Fair 12-20 May, 1998.

(3) Pannel discussion on Drug Abuse Prevention through All India Radio on 26.6.97.

(4) Coverage of Cultural Programme on the occasion of International Day against Drug Abuse and illicit trafficking.

(5) Radio varta, Radio talk on Drug Abuse Prevention on Occasion of International day against Drug Abuse and Illicit Trafficking.

(6) Film on 'Ability India Exhibition, 1998' was produced.

(7) Coverage of 'Ability India Exhibition' on Disability in September, 98 at Pragati Maidan, New Delhi.

(8) Pannel discussion on Disability on 3.12.98.

(9) Radio Varta on Disability on 3.12.98

(10) Coverage of National Award function was done over AIR on the occasion of International Day for the Disabled Persons (312-97)

(11) Coverage of Cultural function of reception of Tribal guests and Tableau Artists on 31st January 1999.

Films/video

(1) Coverage of Social Development Fair, 1998.

(2) Film "Apnapan" on adoption was produced.

(3) Film "Ehasas", Dushman Dost, Sankalp, Mrigtrishna, Yesterday's addict today's counsellor, Paigam Wapsika were telecast on National network w.e.f. 15.6.98 to 30.6.98.

(4) Coverage of cultural Programme through Doordarshan, Zee TV, NDTV, Aaaj Tak on the occasion of International Day against Drug Abuse and Illicit Trafficking (26.6.98).

(5) Coverage of Ability India Exhibition organised at Pragati Maidan in September, 98.

(6) Curtain Raiser on International Day for the Disabled, 98 on 2nd December, 98.

(7) Live Coverage of National Award Function was~ done over National Channel (DD-1) on the occasion of International Day for the Disabled, 98.

(8) Video spots and films on various disabilities were telecast over DD 1, DD 11 and DD III free of cost, w.e.f. , 31st November to 15th December, 1998.

(9) Film Bhor-Bhai on-Disability was screened in theatres in December, 1998.

(10) Coverage of Exhibition in Handicraft items produced by Disabled persons through Doordarshan.

(11) Film 'Apnapan' on adoption was telecast over National channel in January, 98.

(12) Film 'Arpan' and 'Glani' on Drug Abuse Prevention and 'Hamari Beti' on Adoption was produced and telecast over DD I and DD It 5 times.

(13) 13 films on various themes of the Ministry were produced.

(14) One Full length film titled 'SAMAR'- on Dalit Empowerment was produced and screened twice, once for Ministry Official and once for forum of SC/ST Parliamentarian in Siri Fort Auditorium and Films Division Auditorium.

(15) coverage 'of Cultural function of reception of Tribal guests and Tableau Artists on 31st January, 98.

Print media

(1) Slogans/Messages on untouchability, Disability, Scheduled Caste development, Drug Abuse Prevention, Care of the Aged, Adoption, antibeggary and prohibition were printed throughout the year on the following items:

   (i) Computerised Railway tickets on Northern and Eastern Railway.

   (ii) Postal stationery i.e. Inland cards. Post cards, Aero Grammes and POSB Pass Books.

(2) Two Booklets on Scheduled Caste Development were printed and distributed.

(3) Posters, Booklets, Leaflets, Folders on Drug Abuse Prevention, adoption and older persons were printed and Distributed in Social Development fair, 98 NGOs,

(4) Leaflet on Drug Abuse Prevention, adoption and older persons were printed and distributed.

(5) Folder on adoption was Printed and distributed.

(6) 2nd issue of News letter on Disability was released.

Out door media

Messages/slogans on various social welfare issues were on continuous display through the following media:

a. Social Development Fair was organised at pragati Maidan, New Delhi in the Month of May, 98 to publicise the activities of the Ministry.

b. Four cultural evenings were organised during Social Development Fair, 98 for minority and Backward Classes, Disability, scheduled Caste Development and Social Defence Divisions.

c. 8 animation display on themes of Handicapped welfare, Drug Abuse Prevention, prohibition, Care of the Aged, Anti beggary and adoption at Katra in Jammu.

d. 187 Hoardings on Drug Abuse Prevention in Delhi, Pondicherry, Madhya Pradesh, Rajasthan and North Eastern Region.

e. 450 Kiosks on Drug Abuse Prevention and Untouchability in Jaipur, Faridabad, Calcutta, Mumbai, Allahabad, Jalandhar, Ghaziabad.

Press media

(1) One full page advertisement on Dr. B.R. Ambedkar was released on the occasion of birth anniversary of Baba Saheb.

(2) 2 quarter page advertisement released in Hindi and English on Social Development Fair, 1998.

(3) One advt. on National Award for Handicapped welfare was released in National Dailies and Regional News Papers in Hindi, English and Regional languages.

(4) One full page News Paper Supplement on the occasion of International Day against Drug Abuse and Illicit Trafficking (26.6.98) released in Hindi, English and regional languages.

(5) Three quarter page advt. on ability India Exhibition were released all over India In English, Hindi and regional languages in September, 98.

(6) One advertisement on Pre-examination coaching facility for SC/ST students was released in Hindi, English and regional languages on all India basis.

(7) One advertisement on overseas scholarship was released in Hindi, English and regional languages.

(8) One full page News paper supplement was released on the occasion of International day for the disabled persons 97 released in English Hindi and regional languages papers.

(9) One quarter advertisement was released all over India in English, Hindi and regional languages on the occasion of Mahaparinirvan Diwas of Dr. B.R. Ambedkar on 6th December, 98.

(10) Quarter page advertisement was released on reception of Tribal guests and Tableau Artists in January, 1998.

(11) One Quarter page advertisement was released all over India in English, Hindi and regional languages on provisions of 'breading of and Experiments on Animals (Control and supervision Rules 1998).

4

SOCIAL DEFENCE PROGRAMMES

1999 is being observed as the International Year of the Older Persons. Population Ageing which was perceived until recently to be a concern of the industrialised countries only has become an active issue of the developing countries including India. The population of Older Persons (60+) in India ranks the Fourth highest amongst the countries in the world and by the end of the present century, it will be second only to China. Today India is home to one out of every ten senior citizens of the world. The older population which was 56.7 million in 1991 is expected to grow to over 76 million by the year 2001 and 137 million by 2021. The proportion of the population aged 60 years and above was 5.1 per cent of the total population in 1901, this rose to 5.4 per cent in 1951, 6.4 per cent in 1981 and is projected to be 7.7 per cent by the year 2001. The decadal per cent growth in the elderly population for the period 1991-2001 would be 37.2 per cent; more than double the rate of increase in the general population. The old age dependency ratio (number of old persons 60 + years) to the working age group 15-59 years) has increased from 9.8 per cent in

1951 to 11.92 per cent in 1981 and is projected to be 12.6 per cent by the year 2001. The index of Ageing indicates that while in 1971 there were nearly 14.2 older persons for every 100 children, this figure will rise to 24.7 per hundred children by 2001. In sum as per United Nations classification, the Indian society will progress from a "mature society" (i.e. elderly population between 4.7 per cent of the total population) to an "Ageing Society" (i.e. elderly population more than 7.0 per cent) by the turn of the century. By then the world is projected to inhabit 612 million older persons, which would be 9.8 per cent of the world's population. In other words, one out of every seven elderly person would be from India by the year 2001.

The Changing demographic profile of the country has been accompanied by a new societal order. The traditional norms and values of the Indian Society laid stress on showing respects providing care for the aged. Consequently, the aged members of the family were normally taken care of in the family itself. In recent times the rapid socio-economic transformation has affected every aspect of traditional Indian society. Industrialization with resultant urbanisation and migration of population have affected Institutions like the Age old joint family. Technological advancement, impact of mass media and higher degree of mobility have influenced long established life styles, conventional value systems and customary place of women in the society. Thus the society is witnessing a gradual but definite withering of the joint family system as result of which section of the family, primarily the elders, are exposed to emotional neglect and to lack of physical support.

As result of demographic changes and the changing family context, it can no longer be assumed that the older persons live comfortably at home receiving care from members. Given the trend of Population Ageing in

India, the older persons face a number of problems ranging from absence of ensured and sufficient income to support themselves and their dependants, to ill-health to absence of social security, to loss of a social role and recognition, to non-availability of opportunities for creative use of free time. The trend clearly reveals that Ageing will become a major social challenge in the future and vast resources will be required towards the support, care and treatment of the older persons. There is an emerging need to pay greater attention to Ageing issues and to promote holistic policies and programmes for dealing with a future Ageing society.

The Ministry of Social Justice and Empowerment is the nodal Department of the Govt. of India for matters relating to older persons. The Ministry is implementing a Central Scheme of Assistance for Programmes relating to the Aged since November, 1992. Under the Scheme, financial assistance is provided to voluntary organisations for establishing and maintaining Old Age Homes, Day Care Centres, Mobile Medicare Units and for supporting and strengthening Non-Institutional services for the Aged. During 1996-97 a new Scheme of Assistance to Panchayati Raj Institutions/Voluntary Organisation for Construction of Old Age Homes was initiated. The Scheme aims at providing at least One Old Age Home per District. The assistance under the Scheme is one time construction grant.

In keeping with the growing importance of the subject a National Policy for Older Persons was announced by the Government in January, 1999. The principle areas of intervention and action strategies suggested in the policy' for the sector include the following:

(1) Financial Security for Older Persons working in the formal sector as well as those working in the informal sector;

(2) Health Care and Nutrition to enable Older Persons to cope up with health and associated problems commonly associated with old age with particular emphasis upon preventive strategies;

(3) Shelter/housing keeping in view the life style of older persons;

(4) Emphasis upon education, training and information needs of older persons;

(5) Priority attention to especially vulnerable group such as the destitutes, widows and the disabled older persons;

(6) Establishment of a welfare fund for Older Persons:

(7) Special attention to protection of life and property of Older Persons;

(8) Provision of appropriate concessions, rebates and discounts to Older Persons;

(9) Full participation of the Non-Governmental Organisation in the sector;

(10) Formation of self-help groups of older persons;

(11) Productive Ageing;

(12) Strengthening of the family and reinforcing inter-generational relationships between children and Older Persons;

(13) Promotion of research and advocacy in the field;

(14) Development of trained manpower in the sector particularly in medical colleges and schools of social work;

(15) Creative use of media to promote concepts such as life long preparation for old age, productive ageing and building a society for all ages;

(16) Establishment of a separate bureau for Older Persons in the Ministry;

(17) Preparation of sectoral Annual and Five Year Plans on the subject;

(18) A detailed review to be carried out of the implementation of the National Policy every three years;

(19) Establishment of a National Council for Older Persons;

(20) Establishment of a National Association of Older Persons;

(21) Use of Social Justice Committee of the Village Panchayats for giving effect to the policy;

(22) Use of experts of Public Administration to coordinate and monitor the implementation of the policy.

In order to facilitate implementation of the National Policy and to bring about a qualitative improvement in the programme interventions of the Ministry both the ongoing schemes were revised during the year.

The Scheme of Assistance to Panchayati Raj Institutions/Voluntary Organisations for Construction of Old Age Homes was revised and broad based. Under the revised scheme which bears the nomenclature: Scheme of assistance to Panchayati Raj Institutions/Voluntary Organisation/Self Help Groups for Construction of Old Age Homes/Multi Service Centres for Older Persons a one time grant of Rs. 30 lakhs is provided to eligible organisations.

The Scheme aims at providing financial grant for construction of old age home or Service Centre for Older Persons. To this end a one time construction assistance shall be provided to Non-Governmental Organisation/ Self Help Groups/Panchayati Raj Institutions for construction of Old Age Home or a Multi-Service Centre consisting of Day Care Centres for the mobile; reach out units for the home bound and Old Age Homes for the destitute Older Persons.

The day Care Centres will be required to provide various non-institutional support systems to Older Persons such as developmental programmes for preparation for old age, death and bereavement; raising family and community awareness for enriched interactions; health checkup camps; information and awareness for prevention of problems and treatment; continuing education; training and opportunities for income generation, employment exchange and sponsorship; training as volunteers; recreation, cultural and creative programmes; occupational therapy, counselling and legal aid; self/mutual help groups; family assistance; information and referral services and any other programme or service in the best interest of Older Persons.

Besides Mobile Medicare the Reach out units will also run other home/family based services for home bound Older Persons such as Mobile meals, clinics, libraries; volunteer visits for help in home making and running external errands; information and referral services etc.

The Old Age Homes will provide for self fulfilment, health, nutrition and care giving, continuing education and recreation activities to the Older Persons particularly the destitute and the homeless. An effort will be made to ensure that institutional life in the Old Age Homes corresponds to normal conditions in the family and in the community. To this end the homes may keep their health, education and recreation services open to nonresident Older Persons. The residents interaction with their family members and the community would also be encouraged.

Grant in aid under the scheme shall be limited to Rs. 30 lakhs per Home/Centre and this amount shall be used only for the purpose of

(i) Construction of building and for furnishing/ equipping the old age home/multi-service centre;
(ii) Expansion of the existing building, of the existing home/centre;
(iii) Completion of the construction of the building and for furnishing/equipping the home/centre.

Grant will be released in two instalments—the first instalment not exceeding 70% will be released at the time of sanctioning of the project. The second instalment will be released on confirmation that the construction has started and has reached the plinth level. Application for release of second instalment shall be accompanied by a Statement of expenditure incurred so far by the institution/ organisation.

An integrated programme for older persons

The Scheme of Assistance to Voluntary Organisations for Programmes relating to Welfare of Aged was also similarly revised and made flexible so as to be able to meet the diverse needs of the Older Persons and it has been also given a new nomenclature: An Integrated Programme for Older Persons. The basic objective of the revised scheme are to:

(i) Reinforce and strengthen the ability and commitment of the family to provide care to Older Persons;
(ii) Foster amiable multi-generational relationships;
(iii) Generate greater awareness on issues pertaining to

Older persons and enhanced measures to address these issues;

(iv) Popularise the concept of Life Long Preparation for Old Age at the individual level as well as at the societal level;

(v) Facilitate Productive Ageing;

(vi) Promote Health Care, Housing and Income Security needs of Older Persons;

(vii) Provide care to the Destitute elderly.

While the basic thrust of the programme will be on the Older Persons (of age 60, years and above) particularly the infirm, destitute and the widows amongst them, broad based interventions targeting the family and the community shall also be undertaken within the overall context of improving the quality of life of Older Persons.

Within this framework under the scheme the Ministry will provide support and financial assistance to a wide range of programmes including;

(i) Programmes to reinforce and enhance the commitment and ability of the family to take care of Older Persons;

(ii) Programmes to build and strengthen inter-generational relationships particularly between children/youth and Older Persons;

(iii) Programmes emphasising and contributing towards the need to undertake Life Long Preparation for Old Age;

(iv) Programmes facilitating Productive Ageing;

(v) Programmes enabling formation of Self Help Groups/Associations of Older Persons and advancement of their rights and interests;

(vi) Programmes facilitating and improving the Health

care of Older Persons including development of trained manpower/para medicos to provide care and attention to Older Persons;

(vii) Programmes attending to the housing needs of Older Persons particularly shelter to the destitute elderly;

(viii) Programmes aimed at promoting the Income Security needs of Older Persons particularly those engaged in Agriculture, Non Formal Sector and those living in rural areas,

(ix) Programmes for providing Institutional as well as Non Institutional Care/Services to Older Persons;

(x) Advocacy and Awareness building programmes in the field of Ageing;

(xi) Research, Training and Documentation in the field of Ageing; and

(xii) Any other programmes in the best interests of Older Persons.

Under the revised scheme up to 90% of the cost of the project will be provided by the Government of India and the remaining shall be borne by the organisation/ institution concerned. However, in the case of schools, colleges and recognised youth organisations such as Nehru Yuvak Kendra Sanghathan (NYKS) and the National Service Scheme (NSS) undertaking programmes and services for Older Persons 100% cost of the project shall be provided by the Government. In case of State Government/Municipal Bodies undertaking execution of any activity directly the funding pattern will be 90 : 10 between the Government of India and the State Government/Local Body. However, where an activity is taken up by Union Territory Administration 100% of the cost shall be borne by the Government of India. Similarly, if the Ministry of Social Justice and Empowerment itself executes any part of the programme

(Monitoring and Evaluation of the Scheme, Advocacy, Awareness building, Research, Documentation, Training etc.) full cost shall be payable from budgetary allocations made for the programme.

Under the Programme while no predefined cost heads shall be stipulated, at the project formulation stage each implementing agency shall submit a detailed proposal clearly bringing out programme modalities and individual expenditure heads. The Ministry of Social Justice and Empowerment while approving the projects shall indicate the extent of support to the project as a whole as well as to each component of the project which shall not be variable except by prior approval of the Ministry. Normally a ceiling of Rs. 10 Lakhs per annum per project shall be applicable for release of grants-in-aid under the programme. Further for all new projects under the scheme, there shall be a ceiling of 60% on the expenditure to be incurred by a organisation on administrative costs and the balance 40% of the expenditure must be spend directly on the beneficiaries. In exceptional cases however, deviance from these norms may be permitted by the Secretary (SJ&E).

Grants will be given in two equal instalments. The first instalment will cover 50% of the sanctioned amount and will be released on receipt of the prescribed proforma. The remaining 50% will be released as the second instalment on receipt of the prescribed proforma.

Project OASIS

An Old Age Social and Income Security (OASIS) project was also launched during the year to comprehensively examine policy questions connected with Old Age Income Security. The Project OASIS Phase-I report was formally presented by the Minister for Social Justice and Empowerment to the Finance Minister with a plan of action for enhancing the coverage and the rate of returns of the existing Social Security Instruments: Employees Provident Fund, Public Provident Fund, Pension schemes of LIC, UTI etc.,

Partnership between the old and the young

Realising the importance of strengthening partnership between the young and the old a collaborative project was launched with the Nehru Yuvak Kendra Sangathan under which 100 new Day Care Centres for Older Persons were established in different parts of the country. Based upon deliberations with representatives from schools the blueprint of a programme intervention to bring school children and Older Persons together was also prepared.

New projects sanctioned during the year

As a part of the ongoing schemes of the Ministry grants-in-aid were provided to NGOs to establish 44 new Old Age Homes, 164 new Day Care Centres, 12 new Mobile Medicare Units and 1 new project for providing Non-institutional Services to the Older Persons. The Ministry is as a result supporting 230 Old Age Homes, 387 Day Care Centres, 40 Mobile Medicare Units and 3 Projects of Non-Institutional Services for Older Persons,

New performance

In order to improve the quality of feed back on performance of the projects and to ensure better utilisation of funds a new performance appraisal system will be put in place from the next financial year under which in addition to State Governments inspections will be carried out by other authorised agencies such as Schools of Social Work. It is expected that this will go a long way in ensuring full utilisation of funds as well as due to delays on the part of State Governments year after year the Ministry has not been able to use the full quantum of funds provided for the schemes for older persons.

The allocation and expenditure incurred during the preceding years under the Scheme of Financial Assistance to Voluntary Organisation for Programmes related to Aged is given below:

(Rs. in lakhs)

S.No.	*Year*	*Budget*	*Expenditure Estimates*
1.	1992-93	100.00	107.00
2.	1993-94	300.00	305.62
3.	1994-95	480.00	528.50
4.	1995-96	600.00	637.05
5.	1996-97	700.00	720.00
6.	1997-98	1250.00	610.00
7.	1998-99	1500.00	640.00
			(As on 14.2.99)
	Total	4930.00	3548.85

The allocation and expenditure incurred during the preceding years under the Scheme of Assistance to Panchayati Raj Institutions/Voluntary organisations/Self Help Groups for construction of Old Age Homes/Multi Service Centres for Older Persons is given below:

(Rs. in Lakhs)

S.No.	*Year*	*Budget Estimates*	*Amounts Released*
1.	1996-97	500.00	130.00
2.	1997-98	500.00	30.00
3.	1998-99	320.00	68.84
			(As on 14.2.99)
	Total	1320.00	228.84

A statement showing release of grants in aid under the

Scheme of Financial Assistance to Voluntary Organisations for Programmes relating to Welfare of Aged for ongoing projects. A statement showing release of grants in aid under the Scheme of Financial Assistance to Voluntary Organisations for Programmes relating to Welfare of Aged for new projects. A statement showing release of grants in aid State-wise under the Scheme of Assistance to Panchayati Raj Institutions/Voluntary Organisations/ Self Help Groups for~ Construction of Old Age Homes/Multi Service Centres for Older Persons.

Programmes for children

The Social Defence Bureau of the Ministry is responsible for initiating policies and programmes for Street Children, children of sex workers and neglected and delinquent Juveniles. The basic framework for the mandate of the Ministry for neglected and delinquent Juveniles is provided by the Juvenile Justice Act, 1986, a Central Act applicable to the whole country except the State of Jammu and Kashmir. In order facilitate implementation of the Act the Ministry has been operating the Scheme for Prevention and Control of Juvenile Social Maladjustment since 1986. Under the scheme, financial assistance is provided to State Governments to the extent of 50% for establishing and maintaining Observation Homes, Juvenile Homes, Special Homes and After Care Institutions for neglected and delinquent Juveniles. As a part of a Non Institutional approach to the problem of neglect and destitution the Ministry has been Budget Amounts operating since 1992-93 the Scheme for Welfare of Estimates Released Street Children. Under the scheme upto 90% cost of projects is provided as grants-in-aid to NGOs for operating out reach programmes and establishing drop-in-shelters for Street Children. In order to meet the developmental needs of children of sex workers as well as to facilitate their integration in the society the Ministry has been providing grants-in-aid to NGOs under its Scheme of Assistance to Voluntary Organisations for Providing Social Defence Services.

During the year a complete review of all the above programmes for children was undertaken. Based upon available feed back the three schemes were revised and updated.

An integrated programme for street children

The Scheme for Welfare of Street Children was updated and is now called, An Integrated Programme for Street Children. The salient features of the revised programme are as follows:

(i) The basic aim of the programme is to prevent destitution of children and facilitate their withdrawal from a life on the streets.

(ii) Under the programme a wide range of initiatives relating to street children, can be supported including those relating to shelter, nutrition, health care, sanitation and hygiene, safe drinking water, education, recreational facilities and protection against abuse and exploitation.

(iii) In addition to voluntary organisations, under the revised programme State Governments, UT Administrations, Local Bodies and educational institutions are also eligible for financial assistance.

(iv) The target group of the programme are essentially children without homes and families i.e. street children and children specially vulnerable to abuse and exploitation such as children of sex workers and children of pavement dwellers. The revised programme seeks to shift the focus to these children from children living in slums who have hitherto been the main beneficiaries of the programme.

(v) The programme requires participation of organisations having experience of working for children although this clause can be relaxed in special circumstances.

(vi) Up to 90% of the cost of each project will be covered by the Govt. of India although in the case of Union Territory Administrations themselves operating a project 100% cost can be covered.

(vii) While no pro-defined cost heads are stipulated as a part of the programme, at the project formulation stage each implementing agency is required to submit a detailed proposal clearly bringing out individual expenditure heads.

(viii) The maximum amount of grants in aid admissible under the project shall be Rs 15.00 lakhs per annum.

(ix) Both ongoing as well as new projects will require to be inspected and recommended by the State/UT Government or an agency authorised for the purpose by the Ministry.

(x) Grants will be released in two equal half yearly instalments. For the release of the second instalment an organisation shall be required to amongst others submit an Audited Statement of Accounts (in four parts i.e. income and expenditure, receipt and payment, balance sheet, and utilisation certificate).

(xi) For ongoing projects a transitional period of three years effective April 99 will be provided to adjust to the new programme, particularly the shift in the target group. Also under the revised programme grants in aid will be provided to them at the per capita rate of Rs 250/- per child per month. The utilisation of these grants ,in aid shall be left to the discretion of each individual agency. However before the new funding pattern comes into force each NGO will be required to submit a detailed proposal of the manner in which it proposes to utilise the per capita grant in aid. The NGO in its proposal shall clearly specify item wise expenditure to be incurred which shall not be changed without the prior permission of the Ministry.

(xii) In the revised programme existing stipulation regarding minimum size of each project (300 children earlier), qualifications relating to staff (BSW/MSW) an item wise allocation of grants in aid shall not be insisted upon similarly there shall not be any restriction on the cities to be covered under the programme.

It is expected that as a result of revision and board basing the scheme of the Ministry will be able to support innovative and a diverse range of initiatives in favour of children in distress.

Child line service

One of the important initiatives taken under the revised programme during the year was establishment of Child Help Line Service in a number of cities. The Child Line is 24 hour free phone service which can be accessed by dialling the number 1098 on the telephone. Child Line provides emergency assistance to the child and subsequently based upon the child's need, the child is referred to an appropriate organisation for long* term follow up and care. The service focuses on the needs of children living alone on the streets, child labourers working in the un-organised sector, domestic workers and sexually abused children.

The primary objectives of the child Line Service are:

(i) To ensure that every child in the major cities of India can avail of emergency phone assistance through the child Line Service.

(ii) To respond to children in emergency situations and refer them to relevant governmental and non-governmental organisations.

(iii) To provide a platform for networking amongst organisations and to strengthen the support systems which facilitate the rehabilitation of children in difficult circumstances through on going training to develop affective management information systems.

(iv) to, sensitize collateral agencies such as the police, hospitals, municipal corporations and the railways about the problems faced by children in difficult circumstances and to develop necessary intervention strategies.

(v) To document the process of child fine and conduct research to serve as a data bass for lobbying and advocacy on issues related to children in distress.

The Child Line is operated in each city by, a network of NGOs. For the purpose of identifying, cities for initialling the service as well as for selecting participating organisation the Ministry has engaged .the services of the Tata Instituter of Social Sciences. In fact the design of the programme intervention itself was conceived on behalf at the Ministry by the Tata Institute of Social Sciences. This, service is currently available at Mumbai, Deft, Calcutta, Hyderabad, Nagpur, Bangalore, Chennai and, Patna, Additionally preparatory- activities for Child Line have been initiated in, 13 other cities/towns across the country.

An integrated programme for juvenile justice

During the current year the, scheme for Prevention and. Control of Juvenile Social Maladjustment which the Ministry has been operating since 1986-87 was also revised with, a view to strengthening the implementation of the Juvenile Justice Act 1988 in the country and bringing about a qualitative improvement in the services provided under the scheme to both neglected as well as delinquent children. The salient features of the revised scheme which is called, "A Programme for Juvenile Justice" are as follows:

(1) Establishment of a National Advisory Board (NAB) on juvenile justice to advise the government on matters relating to the implementation of the Juvenile Justice Act 1986 in the country including the quality of infrastructure and the staff available under the Act. The Chairperson of the NAB is the Secretary. Ministry of Social Justice and Empowerment and it has representation from other Ministries of the government of India, State Governments, Juvenile Welfare Boards, Juvenile Courts, Schools of Social Work, Law Schools and NGOs.

(2) Creation of a Juvenile Justice Fund.

(3) Establishment of a Secretariat for the National Advisory Board.

(4) Constitution of a Social Audit Pane (SAP) comprising of 5-6 eminent persons to report upon juvenile justice facilities in the country.

(5) Appointment of observers/to report upon implementation of the Act in different States/ UTand

(6) Institution of a Chair on Juvenile Justice at the Child and the Law Centre of the National Law School of India University, Bangalore.

(7) Institution of awards for the best maintained juvenile justice institutions in each State and at the National level.

(8) Training, orientation and sensitization of judicial, administrative, police and NGO personnel responsible for implementation of the Juvenile Justice Act 1986.

(9) Provision of 100% financial assistance to States/ UTs/Voluntary Organisations to facilitate creation of infrastructure prescribed under the Act in hitherto uncovered districts of the country.

(10) Expansion of non-institutional Services such as sponsorship, foster care, probation, etc. as alternates to institutional care.

(11) Provision of scholarships to children being processed under the Act for excelling in academics or in extra curricular activities.

Partnership with the corporate sector

As a part of the Ministry's Plan of Action for strengthening and improving facilities for children a project was launched seeking participation of the Corporate Sector for providing additional facilities in observation/juvenile/special homes. A pilot Project was initiated with the help of an external agency, Advantage India, under which a needs assessment of all the homes in Bihar and Delhi was carried out. The possible areas of intervention and, help by the Corporate Sector in these homes were identified with the help of staff deployed in the homes. A request was thereafter sent out by the Minister for Social Justice and Empowerment to select Corporate Houses for participation in the programme. The first home under the project has already been taken up at Delhi arid follow up action is being taken up with a number of Corporate Houses which have evinced interest in the programme.

Scheme of assistance to voluntary organisations for providing social defence Services

The Scheme of Assistance to Voluntary Organisations for providing Social Defence Services was also revamped. Under this scheme assistance is provided for undertaking programmes which are not covered under the existing schemes of the Ministry. In particular the scheme provides for Pilot Projects in un, chartered areas in which the Ministry may like to formulate independent programmes in due course. Under this scheme currently a number of programmes are being supported for rehabilitation of children of sex workers. Initiatives have also been taken to support projects for rehabilitation of widows and for providing counselling and support to traumatized children and women particularly those who have been victims of physical violence and sexual abuse.

New performance appraisal system

Keeping in view the difficulties faced in obtaining inspection reports and recommendations in respect of both new and on-going projects from State Governments and to obviate the resultant delays as well as under utilisation of funds an interesting irritative taken by the bureau was relating to performance appraisal of NGOs participating in the implementation of the schemes of the Ministry. In order to build alternate channels of feed back, the leading schools of social work in the country were contacted to undertake inspection and evaluation of the schemes for older persons and children. This .programme will be operational from the next financial year.

The allocation and expenditure since the inception - of the Scheme for Welfare of Street Children is given below:

(Rs. in lakhs)

S.No.	*Year*	*Budget allocation*	*Expenditure*
1 .	1993-94	300.00	111.14
2.	1994-95	300.00	301.74
3.	1995-96	550.00	284.48
4.	1996-97	450.00	340.00
5.	1997-98	400.00	348.00
6.	1998-99	800.00	409.32 (As on 14.2.99)
	Total	2800.00	1794.68

The allocation and expenditure since the inception of the Scheme of Assistance to Voluntary Organisations, for Providing Social Defence Services is given below.

(Rs. in lakhs)

S.No.	Year	Budget	Expenditure Allocation
1.	1992-93	50.00	57.00
2.	1993-94	50.00	22.16
3.	1994-95	25.00	25.00
4.	1995-96	38.00	36.86
5.	1996-97	38.00	35.43
6.	1997-98	38.00	31.70
7.	1998-99	200.00	40.16 (As on 14.2.99)
	Total	439.00	248.31

The national institute of social defence

The National Institute of Social Defence (NISD) is a subordinate office under the administrative control of the Ministry.

The NISD serves as the Central Advisory Body in the field of prevention of crime and treatment of offenders. The main areas covered by the Institute are juvenile justice administration, welfare of prisoners, probation and allied measures, suppression of immoral traffic, beggary control and drug abuse prevention. During the year the mandate of the institute was enlarged to cover areas of concern to older persons. A number of expert consultations were organised by the Institute both at the national and at the regional level which provided inputs to the Ministry for formulation of the National Policy for Older Persons. After lapse of more than a decade the practice of holding in house training programmes was revived and a number of programmes were organised in the areas of juvenile justice, beggary prevention, etc.

A major development in the NISD was upgradation of the Bureau of Drug Abuse Prevention into a full fledged National Centre for Drug Abuse Prevention (C-DAP). The basic activities planned for the Centre include conducting of research; establishment of a data base, evaluation of existing approaches; field testing of new and innovative approaches; documentation of scientific material; training of workers; development of information, education and communication material, etc. The CDAP held the first three month Certificate Training Course on De-addiction Counselling and Rehabilitation from 16th November 1998 to 12th February 1998 which invited participation from organisations from all over India as well as from countries of the SAARC region (Bangladesh, Maldives and Srilanka). The curriculum for the course was designed with the help of leading academics and practitioners from India arid abroad.

Realising the growing menance of drug abuse in the north eastern region of the country the NISD launched a project for Training of 'trainers on drug abuse prevention. Under the project a large number of social workers from the north east were attached for theoretical as well as practical training with 1995 leading organisations/institutions working on drug 1996 abuse prevention in the country. The trained workers 1997 are expected in turn to disseminate knowledge the subject in their respective States. The NISD also initiated a programme to sensitize police personnel on different facets of drug abuse by providing training inputs at the police stations themseives.

A working group to review the Probation Services in the country was also constituted to suggest measures for reviving and strengthening this important crime prevention strategy.

Central adoption resource agency (CARA)

It is an accepted fact that for full fledged development of the child-emotionally, physically as well as intellectually it is desirable that the child is given an opportunity to grow within familiar surroundings. It becomes the responsibility of the community, the society and the state to provide the necessary institutional as well as non-institutional infrastructure to the orphaned, abandon relinquished, neglected and destitute children Adoption has been considered the most ideal effective medium of non-institutional rehabilitation for the children.

In India there is no uniform law on adoption. Hindus can adopt a child under the Hindu Adoption and Maintenance Act, 1956, while others can take a child under their guardianship under the Guardians and Wards Act, 1890.

The Ministry of Social Justice and Empowerment grants recognition to both Indian and foreign agencies which are engaged in sponsoring children for adoption abroad. About 85 agencies in the country have been given recognition for doing inter country adoption. In addition, 292 foreign agencies have also been enlisted to sponsor inter country adoption cases in more than 25 countries. During the last 3 year and upto September, 98 the following estimated number of children have founded home through these agencies as per records available with C.A.R.A.

Year	*In country adoptions*	*Inter country adoptions*	*Total*
1995	1424	1236	2660
1996	1623	990	2613

1997	1330	1026	2356
1998	858	665 (Sep. 98)	1523
Total	5235	3917	9152

Guidelines for Foster Family Care as an alternative to Institutional Care for children awaiting adoption has been circulated to Voluntary Social/Child Welfare agency and State Govts. for implementation and these Guidelines is being published in the Gazette of India 5 new agencies in India and 7 new agencies abroad have been given recognition/enlistment by this Ministry for doing inter country adoption.

The Shishu Greh Scheme has been revised and the ceding on Grant in Aid has been raised to Rs. 6.00 lakhs in order to facilitate better services for the children. As far as the Voluntary Coordinating Agencies are concerned, there is no structured scheme and the funds are met from the General Grant in Aid Head of the Ministry where Rs. 41.5 lakhs is earmarked. The Planning Commission has agreed to examine the possibility of considering its inclusion in the Annual Plan proposals for the year 1999-2000. Pending that a separate proposal has already been sent to Internal Finance Division for revising the expenditure norms.

A total of Rs. 76.30 lakhs was provided to 23 NGOs under the Shishu Greh Scheme for the year 1997-98 in the current years, Rs. 82,87,8454 has been spent on 31 NGOs under the Scheme till 24.12.98. Further an amount of Rs. 3.30 lakhs has also been provided to 6 VCAs in the current year.

Prohibition and drug abuse prevention

The problem of drug abuse has emerged as one of the vital concerns of human race with far reaching sociomedical and economic consequences. The changes in the population structure, traditionally operative-control mechanisms and social and ethical values are closely associated with the proliferation of drug abuse in modern society. The process of industrialisation and consequential urban drift, stresses and strains of modern life have -rendered individuals much more vulnerable to substance abuse than ever before.

The use of dependence-producing substances, in some form or the other, has been a universal phenomenon. In India too, the abuse of alcohol, opium and cannabis has been known for long. But, the consumption of drugs like heroin, hashish, LSD etc., is altogether a new trend. Within a decade or so, the proliferation of such lethal drugs in various segments of society seems to have acquired an alarming dimension, India, today, is no more merely as transit country for illicit trafficking in drugs from 'golden triangle' or 'golden crescent'. It is also becoming a consumer in the global scenario. As long as addiction was a problem of certain individuals or socially alienated groups and was well contained by informal social control mechanism, it did not evoke much attention. However, with its seepage and spread among various socio-cultural and economic strata and in increasing perception of its disruptive influence on the individual, the family and society at large, drug abuse has emerged as a vital issue of the quality of life and welfare of the people.

Addiction to drugs is not merely a problem for the physical and mental health of the individual involved. 11 also disrupts his family and social relationship. An addict is not on loss to himself but also to society as a productive individual and to the nation as an asset for development. Trend is most ominous for a developing country like India which is still struggling to overcome its basic problems of poverty, hunger and disease. Drug

Abuse has emerged as a vital issue of the present and future quality of human life for us as much as for other countries.

Experience has shown that the demand' of drugs can be curbed effectively only in a social climate of abstience among the people to be created by propagating -a life style that rejects the Use of dependence producing substances. By and large, abstience is still deeply rooted, in our culture and is strongly supported by the family, the community and the religion.

In order to tackle the problem of drug abuse a two pronged strategy has been adopted by the Govt., of India i.e. (a) supply control (b) demand reduction while supply control aspect is taken care of by the Narcotic Control Bureau and the Police, the Ministry of Social Justice and Empowerment has been given the responsibilities of looking after the social welfare and educational aspects of drug addiction. In fulfilling this objective the Ministry of Social Justice and Empowerment has formulated three pronged strategy with the following components:-

(i) Building awareness and educating people about ill effects of drug abuse.

(ii) Dealing with the addicts through a well rounded up programme of motivation, counselling, treatment, follow-up and social reintegration of cured drug addicts.

(iii) To impart drug abuse prevention rehabilitation training to voluntees having in view to build up an educated cadre of drug abuse control operators.

Assistance to voluntary organisations

In order to counteract the increasing demand for dependence-producing drugs, the Ministry has embarked on, since the Seventh Five Year Plan, a comprehensive scheme for Prohibition and Drug Abuse Prevention. The

Scheme is implemented through voluntary organisations by providing them financial assistance on the basis of 90% of the approved expenditure.

Drug awareness, counselling and assistance centres

These centres provide community based services for awareness building, screening of addicts, counselling to addicts and their families, referral of hardcore addicts to De-addiction-cum-Rehabilitation centres and follow-up assistance to former addicts.

De-addiction-cum-rehabilitation centres

These centres provide community based services for awareness services for the identification, motivation counselling, de-addication, after care reintegration of addicts into the social mainstream. A De-addiction-cum-Rehabilitation Centre may either be a 15 bedded or a 30 bedded facility. While setting up new centres, no such two centres are to be set up within a radius of at least 15 kilometers from each other, Where there is a justification for two 15 bedded centres in the same area, a 30 bedded centre is being provided under the scheme.

De-addiction camps

To give a wider coverage the provision of deaddication camps has been made in the urban and rural areas where de-addication cum-Rehabilitation Centres have not been established yet but there is need for the service.. These camps are organised only by the organisations which are running Deaddiction-cum-Rehabilitation centres.

Awareness generation programmes

There is still a considerable degree of ignorance among the public about the ill-effects of drug abuse on the individual, the family and the community. A deliberate decision has, therefore, been taken by the Ministry of Social Justice and Empowerment to step up awareness generation programmes which include holding of seminars, conferences workshops, corner meetings, essay/debate competitions, publicity through mass media etc. Several radio and TV Programmes have been launched to create awareness about role of parents, teachers and opinion leaders in the prevention and control of drinking and drug abuse. A number of films have been produced and distributed to disseminate knowledge among the masses. Voluntary Organisations are being financially assisted to undertake educational work in various communities and target groups. The experience gained by Voluntary Organisations in selected case studies, is being widely shared with enlightened groups to invigorate their role in educating the public and preventing drug abuse. The utilisation, of community based organisations like \ ıth Clubs, Religious Institutions, Panchayats, I C. D S, I H C is also being explored.

Evaluation of the programme and future thrust areas

Rehabilitation

The ultimate goal of treatment of substance abusers is to help them to enter into society so that they are able to lead healthy and productive life. In other words, the objective is to achieve "Whole person recovery" (WPR) which emphasises the physical, emotional and mental rehabilitation culminating to a physically, socially and economically self-dependent life for the recovering addicts.

It is, therefore, felt imperative that rehabilitation aspect should receive more focus in the programme

Based on the discussions in the core group set up in the Ministry comprising of professionals and representatives of international bodies, the entire scheme is being remodified with emphasis on total recovery/ rehabilitation of the addict and reducing the dependence on the large number of purely medical staff. The Ministry has now undertaken revision of the Scheme based on the past experience and interaction with the NGOs to introduce flexibility in operation, revision of financial norms and encourage innovative approaches. It is desired to solicit greater involvement of voluntary as well as Corporate Sector in implementation of the various programmes.

In order to provide a holistic treatment to the addict which will go long way in helping the rehabilitation process, the possibilities of better utilisation of Indian and traditional systems of' medicines for recovery of addicts is also actively explored. A three day Workshop was held in the month of April, 1997 on this subject. Their recommendations are being examined and suitable modifications are proposed in the Scheme to enable alternative systems of medicines to be utilised for treatment of drug addicts.

Special attention is being given to tackle drug abuse problem amongst socially and economically vulnerable groups as street children, commercial sex workers, destitute women etc. In this connection, all the NGOs and State Governments are addressed for identifying these groups and the facilities that are required to be provided to them. A project on Reducing Risk Behaviours and HIV/AIDS/STD drug abuse among street children has been undertaken by the then Ministry of Welfare, United Nations Drug Control Programme, UNICEF,. WHO, NACO and ODA. City level plan have been prepared for four cities namely Bombay, Hyderabad, Calcutta and Delhi and a national Action Plan has been formulated.

In consonance with, the directives of the Prime Minister of India, special focus is given to the Drug Abuse Prevention Programme in North-East keeping in view the enormity of the problem. A three day Workshop was conducted on Need Assessment Study of the Problem of Drug Abuse in North-East at Imphal from 29—31 January, 1697 to assess the ground realities of the problem and plan future interventions. Accordingly, a three pronged strategy has been adopted for the North-East.

(a) Training and enhancing the capabilities of the NGOs in the area.

(b) Extending the outreach of drug abuse prevention scheme of the Ministry by opening of new centres; and

(c) Awareness and Education Programmes for "he North-East.

Five Training Programmes for trainers, 16 training Courses for Service Providers in the North East and Attachment training of service providers in reputed Centres is also being implemented. A Committee has been constituted by the Ministry to visit the north Eastern States for reviewing the working of the existing NGOs, explore the possibilities for opening of new Centres; and identify service providers for the purpose of training.

The Ministry has established a Centre for Drug Abuse Prevention under the aegis of the National Institute of Social Defence, Now Delhi, a subordinate office of the Ministry to serve as the apex body in the country in the field of training, research and documentation in the field of drug abuse prevention.

Realising that the drug and alcohol addiction amongst the workers in industries is very high, the Work Place Prevention is being given greater importance. In this connection, ILO-UNDCP/Ministry of Social Justice and Empowerment 'Project on Community Rehabilitation and Work Place is already under way for developing modules for work prevention. Beginning with seven Centres established in Delhi in 1985-86 the total number of Centres has reached 414 as on 31st December, 1998 of which 218 are Drug Awareness, Counselling and Assistance Centres and 196 De-addiction-cum-rehabilitation Centres. State/UT wise number of centres and voluntary organisations given grant-in-aid under the Scheme. As a result of the impact of the implementation of the program, me the number of Drug Addicts registered in these Centres was 2.49 lakhs in 1997-98 of which about 0.90 lakhs were detoxified. During the year 1998-99 (upto September, 1998) about 1.29 lakhs drug addicts were registered and 51,164 were detoxified in these centres.

In order to provide for better training and qualified personnel amongst the service providers, the Ministry in collaboration with United Nations International Drug Control Programme (UNDCP), has taken up a number of projects which include Community Drug Rehabilitation and Work Place Prevention Programme. This is in collaboration with ILO and UNDCP.

Under this programme, 20 NGOs have been identified in different parts of the country with an objective to train at least 4000 service providers in rehabilitation of drugs.

Another study was conducted on Reducing Risk Behaviour relating to HIV/AIDS/STD Drug Abuse among Street Children sponsored by the Ministry of Social Justice and Empowerment, WHO, UNDCP, UNICEF and Ministry of Health and Family Welfare. City level action plans have been prepared for 4 cities viz. Bombay, Calcutta, Hyderabad and Delhi and a National Action Plan have been formulated.

Year	*BE (Rs. in crores)*	*Expenditure (Rs. in crores)*	*No. of centres*	*No. of Addicts registered*	*No. of Addicts Detoxified**
1	2	3	4	5	6
1992-97 (VIII Plan)	70.25				
1992-93	6.92	8.06	254	270133	85115
1993-94	7.60	9.87	274	290628	101007
1994-95	14.00	13.50	376	312118	110858
1995-96	15.00	11.00	363	282266	107328
1996-97	14.50	9.57	341	305098	114831
IXth Plan	17.50				
1997-98	(RE 11.52)	11.52	370	249048	90050
1998-99	16.00	11.26 (31st Dec.,) 1998		129639 (upto Sept., 1998)	51164 (Upto Sept., 1998)

* *Source :* Based on the Data received from the centres being funded by the Ministry.

In order to have an exhaustive data regarding the extent of drug abuse problem in the country, the Ministry proposes to take up an extensive survey on the drug abuse scenario in India which interalia will also include a survey on the HV/AIDS infected IDUs for facilitating better planning in future.

Monitoring system

Monitoring forms an integral part of the Scheme. The programme is evaluated on the basis of information and statistics collected in prescribed preform on quarterly and yearly basis from the De-addiction and counselling Centres funded by the Ministry. The feed back enables the Ministry to evaluate the performance of the voluntary agencies. The State Government conducts yearly inspection of the agencies and sends its report to the Ministry of Social Justice and Empowerment.

The grantee organisations are required to 'furnish Utilisation Certificate and audited accounts verified by Chartered Accountant. The second instalment to the NGO is released only on the basis of the Inspection Report and recommendation of the State Government. In order to undertake regular review of the progress of utilisation of funds under the Scheme, Ministry of Social Justice and Empowerment has convened series of meetings with State/UT Social Welfare Secretaries in November, 1997 wherein the need for a proper and intensive evaluation of the working of the Centres was stressed.

5

Employment and Poverty Alleviation

Wage employment programmes

The high incidence of poverty in rural India is directly related to prevalence of unemployment and underemployment on a large scale. Majority of the rural population is landless and sustains entirely on wage employment. While the self-employment programmes are intended to remove poverty on a sustainable basis, there is need to take care of the wage employment needs of the rural poor. The rural workforce continues to suffer due to excessive seasonality of employment, lack of wage employment opportunities and low wage rates. Migration of labour, discrimination between wages paid to men and women, distressed child labour etc. are therefore, common features of rural areas.

Efforts to provide wage employment, as a short-run strategy for alleviation of rural poverty has been a major component of development planning in India. The major programmes under implementation in this direction are the Jawahar Rozgar Yojana (JRY), Employment Assurance Scheme (EAS). The Million Wells Scheme (MWS) is also one such programme which helps the beneficiary to acquire an asset for his/her sustained self-employment on land-based activities.

Jawahar Rozgar Yojana

The Jawahar Rozgar Yojana (JRY) was started in April i 1989 by merging the on-going National Rural Employment Programme (NREP) and Rural Landless Employment Guarantee Programme (RLEGP) into a single rural employment programme.

Objectives

The main objective of JRY is generation of additional gainful employment for the unemployed and underemployed persons, both men and women, in rural areas. The secondary objective of the Yojana is creation of durable community and social assets. The Yojana has been designed to arrest the seasonality of wage employment and provide a positive impact on the prevailing wage rates in rural areas. It also contributes to improvement in the quality of life of the rural poor by providing supplementary source of income through wage employment and by creating community and social assets.

Target group and special safeguards for certain sections

The JRY is targeted to benefit people living below the poverty line in rural areas. Preference, however, is given to the Scheduled Castes, the Scheduled Tribes and freed bonded labourers. At least 30 % of employment is to be provided to women under the Yojana. 22.5% of funds have to be to spent on individual beneficiary schemes for the direct benefit of SCs/STs.

Allocation procedure

JRY is a Centrally Sponsored Scheme. The expenditure under the programme is shared between the Centre and the States in the ratio of 80:20. Central assistance is provided to the States on the basis of proportion of rural poor in a State/UT to the total rural poor in the country. From the States to the districts, the allocation is made on the index of backwardness formulated on the basis of equal weightage to the proportion of rural Scheduled Caste/Scheduled Tribes population in a district to total rural SC/ST population in the State and the inverse of per capital production of agricultural workers in that district.

Implementing agencies

JRY is implemented in a decentralised fashion by the Panchayati Raj Institutions. The major share of funds are utilized at the village level by the Gram Panchayats. At the district level the responsibility of co-ordination, guidance and monitoring is vested with the DRDA/Zilla Parishad (ZP). Funds under JRY are distributed among DRDAs/ZPs, Intermediate Panchayats / Village Panchayats in a district in the ratio of 15:15:70.

The resources allocated to DRDA/ZP, intermediate panchayats and gram panchayats are to be spent within the geographical boundaries of each unit. These funds cannot be diverted under any circumstances except where two or more intermediate level panchayats / Gram Panchayats decide to pool the resources together to take up a work for their common benefit.

Financial and physical performance under JRY

Since inception in 1989-90 upto 1997-98, the Yojana has been able to generate a total of 70003.32 lakh mandays, of employment. The expenditure during this period was Rs. 27649.00 crores. The year-wise financial and physical performance under JRY since 1989-90 is given in Table- 1. 1 and 1.2 respectively.

Performance during 1998-99

In 1998-99, the Central allocation for the Yojana was Rs. 2078.44 crores. Against this, releases made to the States/ UTs are Rs. 1398.19 crores upto November, 1998. The total availability of funds with the States/ UTs, however, is Rs 2222.16 crores which included States, UTs, matching share of Rs. 347.67 crores and opening balance of Rs. 476.30 crores. Against this the expenditure reported is Rs. 1243.71 crores upto November, 1998. The employment generated is 1902.80 lakh mandays during this period against the target of 3966.57 lakh mandays for 1998-99. The State-wise details are given in Annexures - III & IV.

Monitoring of JRY

The performance of JRY is monitored regularly by the Centre and the State Governments. To facilitate proper monitoring, emphasis is laid on building a strong data base and periodical feedback through monthly and annual progress reports. The physical and financial achievement under the programme is monitored at the Central level through monthly and annual progress reports received from the States. The Department of Rural Employment and Poverty Alleviation has evolved a system to ensure that the guidelines are followed strictly. The utilisation certificates, audit reports and other parameters such as matching grants from the States, minimum expenditure etc. are examined before the release of second instalment. Periodical reviews are carried out by the Central Government in the meeting of Secretaries of the State Governments. Senior officials of the Ministry also see operation of various Rural Development programmes during their visits to the States under the Area Officers Scheme. The scheme is supervised by officials of DRDA/ZP at the district level. The State Level Coordination Committee (SLCC) for the rural development programmes monitors the programmes at the State level. State Government officials also inspect the programmes.

For better monitoring and to check diversion, embezzlement and misappropriation of rural development funds including JRY, Government of India has issued instructions to all the State Governments for constitution of Vigilance and Monitoring Committees at State/district and block level. In many States these committees have been constituted and have started functioning.

Concurrent evaluation of JRY

The Ministry of Rural Areas and Employment had undertaken concurrent evaluation of JRY from June, 1993 to May, 1994 covering 470 districts, 933 blocks and 4700 Village Panchayats. The findings of the Report in brief are as follows:

Among the positive aspects highlighted in the Evaluation Report are that nearly 82.16% of available funds were spent on community development projects; construction of rural link roads received the highest priority; average wages paid per manday of the unskilled workers were more or less on the lines of minimum wages prescribed under the Act; the wage and non-wage component of the expenditure was 52.84:47.16; by and large, payment of wages to workers was made either on a daily basis or weekly basis; muster rolls were maintained; of the total assets created, 76.11 % were found to be in good/satisfactory condition; the share of SCs/STs in generation of employment was satisfactory; roughly, 11 mandays of employment were created during the reference period; family members of the workers also received employment during the last 30 days preceding the date of survey and 76.96% of the assets were created by village panchayat.

The evaluation, however, has highlighted some inadequacies. More than 50% of elected panchayat heads were not imparted training for implementation of JRY works. The share of women in employment generation was less than the prescribed 30%. 49.97% of the works could not be completed on account of shortage of funds. Some discrepancies were observed between payment of wages to male and female workers. The use of locally available material in various works undertaken by Panchayats was not appreciable.

Recently introduced important changes in the yojana

The Yojana is reviewed regularly. In light of the outcome of these reviews and experience gained through time in implementing the Yojana, changes are brought about in the guidelines to sharpen it's focus on the genuinely needy and deserving in tune with the social and moral commitments towards socially deprived sections of the society. Some recently introduced changes are as follows:

- preference in employment under the Yojana to the parents of child labourers withdrawn from hazardous/non-hazardous occupation;
- foodgrains to be given as a part of wages under JRY at the rate of 1 kg. per person-day at the same price fixed for the people below the poverty line under Targeted PDS. Distribution of foodgrains, however, is optional on the part of the State Governments;
- earmarking of three per cent of the funds to create barrier free infrastructures like a pucca path or a street connecting the house of the beneficiaries or a sloped entrance in the house of the beneficiaries or in public places like Panchayat Ghar, schools, hospitals, park etc. in favour of physically handicapped persons living below poverty line in rural areas;

- keeping of funds under JRY in separate saving bank accounts of ZP/DRDA.

New initiatives and looking to the future

JRY is implemented by the village panchayats with active participation of people. The programme, therefore, empowers the village panchayats and the people. The programme also contributes significantly in creating social and community assets and economic infrastructures at the village level. In order that the panchayats have reasonable autonomy in implementation of the programme and have freedom from bureaucratic control in approval and technical scrutiny of the works and at the same time become effective in development of the basic infrastructures at the village level, steps are being taken to restructure and entrust the implementation of JRY entirely to the Village Panchayats.

Employment assurance scheme

The Employment Assurance Scheme (EAS) was introduced w.e.f. 2nd October, 1993 in the rural areas of 1778 blocks of 261 districts in which the Revamped Public Distribution System (RPDS) was in operation. The blocks selected were in the drought prone areas, desert areas, tribal areas and hill areas.

Expansion of EAS

During 1994-95, EAS was extended to 409 blocks under DPAP/DDP and Modified Area Development Approach (MADA) blocks having larger concentration of tribal population. In March, 1995 the scheme was further extended to 256 blocks (233 flood prone blocks in the States of Uttar Pradesh, Bihar and Assam, and 23 blocks of Jammu and Kashmir in view of the special conditions prevailing there). The Intensified Jawahar Rozgar Yojana (IJRY) was merged with EAS w.e.f. 1.1.1996. Consequently, 722 non-EAS blocks in 120 IJRY districts were also covered under EAS. On universlisation, the remaining blocks were covered under the scheme in two phases Le 1123 blocks in 1996-97 and 1121 blocks in 1997-98. At present, the scheme is being implemented in all the 5448 rural blocks of the country.

Objectives

The primary objective of the Employment Assurance Scheme is to provide gainful employment during lean agricultural season in manual work to all able bodied adults in rural areas who are in need and desirous of work, but cannot find it. The secondary objective is the creation of economic infrastructure and community assets for sustained employment and development.

Salient features

- The scheme is operative in all the rural blocks of the country.
- It is a demand driven scheme with no fixed earmarking of annual funds for any district or block.
- Expenditure is shared between the Centre and the States on 80:20 basis.
- The Central assistance under the scheme is directly released block-wise to DRDA/ZPs based on the demand for wage employment and expenditure.
- All adult rural poor normally residing in the villages are covered.
- A maximum of 2 adults per family are *provided* the assurance of up to 100 days of employment. New works will not be opened under this scheme if employment potential is available through plan and non-plan works already in progress and the assurance could be fulfilled by utilising the same.
- Works should be labour intensive which result in the creation of durable productive assets.

- As an individual beneficiary oriented scheme, on the lands of BPL families, horticulture development is a permitted activity.
- Implementing agencies are Block Development Officers, District Officers of various line Departments and PRIs at all three levels.
- The desirous workers have to get themselves registered with village level workers or Gram Panchayats and are issued a family card.
- When about 10 workers demand work, new projects can be started by the block level officer for providing employment.
- The State Level Coordination Committee for the Rural Development programmes is responsible for the overall supervision, guidance and monitoring of EAS.

Block-wise entitlement of funds under EAS

As per the present classification of blocks into 'A', '13' and 'C' categories, the central share of each instalment to the blocks is Rs. 40 lakhs, Rs. 30 lakhs and Rs. 20 lakhs respectively. The State share is Rs. 10 lakhs, Rs. 7.50 lakhs and Rs. 5 lakhs respectively. The shelf of projects for new works to be taken up in each of the categories should not exceed 150% of the funds expected by a block in two installments.

The classification of the blocks into 'A', '13' and 'C' categories was made earlier on the basis of the criteria of backwardness and size of the population. These were mostly blocks in hilly, tribal, drought prone and desert areas. These criteria were followed upto the merger of IJRY with EAS. As per this criteria blocks with population above 196287 were put in 'A' category; blocks with population between 196287 and 65585 were put in '13' category and blocks with population below 65585 were put in 'C' category. Consequent upon universalisation of EAS all the remaining blocks have been put in 'C' category for the purpose of determining the entitlement of funds by each.

Financial and physical performance under EAS

Since inception of EAS in 1993-94 to 1997-98, a total of 15447.33 lakh mandays of employment have been generated by utilising Rs. 8205.20 crores.

Performance during 1998-99

During 1998-99, the Central allocation for EAS is Rs. 1990 crores. Against this, releases made to the States/UTs are Rs. 1564.21 crores upto November 1998. The total availability of funds with the States/ UTs, however, is Rs. 2816.93 crores which includes States/UTs matching share of Rs. 391.05 crores and opening balance of Rs. 861.67 crores. Against this, the expenditure reported is Rs. 1571.97 crores (upto November, 1998). The employment generated is 2376.14 lakh mandays during the period. The State-wise details are given in Annexures - V & VI.

The year-wise financial and physical performance under EAS since 1993-94.

Number of persons registered under EAS

A total of 4.12 crore persons have been registered under EAS in various States/UTs since inception of the scheme upto November, 1998.

Evaluation

The Programme Evaluation Organisation (PEO) Wing of Planning Commission is in the process of evaluating the programme.

Some recently Introduced changes In EAS

- Panchayati Raj Institutions of all three levels have been included as Implementing Agencies.

- The shelf of Projects would be prepared based on suggestions of Gram Sabhas and Panchayats as well as from other sources like line departments, people's representatives etc. as per felt needs of the people.
- Registration of wage-seekers would be done in Gram Panchayats and work-site etc.
- The implementing agencies have been permitted to utilise one person from among the beneficiaries group as animator/leader/ facilitator in maintenance of muster roll, payment of wages, monitoring of quality of works etc. Such person will be eligible to receive wages applicable to unskilled labourers.
- The States have been requested to evolve and publish "Rural Standard Schedule of Rates" as has already been done by some States to eliminate the role of contractors in EAS works.
- To make the implementation of the programme more transparent instructions have been issued to all the states to exhibit prominently the details of funds received, works sanctioned, estimated cost, quantity of material used, workers engaged and wage rates etc. in the Panchayat Office/work site. The accounts of the Gram Panchayats are also open for scrutiny by the Gram Sabha.
- To avoid multiplicity of Committees and as per the recommendation of the Standing Committee of Parliament a decision has been taken to merge District and Block level EAS Committees with the existing Vigilance and Monitoring Committees.
- In case of Karbi-Anglong and North-Kachar hill districts of Assam the Principal Secretaries of the respective Autonomous Hill Councils have been declared as Implementing Agencies of EAS in place of the Deputy Commissioners.

Million wells scheme

Million Wells Scheme (MWS) was launched as a sub-scheme of National Rural Employment Programme (NREP) and Rural Landless Employment Guarantee Programme (RLEGP) during 1988-89. It continued as a sub-scheme of Jawahar Rozgar Yojana from April 1989 to 31.12.95. From 1.1.96, MWS is an independent scheme.

Objectives

The objective of the scheme is to provide open irrigation wells free of cost to poor, small and marginal farmers who are below the poverty line and freed bonded labourers.

Target group

Up to 1992-93, the target group for MWS comprised of small and marginal farmers belonging to SCs/STs and freed bonded labourers. From 1993-94 onwards, MWS has been extended to include poor small and marginal farmers belonging to non-SC/ST category as well, who are below the poverty line and are listed in the IRDP register of the village. The financial assistance provided to SC/ ST poor, small and marginal farmers under MWS, however, must not be less than two-thirds of the total funds utilised under the scheme in any year.

Allocation of funds

The MWS is a Centrally sponsored scheme. Funds under the scheme are shared between the Centre and the States on 80:20 basis. State-wise allocation is arrived at on the basis of the proportion of rural poor in a State to the total rural poor in the country. State Governments fix the district-wise allocation and physical targets keeping in view the size of the un-irrigated land in a district, potential for well irrigation and need for improvements of land held by the rural poor.

Works to be taken up under MWS

MWS is primarily intended to provide open wells. Tube wells and bore wells are not to be taken up under this scheme. However, where wells are not feasible due to geological factors, funds under the scheme could be utilised for other works of minor irrigation like irrigation tanks, water harvesting structures and also for the development of lands belonging to the target group. The fund cannot be diverted for any other purpose.

Each well/irrigation source constructed under MWS has to be located in the holding of the beneficiary and an entry to that effect should be made in the revenue records.

The beneficiaries themselves undertake the construction of wells through their own labour and by hiring local labour for which they are paid. Engagement of contractors is strictly prohibited under the scheme.

Cost/area norms

The cost/area norms in regard to works under MWS is decided by a committee comprising of Chief Secretary/ Secretary (Rural Development), Secretary (Planning), Secretary (Irrigation) and Chief Engineer, Minor Irrigation of the State.

Implementing/executive agency

At the district level DRDA/ZP is the implementing agency of the scheme. But the beneficiaries themselves execute the construction of wells under MWS through their own labour for which they are paid or by hiring local labour. In no case the work should be entrusted to contractors.

Performance under million wells scheme

Since inception of the scheme in 1988-89 till 1997-98, a total of 12,63,090 wells have been constructed under

MWS with an expenditure of Rs. 4728.17 crores. The total number of beneficiaries is 12,63,090. The year-wise resources allocated, utilised and wells constructed since inception under MWS is given in table 1.4.

Performance during 1998-99 (Upto November, 1998)

The Central allocation under MWS for 1998-99 is Rs. 448.97 crores. Against this, Rs. 228.14 crores have been released to States/UTs upto November, 1998. During this period, a total of 49821 wells have been constructed with an expenditure of Rs. 225.89 crores. The State-wise details of allocation and releases, category-wise expenditure and number of wells constructed are given in Annexure VII, VIII and IX

Monitoring and supervision

The DRDA/ZP is also responsible for monitoring and supervision of the scheme in the district. The state level monitoring is the responsibility of the State Level Coordination Committee of the State. At the State level, Secretary, Rural Development is the nodal agency for implementation of the scheme. Apart from the above, the implementation of the scheme is also supervised by the Monitoring and Vigilance Committees set up at the State, District and Block levels for all the programmes of the Ministry.

At the Central level, the MWS is regularly monitored through monthly and annual progress reports from the districts/states. The Area Officers of the Ministry of Rural Areas and Employment also provide feedback on the implementation of MWS.

Evaluation

A regular Concurrent Evaluation of MWS by this Ministry is under process. However, some State specific Concurrent Evaluation (September-December, 1995) by the Lal Bahadur Shastri National Academy of Administration (LBSNAA), Mussoorie has revealed that the scheme is definitely a success as it has provided water sources for agriculture and other activities. Similarly, in an evaluation of Rural Development Programme in Andhra Pradesh conducted by the Institute of Resource Development and Social Management, it has been brought out that MWS has helped the farmers by providing an assured irrigation facility for agriculture. The farmers raise mostly commercial crops. The scheme has helped the farmers to enhance both crop production and productivity. As a result of this the beneficiary household income has gone up from Rs. 750 to Rs. 2500 per month. These findings of the evaluation studies show that MWS has been useful and effective in alleviation of poverty particularly of the rural SC/ST poor, marginal/small farmers and providing income appreciation on a long term basis.

These evaluations, however, also reveal some weaknesses of the scheme. In many cases, the land of the beneficiary continues to be single cropped area. Motivation to procure pump sets and use it for a second crop has been found to be inadequate. The beneficiaries are not able to make optimal utilisation of the wells because of lack of complementary facilities like lifting devices (pump sets) and power to energize.

Recently introduced changes in MWS

Some recently introduced changes in MWS are as follows:

- Strict compliance to ensure 2/3rd of MWS expenditure for the benefit of SCs/STs;
- Providing lifting device to the beneficiaries wherever needed under IRDP/SC/ST Finance Corporations etc.;

- Educating beneficiaries in improved farm practices through agricultural extension programmes;
- Active involvement of the Panchayati Raj Institutions in planning and selection of MWS beneficiaries. The village Panchayat has to select the beneficiaries which have to be then approved by the DRDA/ZPs;
- Reservation of 3% allocation for the year for disabled persons. This reservation would be horizontal reservation Le disabled persons belonging to SCs/STs and others would fall in their respective categories;
- Fixation of district-wise physical and financial targets from 1997-98 onwards which was not done earlier;
- Priority to be given to MWS beneficiaries under the horticulture development component of Employment Assurance Scheme.

Rural housing

Housing is one of the most serious challenges facing India's sociopolitical economy today, While food security has been largely achieved and clothing today is not a serious problem for the poor, shelter remains beyond the reach of millions in India even after 50 years of the country's independence. This is a matter not merely of deep concern but also a matter that requires immediate attention and urgent action. For a normal citizen, owning a house provides significant economic security and status in society. For shelterless persons, a house brings about a profound social change in their existence, endowing them with an identity, thus integrating them with their immediate social milieu.

Housing shortage

According to the 1991 Census, the rural housing shortage

was 13.72 million consisting of 3.41 million households without houses and 10.31 million living in unserviceable kutcha houses. It has also been estimated that another 10.75 million houses would be needed to cover the population growth during 1991-2002, at the rate of an annual growth of 0.89 million houselessness. Thus, a total of 24.47 million houses need to be constructed or upgraded to achieve the target of providing shelter to all in the rural areas by 2002 A.D. Of the above 24.47 million houses, 5.7 million houses have been added by various agencies until 31.3.1997. It is anticipated that around 6.17 million houses will be added by different agencies by 2002. Thus the housing shortage to be tackled is 12.60 million houses, of which 10.31 million houses need up-gradation and 2.29 million new houses will need to be constructed.

Indira Awaas Yojana

The Government of India Is implementing Indira Awaas Yojana (IAY) since the year 1985-86 with the objective of providing dwelling units free of cost to the members of Scheduled Castes, Scheduled Tribes and freed bonded labourers living below the poverty fine in rural areas. From the year 1993-94, its scope has been extended to cover non-scheduled castes and scheduled tribes rural poor subject to the condition that the benefits of the scheme have also been extended to families of servicemen of the armed and paramilitary forces killed in action. 3% of the houses are reserved for the below poverty line disabled persons living in rural areas.

IAY operates as a 100% subsidized centrally sponsored programme with the resources being shared on 80:20 basis between Centre and the States. Funds under the scheme allocated to the States/UTs are further distributed to the districts in proportion to the SC/ST population in the district.

The allotment of house under the scheme is done in the name of the female member of the beneficiary household. Alternatively, it can be allotted in the joint name of both the husband and wife. The beneficiaries are to be involved from the very beginning in construction work and, have to make their own arrangements for construction to suit their requirements. As far as possible houses are built in dusters so as to facilitate provision of common facilities. The permissible construction assistance per house is Rs.20,000 in plain areas and Rs.22,000 in hilly or difficult areas.

District Rural Development Agencies/Zilla Parishads on the basis of allocations made and targets fixed shall decide the number of houses to be constructed Panchayatwise under IAY during a particular financial year. The same is intimated to the Gram Panchayat. Thereafter, the Gram Sabha select the beneficiaries from the list of eligible households according to IAY guidelines and as per priorities fixed, restricting this number to the target allotted. No approval of the Panchayat Samiti is required. The Panchayat Samiti is however, sent a list of selected beneficiaries for their information.

The nutritional status of women and children in rural areas is a matter of concern. Most of the rural women and children belonging to families below poverty line are found to be suffering from various ailments related to malnutrition. It is, therefore, necessary to focus attention on the need for improvement in nutritional status of our rural population by encouraging the cultivation of fruits and vegetables which can be grown easily in the backyard of rural houses. Accordingly instructions have been issued to implementing agencies for popularising the production of fruits and vegetables at household level particularly in houses constructed under IAY.

The IAY is implemented through District Rural Development Agencies specially set up in each district of the country for the implementation of Rural Development Programmes or through Zilla Parishads. At the field level the Block machinery is entrusted with the responsibility for implementing the programme. At the village level the Gram Sabha is responsible for selection of beneficiaries.

Fuel efficient chullahs have been developed and are being manufactured at several places. The Department of Non-Conventional Energy Sources is encouraging installation of such chullahs. It is ensured that every house constructed under the Yojana is provided with the fuel efficient chullah.

Construction of sanitary latrines forms an integral part of IAY house. It has, however, been observed that in a large number of cases either the sanitary latrines in these houses are not constructed or if they are constructed, these are not put to proper use which is mainly due to the old habits of the people.

While fixing technical specifications, efforts are to be made to utilise to the maximum extent, local materials and low cost technology developed by various institutions. Technology using bricks, cement and steel on large scale is not to be encouraged. As far as possible, cement is substituted by lime and lime surkhi manufactured locally. Due to increase in price of bricks, it is considered desirable to substitute burnt bricks with sun dried bricks of earth-soil-cement. Bricks manufactured by the beneficiaries themselves instead of its purchase may also be undertaken for reduction of cost and better wage employment.

Programme performance

The IAY has proved to be a popular programme and targets have exceeded in almost every year since its inception. A total of around 48 lakh houses have been constructed from 1985-86 till date under the scheme.

During 1998-99 allocation under IAY is Rs. 1484 crores with a target of constructing 987022 houses under the scheme. An amount of Rs. 1004 crores has been released to various States/UTs upto November, 98 and about 354683 houses have been constructed with reported expenditure of around Rs.769.54 crores till date. Financial and Physical performance under IAY during the current year (up to November, 98).

Year	*Expenditure (Rs. In crore)*	*No. of houses built*
1985-86	57.93	51252
1986-87	149.18	160197
1987-88	235.37	169302
1988-89	149.65	139192
1989-90	188.50	186023
1990-91	213.07	181800
1991-92	263.01	207299
1992-93	238.84	192585
1993-94	481.00	372535
1994-95	500.38	390482
1995-96	1166.36	863889
1996-97	1385.92	806290
1997-98	1596.44	767649
1998-99*	769.54	354683
Total	7395.19	4843178

In addition to regular monitoring of the programme by the Ministry, the programme has been evaluated by the Programme Evaluation Organization of the Planning Commission which carried out a Quick Study of the IAY in 1992-93. According to the evaluation done by the Planning Commission, 86.4% of the houses constructed under the Yojana were occupied and lived in. Again about 84% of the households expressed satisfaction/ partial satisfaction with the houses given to them.

Organisation of training course/study tours

The Ministry of Rural Areas and Employment along with the Human Settlement Management Institute (HSMI) of Housing and Urban Development Corporation Ltd. (HUDCO) has organised two Training Programmes on "Rural Housing Project Formulation" of one week duration each in Hyderabad and Guwahati. The course is meant for middle level executive and professionals working in DRDAs, Zilla Parishads, Housing Boards, Financial Institutions, Planning and Development authorities, engineers, architects, NGOs etc. involved in implementation of rural housing and rural infira-structural development projects.

Besides, the Ministry of Rural Areas and Employment in coordination with Nirmithi National Institute of Habitat Management, Thiruvananthapuram organised a Study Tour to Kerala State Nirmithi Kendra (KESNIK) from 7th - 9th October, 1998 in order to sensitize the State Secretaries of Housing Heads of Housing Departments etc. about alternative cost, effective environment friendly technologies, materials and designs.

New initiatives

Government has recognized shelter as a basic human requirement which needs to be met on a priority basis. It has announced a National Housing and Habitat policy which aims at providing 'Housing for All' and to facilitate construction of 13 lakh additional housing units in rural areas annually with an emphasis on extending benefits to the poor and the deprived. An Action Plan for Rural Housing has accordingly been prepared. The Action Plan comprising of a series of recommendations for policy, Institutional and Schematic interventions has attempted to address the various issues related to Rural Housing in a holistic fashion and yet emerge with workable and practical interventions. Among the highlights of the Action Plan for the construction of 13 lakh additional houses in rural areas are:

Conversion of unserviceable Kutcha houses into semi-pucca/ Pucca houses

There are 103.1 lakh unserviceable kutcha houses requiring upgradation in the rural areas. It is therefore, proposed to convert unserviceable kutcha houses to semi-pucca/pucca houses under this scheme with an assistance of Rs. 10,000 per unit utilising the 20% of available funds for IAY. Conversion will necessarily include a provision of sanitary latrine and smokeless chullah.

Credit-cum-subsidy component of IAY

There are a large number of households in the rural areas who have not been covered under IAY, since they do not fall within the Below Poverty Line category. They also do not have high repayment capacity to take benefit of loan based programmes as offered by housing finance institutions. The needs of this large majority located just above the poverty line can be met through a sub-scheme of IAY, which is part credit and part subsidy based. The Finance Minister in his Budget Speech had also announced the credit-cum-subsidy scheme. Furthermore, the introduction of a part Credit and part Subsidy based sub-scheme would be an important step in the direction of redefining the role of Government from that of a 'provider' to a 'facilitator' as envisaged in the new National Housing and Habitat Policy, 1998. It is, therefore, proposed to initiate a Credit-cum-Subsidy component of IAY, which will be targeted to the group just above the poverty line having income limit of Rs. 32,000 annually. It is proposed that the upper ceiling limit of assistance will be restricted to assistance limit under Indira Awaas Yojana (presently Rs. 20,000 for plain areas and Rs. 22,000 for hilly/ difficult areas). The subsidy will be restricted to a maximum of 50% of IAY assistance limit.

Innovative stream for Rural housing and habitat development

Presently under IAY, it is left to the beneficiary to select building/ housing design technology and materials. In fact houses being built under IAY suffer from inadequacies such as the use of expensive materials, technology and design, lack of thermal comfort and the inability to withstand natural calamities. An important and collinear area of concern which needs to be tackled along with housing is the deteriorating habitat and non availability of quality infrastructure support services. In view of this, an Innovative Stream for Rural Housing and Habitat Development is proposed to be initiated.

Under this scheme it is proposed to provide financial assistance for efforts initiated on a project basis by organizations such as HUDCO/Building Material Technology Promotion Council (BMTPC)/Central Building Research Institute (CBRI)/NGOs etc.

Institutional mechanisms for improved shelter delivery

At present there are virtually no institutional structures available in the country to support rural housing initiatives, whether we consider housing finance or the areas of housing construction technology, designs or habitat. A series of initiatives are therefore being proposed to address these glaring inadequacies.

Setting up of Rural building centres.

The primary objectives of setting up of a building centre are:

i) Technology transfer and information dissemination

ii) Skill up-gradation through training and

iii) Production of cost effective and environment friendly material components

In other words, a building centre will be involved in transfer of technology from 'lab to land', production of cost effective building materials for sale and providing training to carpenters, masons, etc.

The Rural Building Centre Programme is proposed to be implemented through one or more agencies contributing to the rural housing/rural development programmes such as HUDCO, BMTPC or well known State organisations involved in setting up of such centres. These rural building Centres are intended to be located within the close reach of rural populations. It is proposed to provide one time grant for setting up of a building centre at the State of Rs. 5 lakhs.

National mission for rural housing

The National Housing and Habitat Policy, 1998 states: "At present the rural housing and to a large extent informal housing do not benefit from the outcome of research and development. Efforts will be made to disseminate information about new technologies and provide training to construction workers in the use of new technologies. In this regard a mission approach may be adopted." Adoption of a 'mission' approach will significantly alter the Rural Housing scenario, by enabling the induction of Science and Technology inputs on a continuous basis into the sector and providing convergence to technology, habitat and energy related issues. Moreover, this will sought to be achieved within a specified timeframe and through community intermediation. It is, therefore, proposed to set up a National Mission for Rural Housing.

Construction designs, materials and technologies are culturally rooted and region specific, these need to be documented/located with reference to past practice and accumulated knowledge systems and thereafter disseminated through a people centered, region specific information, education and communication strategy. Hence housing and habitat related problems would be dealt with through the coordinated effort of various agencies and local communities, within specified time frames and low cost, replicable solutions evolved. A threefold strategy of strengthening of supply lines for technologies, materials, awareness creation among the rural populace and improvement in skills of rural sector professionals will be its centrepiece. This will enable a qualitative improvement in both quality of construction techniques, habitats and in maintenance practices.

Setting up of rural housing and habitat development corporation

Presently the outreach of housing finance institutions in the rural areas is negligible. There is virtually no institutional finance going in for the creation of infrastructure support services in the rural areas. For instance, the definition adopted by the National Housing Bank for rural areas, enables it to extend loaning under the Golden jubilee Rural Housing Finance Scheme to residents of townships having population up to 50,000. It would be pertinent to mention that about 83% urban local bodies fall in this category.

To facilitate and coordinate the rural housing programme, through a multi-pronged approach of evolving strategies for extending the outreach of housing finance in the rural areas, sourcing of capital from both internal and external sources and the development of a menu approach for housing and habitat development, it is proposed to set up a Rural Housing and Habitat Development Corporation under the administrative control of the Ministry of Rural Areas and Employment. The setting up of a separate Rural Housing and Habitat Development Corporation dedicated to the cause of enabling the creation of quality and cost effective rural human settlements will go a long way in achieving the set goals of 'Housing for All'.

Special area development programmes

Drought Prone Areas Programme (DPAP) is one of the area devélopment programmes launched by the Government in 1973-74 to tackle the special problems faced by those fragile areas which are constantly affected by severe drought conditions. These areas are characterized by large human and cattle populations which are continuously putting heavy pressure on the already fragile natural resource base for food, fodder and fuel. This continuous biotic pressure is leading to fast and continuous depletion of vegetative cover, less and less rainfall, increasing soil erosion and fast receding ground water levels due to continuous exploitation without any effort to recharge the under ground acquifers.

Though the Programme created some positive impact in terms of creating durable 'public assets in the programme areas, the overall impact of the programme in effectively containing the adverse effects of drought was found to be not very encouraging. In addition, many of the programme States had also been demanding inclusion of additional areas under the programme. Keeping this in view a High Level Technical Committee under the Chairmanship of Prof. C.H. Hanumantha Rao, Ex-Member, Planning Commission critically reviewed the contents, methodology and implementation processes of all area development programmes and suggested suitable measures for improvement. Based on the recommendations of the Hanumantha Rao Committee, comprehensive Guidelines for Watershed Development commonly applicable to the DPAP, DDP IWDP, EAS (50% allocation in DPAP and DDP areas) were issued in October, 1994 which came into effect from 1995-96.

Objectives

The basic objective of the programme is to minimise the adverse effects of drought on production of crops and livestock and productivity of land, water and human resources ultimately leading to the drought proofing of the affected areas. The programme also aims to promote overall economic development and improving the socioeconomic conditions of the resource poor and disadvantaged sections inhabiting the programme areas.

Strategy

The common Guidelines for Watershed Development provide for a uniform strategy in the implementation of all area development programmes viz. DPAP, DDP IWDP and EAS. The main features of this strategy are:

- Area development programmes to be implemented exclusively on watershed basis.
- Programme activities to be confined to the identified watershed of about 500 hectares and are to be executed on a project basis spanning over a period of four years.
- Watershed project to cover a village, as far as possible.
- Elaborate institutional mechanisms at various levels clearly defined for effective participation of the local people and the Panchayati Raj institutions in all stages of project management.
- DRDA/ZP to be the nodal Government agency at the district level to act as a facilitator and provider of finances and technical assistance to the people's organizations executing the watershed projects.

Coverage

At present, DPAP is in operation in 947 blocks of 155 districts in 13 States. The corresponding physical area for treatment under the programme works out to approximately 7.45 lakh square kilometers. The States where DPAP is under implementation along with number of districts and blocks may be seen in the Table.

S.No.	Name of State	Districts	Blocks
1.	Andhra Pradesh	11	94
2.	Bihar	16	121
3.	Gujarat	10	52
4.	Himachal Pradesh	3	9
5.	Jammu & Kashmir	2	22
6.	Karnataka	11	81
7.	Madhya Pradesh	25	134
8.	Maharashtra	22	148
9.	Orissa	8	47
10.	Rajasthan	10	32
11.	Tamil Nadu	15	80
12.	Uttar Pradesh	18	91
13.	West Bengal	4	36
	Total	155	947

Funding pattern

The programme allocation is shared on 50:50 basis between the Centre and the State Governments. The cost norms adopted under DPAP for various ecosystems depending on the severity of the problem are as below :

S. No.	Ecosystem type	Per Ha. cost Average (Rs.)	Watershed project cost (Rs. In lakhs)
1.	Semi-Arid Region	4,000	20.00
2.	Dry-Sub-Humid Region	3,000	15.00
3.	Dry Sub-Humid (Hill) Region	4,000	20.00

Physical and financial performance

Under DPAP, 6454 Watershed Projects have been sanctioned in four different batches-two batches in 1995-96 and one batch in 1996-97 and 1997-98. Against this, 5956 Watershed Projects have so far been taken-up by the programme States and were under various stages of implementation during 1998-99. Table-2 shows the number of Watershed Projects sanctioned and taken up during the last four years since the introduction of the new Guidelines.

In addition, financial assistance of Rs.10 crores was provided to CAPART during 1997-98 for execution of 400 watershed projects through the voluntary sector. Against this provision, CAPART had so far sanctioned 41 watershed projects at a total cost of Rs. 183.50 lakhs and released Rs. 69.59 lakhs to the implementing agencies.

There are two districts, Doda and Udhampur, in Jammu and Kashmir where DPAP is being implemented. But the State does not figure in the above table as the Government of Jammu and Kashmir continues to follow the old Guidelines in the implementation of DPAP during 1998-99 also due to the disturbed conditions prevailing in these districts. The State is expected to operationalise the new watershed guidelines from the next financial year.

Desert development programme

Over the years, the increase in human and livestock population in desert areas has placed the natural resources of the region under great stress. The major problems are continuous depletion of vegetative cover, increase in soil erosion and fall in ground water table. All these factors account for diminishing productivity of land and loss of natural resources.

The problems would have been worse but for the introduction of some specific highly focused area development programmes in these areas. On the recommendations of the National Commission on Agriculture in it's Interim Report (1974) and Final Report (1976), the Desert Development Programme (DDP) was started in the year 1977-78. The programme was started both in the hot desert areas of Rajasthan, Gujarat and Haryana, and the cold desert areas of Jammu & Kashmir and Himachal Pradesh. The objective of the programme has been to mitigate adverse effects of desertification and adverse climatic conditions on crops, human and livestock population, combating desertification and restoring ecological balance of the area.

In hot sandy desert areas, sand dune stabilization and shelter belt plantations were given greater weightage. On the other hand, in cold desert areas, since rainfall is negligible, crop cultivation and afforestation could be taken up only through assured irrigation. In these areas, the main activity was water resources development by construction of channels for diversion of water flow from the glacier and springs to the fields and lift irrigation works in the valleys.

Though the Programme created good impact in the areas treated, overall impact in the identified areas in the country was not very encouraging. Some State Governments had also been requesting this Ministry for inclusion of additional areas under the programme. With a view to identifying the infirmities in the programme and also to consider the cases for inclusion of additional areas, a Technical Committee on the DPAP and the DDP was constituted in 1993-94 under the Chairmanship of Prof. C.H. Hanumantha Rao, Ex-Member, Planning Commission. The Committee submitted its Report in April, 1994.

The main reasons identified by the Committee for the far from satisfactory results under the programme was that area development was not taken up on watershed basis and the involvement of the local people both in planning and execution of the programme was virtually nonexistent. Besides inadequacy of funds, non-availability of trained personnel and taking up of too many activities, which were neither properly integrated nor necessarily related to the objectives of the programme, were also identified as contributory factors towards reducing the impact of the programme.

Based on the recommendations of the Committee, new districts/blocks were included under DDP and a fresh set of Guidelines for Watershed Development applicable to DPAP, DDP, IWDP and EAS (50%) were issued in October, 1994. These Guidelines were made applicable from the year 1995-96.

Objectives

In a broad sense, the objectives of the programme are to promote the economic development of village community, restore ecological balance and improve the economic conditions of resource poor and disadvantaged section of society through creation, widening and equitable distribution of resources and increased employment opportunities. DDP has been envisaged as an essentially land-based activity and conceived as a long-term measure for restoration of ecological balance by conserving, developing and harnessing land, water, livestock and human resources. Objectives of the programme have been recast as under :-

- Combating drought and desertification.
- Encouraging restoration of ecological balance.
- Mitigating the adverse effects of drought and adverse edapho-climatic conditions on crops and livestock, and productivity of land, water and human resources.
- Improving socioeconomic conditions of the resource poor and disadvantaged sections of village community viz. assetless and women.

Strategy

Although the DDP has been under implementation in several areas, its impact had been felt only in the areas actually treated by core activities. Growing population and poverty compounded the problem by increasing pressure on fragile ecosystems. On the basis of lessons learnt, the major elements of new strategy are :-

- Area development under the programme will be on watershed basis only and a watershed project of about 500 hectares would be the field unit for implementation and it will be developed in four years.
- The strategy adopted to achieve these objectives involved development of the programme area on watershed basis. However, in some sandy areas where it is not physically feasible to demarcate a watershed, programme is to be implemented by adopting either a cluster of village or an Index Catchment as the unit of planning.
- There would be direct participation of the local people in planning and development of watersheds and maintenance of assets after the project is completed through Watershed Association (WA) comprising of all adults residing within watershed project area and its executive body named as Watershed Committee (WC).
- The Zilla Parishads, Panchayat Samitis and Gram Panchayats have the right to monitor and review the programme at district, blocks and village levels. The Panchayati Raj Institutions can also function as Project Implementation Agencies (PIA) if they so desire.
- Similarly, in the new system of programme implementation a voluntary agency can be selected as a Project Implementation Agency by the DRDA/ Zilla Parishad. The voluntary agencies have an effective role particularly in motivating people, community organizations and training.

- Keeping in view the problem of sand dune stabilization in 10 districts of Rajasthan, 50% of funds under DDP for implementation of watershed projects allocated to each concerned district, has been permitted for three activities namely; sand dune stabilization, shelter belt creation and afforestation.

Coverage

Under DDP 227 blocks of 36 districts having an area of 457,432 sq.kms. in 7 States are covered. The States where DDP is under implementation are Andhra Pradesh, Gujarat, Haryana, Himachal Pradesh, Jammu and Kashmir, Karnataka and Rajasthan.

Number of districts and blocks covered under DDP

S.N.	*Name of the State*	*District*	*Blocks*
1.	Andhra Pradesh	1	16
2.	Gujarat	6	47
3.	Haryana	6	44
4.	Himachal Pradesh	2	3
5.	Jammu & Kashmir	2	10,
6.	Karnataka	3	22
7.	Rajasthan	16	85
	Total	36	227

Guidelines for watershed development

Main features of new Guidelines for Watershed Development are :

- At the district level the District Rural Development Agency/Zilla Parishad will be in overall charge of implementation of the programme. The DRDA/ZP will be advised in regard to selection of Project Implementation Agencies (PIAs), approval of Watershed Plans, training, publicity etc., by a district level Watershed Development Advisory Committee under the chairmanship of Project Director, DRDA/CEO, ZP.

- The DRDA/ZP will select the PIAs which could be besides DRDA/ZP itself, other line departments, autonomous organizations, public sector undertakings, voluntary organizations, cooperatives, banks, etc. The PIA will remain in-charge of implementation of the Watershed Projects (WPs). A multi-disciplinary team designated as Watershed Development Team (WDT) shall assist each PIA in the implementation of these WPs.
- Planning and implementation of the Watershed Project will be done with the technical support of multi-disciplinary Watershed Development Team by the WA comprising all adult members of the village(s) in the watershed area. 75% of the project fund will be spent directly by the Watershed Association on the development works of each project.
- The Watershed Committee comprising of 10- 2 nominated members by the Watershed Association from amongst the user groups, self-help groups, with representation from Gram Panchayat, Watershed Development Team, women, Scheduled Castes, and Scheduled Tribes will be the executive body of the Watershed Association.
- As per Guidelines for Watershed Development issued by this Ministry, 10% of the total project cost is earmarked for administrative expenditure, 5% for community organization works, another 5% for training to people associated with the implementation of Watershed Projects and 80% for works.
- As regards the Panchayati Raj Institutions (PRIs), the Zilla Parishad at the district level may remain

overall in-charge of implementation. The Panchayat Samiti and Gram Panchayat will have the right to monitor and review the implementation of programme and can take the responsibility of implementing the projects as PIAs.

The Guidelines also provide for an elaborate institutional arrangement at the, Centre for monitoring, review and policy making, at the State level for monitoring and review of programmes and at the district level for selecting Watershed Projects and Project Implementation Agencies, monitoring and review of the implementation of the programme.

Problem of inadequacy of funds has been tackled by allowing utilization of 50% of the Employment Assurance Scheme (EAS) funds for the development of watersheds. Training has been made a continuous process and 5% of the funds of each project has been earmarked for training of the WDT members, field functionaries and the local people. There is an inbuilt provision in the guidelines for maintenance of assets created under the watershed development projects.

People's participation

The guidelines for Watershed Development issued by this Ministry is an instrument, which provides an opportunity to local people to not only involve themselves in the implementation of the programme but is a tool for capacity building and empowerment of participating village community.

The critical key factor in the implementation is people's participation in all aspects of the programme. It has been envisaged under the Guidelines that the local people through User Groups and Self-help Groups formed by the Watershed Association shall execute the whole work of Watershed Development Projects. Under the new Guidelines, area development on watershed basis has been made mandatory. To ensure people's participation, an elaborate institutional mechanism at various levels has been prescribed which include the formation of Watershed Association and a Watershed Committee for each watershed project. Watershed Association comprises of all adults residing within a watershed project area. Watershed Committee is the executive body of the Watershed Association constituted by it by nominating 10-12 members from amongst the Self-help Groups (3-4), User Groups (45), Gram Panchayat (2-3) and a member of the Watershed Development Team (WDT). This Committee has been made responsible for planning and development of Watershed Projects with the technical assistance from the Project Implementation Agency.

PIA provides technical input through a Watershed Development Team having four experts in the disciplines of Animal Sciences, Plant Sciences, Civil/ Agricultural Engineering and Social Sciences.

Role of Panchayati Raj institutions

Panchayati Raj Institution have been assigned very active role at the district, block and village levels in the programme. The State Governments have been authorized to empower the Zilla Parishads to discharge all functions of the District Rural Development Agencies (DRDAs) for planning and development of the watershed projects. In that capacity, the Zilla Parishad will select the Watershed Projects and the Project Implementation Agencies, approve Watershed Plans, release funds to the PIAs and the Watershed Committees and monitor and review the implementation of the programme.

The Panchayat Samitis have been given the right to monitor the implementation of the programme at the block level and give guidance for integration of other area development programmes. At the village level, the Gram Panchayat is to be fully involved in mobilizing the community, training, dovetailing of other programmes and maintenance of common property resources such as pasture lands, fisheries tanks, plantation etc. The Gram Panchayat has been entrusted with the task of monitoring the implementation of the programme.

In addition to the above mentioned functions, the Panchayati Raj Institutions are also entitled to take on the responsibility of planning and development of a cluster of watershed projects. In the capacity of a Project Implementation Agency, the Zilla Parishad/ Panchayat Samiti/Gram Panchayat concerned shall be subjected to the complete discipline and control of DRDA as any other PIA.

Finding pattern

The DDP is a Centrally Sponsored Programme and funds are released to DRDAs/ZPs for implementation of the programme. The Central share under each type of project area based on the ecosystem type is as under :-

S.No.	*Type of ecosystem*	*Central share*
1.	Hot arid (non-aandy) areas	75%
2.	Hot arid (sandy) areas	100%
3.	Cold arid areas	100%

The State-wise number of Watershed Projects to be taken up has been arrived at on the basis of the following criteria fixed at block level.

Area of block (Sq.kms.)	*No. of WPs to be taken up*	*Block allocation (Rs. in lakhs)*
Upto 400	3	16.86
401-800	5	28.10
Above 800	6	22.72

In different ecosystems, project cost has been fixed according to the severity of the problems. At present the following rates are applicable in different areas:-

S. No.	Ecosystem Type	Per ha. cost (Rs.) Average	Watershed project cost (Rs. in lakhs)
1.	Hot sandy aricl region	5,000	25.00
2.	Hot arid region	4,500	22.50
3.	Cold arid region	5,000	25.00

Achievements

Under DDP, a number of projects have been targeted and sanctioned for implementation in identified areas. All these projects are envisaged to be completed in a 4-year period and are at different stages of implementation.

The year 1995-96 was the first year of implementation under the new Guidelines for Watershed Development. A considerable amount of time was therefore, spent on preparatory works, making institutional arrangement viz. selection of watersheds and PIAs, imparting training, community organizations and planning before commencement of actual works. This led to slow down in expenditure. The details of budgetary provision and expenditure incurred during in the last three years are given below :-

(Rs. in lakhs)

Year	Budget	Release
1994-95	8,400.00	8,459.55
1995-96	10,000.00	10,100.00
1996-97	65,00.00	6,536.38
1997-98	7,000.00	7,000.00

Since inception till 1994-95 as core sector activities, 1.85 lakh ha. under land resource development, 0.83 lakh ha. under water resource development and 2.85 lakh ha. under afforestation and pasture development have been developed. Since inception till 31st March' 1998, a total sum of Rs.845 crores has been spent on the programme. In 1997-98, a sum of Rs.70 crores was released to different DRDAs/ZPs. During 1998-99, a provision of Rs. 90 crores has been made. In the Ninth Five Year Plan (1997-2002), a sum of Rs. 1,430 crores has been proposed.

6

SELF-EMPLOYMENT AND DEVELOPMENT PROGRAMMES

Integrated rural development programme

Poverty eradication has been one of the major objectives of planned development. The strategy and policy of direct attack on poverty by way of target approach for rural poor came into being in the Fourth Five Year Plan. With the main objective of improving the asset base of the poor and to involve the poor in the production/income generation processes of the economy, Integrated Rural Development Programme (IRDP) was initiated. IRDP was taken up initially in 2300 blocks and has been extended to all the blocks of the country since 2nd October, 1980.

Programme implementation

Programme

IRDP aims at providing income generating assets and self-employment opportunities for the rural poor. Assistance under IRDP is given to a target group of rural poor belonging to families Below Poverty Line (BPL), in the form of subsidy by the Government and term credit by financial institutions.

Criteria for allocation of funds to the states

Allocation of funds to States is being made by the Central Government in proportion to the poverty levels in each State on the basis of official estimates of the Planning Commission. These official estimates of poverty are arrived at by the Planning Commission based on the National Sample Survey Organisation Consumer Expenditure Surveys conducted every five years.

Devolution of funds to districts is based on a formula evolved by the respective State Government. Further devolution to the Blocks is done by the Governing Body of the DRDA based on the criteria approved by it.

Target group

The target group consists of families of small and marginal farmers, agricultural labourers and rural artisans etc. whose per capita monthly expenditure does not exceed the poverty line (ranging between Rs. 216.65 and Rs. 327.48 for different States/UTs) as estimated by the Planning Commission. Currently, the Below Poverty Line census is being carried out in all the States and the revised poverty line will be used to categorise BPL families. Within the target group, special safeguards have been provided by reservation of

- 50% benefits for SCs/STs,
- 40% for women and
- 3% for physically handicapped persons.
- Priority is also to be given to women headed households, assignees, of surplus land, freed bonded labourers and acceptors of small family norm. However, this should not in any way adversely affect the safeguards provided for SCs/STs, women and physically handicapped persons.

- The flow of financial assistance (subsidy + credit) to the categories described above should be commensurate with the percentage of the physical coverage.

Pattern of subsidy

The pattern of subsidy is

- 25% for small farmers;
- 33 1/3% for marginal farmers, agricultural labourers, and rural artisans; and
- 50% for SCs/STs beneficiaries and physically handicapped persons.

The ceiling on subsidy in respect of individuals is

- Rs. 4000 in normal areas;
- Rs. 5000 in DPAP/DDP areas;
- Rs. 6000 for SC/ST families and physically handicapped persons;
- Rs. 7,500 or 50% of the project cost, whichever is less for unemployed educated youth; and
- For activities involving at least 5 persons, the ceiling has been fixed at Rs.1.25 lakhs or 50% of the project cost, whichever is less.

Implementing agency

District Rural Development Agency/Zilla Parishad is the implementing agency for this programme. The Governing Body at the district level provides guidance and directions to DRDAs. It includes local MPs, MLAs, and Chairman of Zilla Parishad, Heads of District Development Departments and representatives of SCs/STs, women and NGOs. At the grassroots level, the programme is carried out by Block Development Officer, and the other block staff with the help of the village level functionaries.

Funding pattern and release of funds

IRDP is financed on a 50:50 cost-sharing basis by the Centre as well as by the States. The funds are released directly to the DRDAs.

BPL census and selection of beneficiaries

In order to target assistance to poor families, a BPL census is conducted at the beginning of each Plan period by the States, at the behest of Ministry of Rural Areas and Employment. The Gram Sabha is involved in the identification and selection of beneficiaries under IRDP from the initial stage itself. After the survey/census is completed, the same is verified in the Gram Sabha and once it is approved, such a list is drawn up. The same is sent to the Panchayat Samitis/blocks and DRDAs for record.

Identification of thrust areas and selection of projects for beneficiaries

The project profiles to be taken up for beneficiaries, take into account the beneficiary's needs and aptitudes and the local resource endowment. The investment target for the year, the choice of the BPL family for the activity, forward and backward linkages and infrastructural support, etc. are also taken into account while making a project profile. The activities can be taken up in Primary sectors, Secondary sectors and Tertiary sectors.

District credit plans

The District Credit Plan and the Annual Action Plan are formulated by the Lead banks according to the guidelines issued by Reserve Bank of India (RBI) from time to time. The District Credit Plans are prepared normally for a period of three to five years. Action plans are prepared for each year. While preparing the District Credit Plans, the targets laid down by Government of India and RBI with regard to the share of lending to the priority sectors, weaker sections, small scale industries etc. are to be kept in view. It is also ensured by the DRDAs that the Annual Plans prepared by them for IRDP are integrated into the District Credit Plans and Annual Action Plan prepared by the Lead banks so that necessary credit support for IRDP is made available.

Credit target

At the beginning of the year target for credit for IRDP at the all-India level as well as at the State level are fixed. This is done in consultation with the RBI, NABARD and the participating banks. Credit should normally flow in the ratio 2:1 to subsidy. However, the effort is to see that credit-subsidy ratio exceed 2: 1. The ceiling limit for collateral free loans is Rs. 50,000.

Acquisition of assets and cash disbursement scheme

The assets procured should be of standard quality, at economic prices and to the satisfaction of the beneficiary. Beneficiaries under IRDP are generally given assets and not the cash. However, sometimes the quality or the price is not to the satisfaction of beneficiaries. It provides greater freedom to the beneficiaries for the purchase of quality assets and to minimize the leakage in its disbursement if the assistance is given to the beneficiary in cash. Experience has shown that reliance can be placed on the good sense of the beneficiaries in purchasing of assets subject to some safeguards.

Disbursement of money in cash to a beneficiary improves his/her bargaining power and has the added advantage of reducing delays and other malpractices prevalent in disbursement in kind. Hence, with effect from the year 1991-92 it was decided to permit disbursement of assistance in cash under the Cash Disbursement Scheme with a view to giving greater choice to beneficiaries in purchasing assets. Initially it was implemented in 50% of the blocks. With effect from the year 1996-97, it is extended to all the blocks of the country.

Release of subsidy (back-end subsidy)

Earlier, simultaneously with the disbursement of loan by the bank, the subsidy amount was debited from the DRDA account and credited to the account of the beneficiaries. Thus in effect, the beneficiary was burdened only with the bank credit portion. This adjustment of subsidy at the beginning itself was termed as Front-End subsidy. It was, however, found that the beneficiaries were repaying the loan immediately, thereby availing of amount of the subsidy. This in effect meant misuse of subsidy. To make beneficiary utilise the loan for sustainable income generation, the system of Front-End subsidy has been replaced by the Back-End subsidy.

The subsidy would be adjusted only in the last few instillments. At the same time a lock-in period for subsidy has also been stipulated and the subsidy would be adjusted only in the last few installments and it will not be allowed in the event of the repayment made before the stipulated lock-in period. The loan document would be taken by the bank for the full project cost and it would be inter-alia stipulated that in case of misutilisation of the loan, the entire amount of subsidy would be forfeited. Such forfeited amount of subsidy will be available to the bank for adjustment against the borrower's dues.

Family credit plan

A new project of Family Credit Plan (FCP) has been launched in the year 1994-95. It is in operation in 316 selected districts. Under this scheme, more than a single member of the family can be given assistance, subject to the normal subsidy limits for the family. The banks mobilize higher credit for families selected under this scheme. The current levels of investment under FCP have crossed Rs. 26,110 at the all-India level.

Monitoring and supervision

IRDP is being monitored from the Central level down to grassroots level. At the State level, a State Level Coordination Committee (SLCC) monitors the programme. At the Central level, the Central Level Coordination Committee (CLCC) monitors and reviews the implementation of the scheme and lays down policy guidelines. A High Level Coordination Committee on credit support to IRDP also functions at the Central level to monitor and review all aspects relating to credit linkage for IRDP.

The progress under IRDP is being monitored on a monthly, quarterly, half yearly and annual basis through reports and returns submitted by DRDAs/States. The shortfall, if any, in the performance under IRDP has been brought from time to time to the notice of all concerned States/UTs for corrective measures. Over and above, the implementation of the Programme is monitored through the annual Project Directors' Workshop and periodic meetings with the State Secretaries. At the Block/DRDA level monitoring is done through field visits and physical verification of assets for which an inspection schedule for the district and block functionaries has been laid down.

Programme support

Absence of linkages has long been identified to be one of the important reasons for lack of sustainability of IRDP schemes. IRDP infrastructure funds are spent for filling critical gaps in infrastructure requirements and to enable IRDP beneficiaries full utilisation of their assets. Marketing linkages/infrastructure are given priority.

Recognizing that infrastructural gaps often lead to difficulties in sustaining IRDP projects, the sanctioning powers for infrastructural projects were considerably decentralised with effect from 1994-95. Currently, projects upto Rs. 10 lakhs can be sanctioned with the approval of the Governing Body of the DRDA and upto Rs. 25 lakhs with the approval of the Divisional Commissioner or Secretary, Rural Development at the State level. Only infrastructural projects beyond Rs. 25 lakhs need to be approved by the State Level Sanctioning Committee. Similarly, the ceiling on permissible expenditure on infrastructure has been raised to 20% from the present level of 10%. For States in the North-Eastern region, including, Sikkim, this has been enhanced to 25%.

Institutional Arrangement For Credit Financing

High level committee at central level

A High Level Committee on Credit (HLCC) for IRDP, headed by the Secretary, Department of Rural Employment and Poverty Alleviation, Government of India and including senior representatives from the Government of India, State Governments, Commercial Banks, NABARD and RBI has been constituted to consider the various problems arising from time to time in the course of implementation of the programme and review the credit arrangements to recommend changes and improvements as and when necessary. This Committee meets regularly.

State level bankers' committee

State Level Bankers' Committees (SLBCs) have been set up for inter-institutional coordination and joint implementation of development programmes. The meetings of this committee are convened by the designated convenor bank (which is usually the bank with substantial lead responsibility in the State). The agenda items discussed by SLBC relate mainly to branch expansion, implementation of Annual Action Plan/ District Credit Plans, support from government agencies, inter-bank differences, problems raised at District Consultative Committee which require attention at State level etc.

District level consultative committee

At the District Level a District Level Consultative Committee (DLCC) has been constituted under the Chairmanship of the District Collector. All the banks and the District level officers of the Government, NABARD, DRDA and DIC are represented on this Committee. This forum should be utilised for allocating share of Credit disbursement to various banks, monitoring and reviewing the overall progress in physical and financial terms, ironing out inter-agency differences and to prepare items for consideration of State Level Committee.

Block level consultative committee

The Block Level Consultative Committee (BLCC) has been constituted at the block level under the chairmanship of the Sub-Divisional Officer. Meetings are to be attended by Block Development Officer, Branch Managers of all commercial banks and Chairman/ Secretary of the Primary Land Development Bank, District, Tehsildar and APO (Credit). The project officer DRDA, the Lead Bank Officer and the Lead District Officer may attend the meetings as special invitees.

Block level bankers' committee

Under Service Area Approach, a Block Level Bankers Committee (BLBC) is to be constituted in each block. All the banks operating in the Block including the District Central Cooperative Bank and RRB are members of the committee. The BDO and other technical officers in the Block such as Extension Officers for agriculture, industries and cooperatives will also be its members. The Chairman of the committee will be the Lead Bank Officer. Lead Bank Officer will also be the convenor.

Risk fund for consumption credit

To meet the small consumption needs of weaker sections of society, a scheme of Risk Fund for Consumption Credit has been in operation as a non-Plan scheme since 1977-78. The scheme is intended to enable Commercial banks, Cooperative banks and Regional Rural Banks to provide consumption loans, not exceeding Rs. 1000 per borrower to weaker sections of society.

Insurance cover for various assets

Insurance Cover is available for livestock assets given under the programme. The General Insurance Corporation provides this cover on certain terms and conditions.

Performance During the Eighth and Ninth Plan

During the Eighth Five Year Plan, more than 108 lakh families have been assisted. There has been a shift of emphasis from mere coverage of families to qualitative aspects of the programme through enhancement of the average level of per family investment. Credit targets have been fixed from 1995-96 onwards. As a result of these interventions, the average level of investment per family which was Rs. 7889 at the beginning of the Eighth Plan period rose to more than Rs. 14,950 during 1996-97 and further increased to Rs. 17,771 during the current year.

Performance during 1997-98

During 1997-98, total allocation was Rs. 1133.51 crores against which Rs. 1109.54 crores have been utilized. The Ministry has fixed a credit target totalling Rs. 2,700 crores for the programme of which Rs. 1996.64 crores have been mobilized during the year. A total of more than 17.07 lakh families have been covered during this period of which SC/ST account for 46.40% and women 34.33% of total coverage. The lower coverage of families is due to a shift of emphasis to qualitative aspects of the programme such as enhancement of average level of investment per family.

Strategy

The basic unit under DWCRA is a group of 10- 15 poor women who have come together to help each other in order to use their collective strength to break social bonds that have denied them income generating and self-fulfilling opportunities. The group size may be smaller in difficult terrain and far-flung areas. One woman amongst the members functions as the group organiser who helps in the choice of activity, procurement of raw-material, marketing of products. Before undertaking the activities women are made aware of the objectives and benefits of group formation under the scheme; understanding their potential and recognising their strength. At the operational level inputs/coaching for such an exercise by the group is given by Gram Sevika for a period of two years, who not only creates a group but also nurtures the group and orients them in availing of benefits of various other programmes/schemes.

Implementing agency and staffing pattern

DWCRA is being implemented by the District Rural Development Agencies. To facilitate the implementation of the scheme, one post of Assistant Project Officer (Woman) has been sanctioned to be part of the DRDA team. One additional post of Gram Sevika has also been sanctioned at the block level to look after the activities of the groups. This is in addition to the two Gram Sevikas in the normal Block pattern.

The Assistant Project Officer (APO), the additional Gram Sevika along with two Gram Sevikas and Mukhya Sevika already available with the CD Block form a team to help in the implementation of DWCRA. They conduct preliminary surveys of the area, and establish contacts with the rural women, identifying their constraints and needs. The team is responsible for monitoring and follow up.

The APO is to help in establishing contacts with different agencies, in moblization of resources and training facilities, marketing of the products of the DWCRA groups and also to look after the day to day administration of the scheme within the DRDA. Implementation of DWCRA is the overall responsibility of the entire DRDA team headed by the Project Officer or Project Director.

Community based convergent services

The Community Based Convergent Services (CBCS), as a component of DWCRA was started in 1991 in a few districts of the country as a pilot programme. The objective was to create greater awareness among the village communities to enable them to demand social services provided by the State in a better manner and also share responsibilities in the management and implementation of these services, thus leading to sustainable development.

Traditional methods like visuals, role play, folk art, puppetry dance and drama etc. are some of the means employed for sensitizing the community to the basic needs. The programme seeks to strengthen existing organizations of rural poor women, encourage women's groups to articulate their felt needs, raise the level of social consciousness, orient the community and formal community organization towards DWCRA and thereby improve the social and economic status of women. The programmes of ICDS, Rajiv Gandhi National Drinking Water Mission, National Literacy Mission are some of the programmes which are sought to be converged at the grassroots level. 298 districts have been covered so far under the scheme of Community Based Convergent Services (CBCS) with cent per cent Central assistance at Rs.5.00 lakhs per district.

Child care activities

Child Care Activities (CCA) has been incorporated in DWCRA programme during 1995-96 with the following objectives :-

- To provide creche services for children of working DWCRA women.
- Setting up of literacy centres for DWCRA women with specific emphasis on girl child dropouts and illiterate members of the DWCRA groups.
- Filling up critical gaps in the areas of immunization, nutrition etc. for the children of DWCRA members with special focus and emphasis on the girl child to reduce gender disparities in the infant girl child care.
- To provide some relief to the physically handicapped children of DWCRA members.
- To provide immediate relief and pay for legal assistance in case of redressal of physical abuse of the girl child.

Children below 6 years are the target group under Child Care Activities. Each DRDA is to receive Rs. 1.50 lakhs (Rs. 1.00 lakh as Central Share and Rs.50,000 as State Share) for Child Care Activities.

Funding pattern

Each DWCRA group gets Rs.25,000 as Revolving Fund to meet capital expenditure requirement of economic activities. Expenditure on revolving fund was being shared equally by the Central Government, State Government and UNICEF till 1994-95. UNICEF assistance was not available from 1.1.96. The Revolving Fund has been increased from Rs. 15,000 to Rs.25,000 from 1995-96. Presently, the expenditure for Revolving Fund is being shared by the Centre and State on 50:50 basis.

Marketing of products

Since the focal point of the scheme is income-generating activities for women, it is necessary that their activities must be economically viable. Marketing of products of the women's group is, therefore, very important. The interest of women in the programme can be sustained only when a proper market outlet is available for their products. Some State Governments like Haryana, Andhra Pradesh have issued orders declaring the DWCRA groups as approved sources for the supply of bulk articles required by the Government Departments.

The Gram Shree Melas organised by CAPART are also used as outlets for the sale of DWCRA products. Setting up of supportive institutions for marketing like District Supply and Marketing Societies (DSMS) are being encouraged by the States. These district level agencies must be multifaceted and also support non-credit inputs like purchase of raw materials and sale of goods where sectoral linkages cannot be established. Recently, efforts are also on at state level to create market for the products manufactured under DWCRA/ Integrated Rural Development Programme.

The State of Kerala and Orissa have created State Level organizations like KERAMS and ORAMS. The State of Andhra Pradesh is encouraging organization and melas. A DWCRA Mela was organised, with the State Government support at Hyderabad which has reported very good response. The State of Haryana encourages

DWCRA groups for supply of nutrition providers for ICDS programme. The momentum has to be sustained if the money invested through DWCRA groups has to receive significant returns. A wide range of DWCRA products need improvement in designing and packaging. Such improvements need to be carried out by involving professional bodies. The supply of raw material and its quality, quality control of finished products is an area of concern.

Allocation and release of funds under DWCRA for the year 1998-99

The BE for the programmes is Rs. 100 crores. Central allocation has been made to assist 61850 groups. Accordingly, an amount of Rs.77.97 crores has been allocated for Income Generating Activities. By the end of December, 1998, an amount of Rs.31.9053 crores has been released to 401 districts as first instalment and an amount of Rs.5.7273 crores to 60 districts as second instalment as per each DRDA fulfilling eligibility conditions such as submission of audit reports, utilization certificate and certain minimum percentage of expenditure against available funds with them. Thus a total of Rs.37.6286 crores has been released for Income Generating Activities during the year 1998-99 by the end of December, 1998.

Similarly an amount of Rs. 1.4 crores was released for CCA to those DRDAs who have submitted statements of expenditure for the funds released earlier. An amount of Rs. 1 crore has been released to CAPART to support NCO activities.

Coverage

Initially no specific coverage of vulnerable groups such as SC/STs was fixed. However, during the year 1997-98, it has been made compulsory that 50% of the groups have to be women belonging to SC/ST. Priority has to be given to physically handicapped persons and also girls and women rehabilitated from prostitution. The coverage achieved during each plan period is shown as below :

Training of Rural Youth For Self-Employment

Started as a Centrally sponsored scheme on 15th August, 1979, Training of Rural Youth for Self-Employment (TRYSEM) aims at providing basic technical and entrepreneurial skills to the rural youth from families below the poverty line to enable them to take up self employment in the broad fields of agriculture and allied sectors, industries, services and business activities. This objective was subsequently enlarged in the year 1983 to include taking up of wage employment also to the trained youth. TRYSEM plays an important role in facilitating diversification of activities taken up under IRDR Diversification away from the primary sector to secondary and tertiary sectors requires acquisition or upgradation of skills relevant to industries and business enterprises. TRYSEM seeks to impart new skills and upgrade existing skills of beneficiaries who are by and large attuned only to stagnant levels of agricultural or artisan skills.

Salient features

The rural youth in the age group of 18-35 years from families below poverty line are enlisted for training under the scheme. The minimum age for providing training under TRYSEM is relaxed to 46 years for inmates of orphanages in rural areas. The upper age limit of 35 years is relaxed to 45 years in case of widows, freed bonded labourers, freed convicts, persons displaced due to large development projects and cured leprosy patients. There is no age limit for rural artisans. A minimum of 50% of selected youths should belong to the Scheduled Caste and Scheduled Tribe communities, 40% should be women and 3% of the trainees should be physically handicapped persons.

The duration of training courses is normally six months. However, the State Level Co-ordination Committee (SLCC) can change the duration and prescribe duration for new trades. There are no educational qualifications prescribed for selection of trainees.

The TRYSEM trainees are paid a stipend varying from Rs. 200 to Rs. 500 per month during the training. To enable the participants to take up employment there is a provision of Rs. 800 as an allowance for purchase of toolkits by the trainees.

Pattern of assistance

The share of the Centre and States is on 50:50 basis. In case of UTs the funding is 100% by the Centre. The assistance is released to the DRDAs in two instalments.

Non recurring expenses for TRYSEM training infrastructure

The assistance to the State Government is on 50:50 basis and the Central share is limited to Rs. 20 lakhs per Exclusive TRYSEM Training Centre (ETTC) or 50% of the total cost of the centre whichever is less. The funds are released directly to the State Governments.

Performance during the eighth five year plan

During the Eighth Plan Period (1992-93 to 1996-97) total releases by the Centre and State Governments were Rs. 353.94 crores out of which Rs. 365.80 crores have been utilised which is 103.35%. During the same period against the target of 16.12 lakhs rural youth, 15.17 lakhs youth have been trained which is 94.10%. Details are given below :

Performance during 1998-99

Total allocation under the scheme of TRYSEM (Recurring

Expenses) during 1998-99 is Rs. 89.76 crores out of which Rs. 45.00 crores, is the central allocation. As per the reports received from the States/UTs 0.66 lakh rural youth have been trained upto November, 98. Details are given in the Annexure-XII and XIII. No funds under TRYSEM (infrastructure) have been released during 199899 up to December 1998.

Monitoring and supervision

At the State level a sub-Committee of the SLCC, is constituted exclusively for TRYSEM. An official of the rank of Project Director (DRDA), designated as Director (TRYSEM) functions at the State Headquarters as part of IRDP monitoring cell. At the District level there is TRYSEM Committee under the Chairmanship of the Chairman of the DRDA. Regular monthly monitoring is done by the Ministry of Rural Areas and Employment. Area Officers nominated for various States by this Ministry also regularly inspect the implementation of the scheme in the field during their visits to the States.

Steps for strengthening the scheme of TRYSEM

1. The stipend rates, honorarium and other allowances etc. under the TRYSEM Recurring expenses have been enhanced appreciably from I June 1994 with a view to make the training more effective and meaningful.
2. States and Union Territories have been asked to set up a subcommittee under the SLCC exclusively for TRYSEM. A District Level Committee exclusively for TRYSEM already exists.
3. The State/Union Territories have been advised to explore the possibilities of setting up of production groups from amongst TRYSEM trainees for undertaking the ancillary activities like manufacture and assembly of modern items of production.

4. A scheme regarding setting up of Exclusive TRYSEM Training Centres in each block, where no organised training facility exists, to strengthen training infrastructure under TRYSEM for imparting training to the rural youth in different traditional trades has been introduced.

Linkage with IRDP

The linkage forged between TRYSEM and IRDP has so far been weak. The fourth round of IRDP Concurrent Evaluation revealed that only 3.88% of IRDP beneficiaries received training under TRYSEM. The findings of the 'Quick Evaluation of TRYSEM (June-August 1993) also indicate that of the total number of beneficiaries who got training under TRYSEM roughly 53.57% trained youth did not apply for assistance under IRDP and of the remaining youth only about 50% were given assistance under IRDP. To ensure proper linkage of TRYSEM with IRDP, it has been made incumbent on the DRDAs, the block authorities and the training institutions to complete all the required formalities for sanction of IRDP loans to TRYSEM trainees. During the training period itself, the loan application forms will be sent to the banks so that the bankers in turn can interact with the trainees. This will significantly reduce the chances of such sponsored applications being rejected later and generate interest in the trainees to take up self-employment.

Supply of improved toolkits to rural artisans

The scheme was launched as a sub-scheme of IRDP in July, 1992, with the objective to enabling the rural artisans Below Poverty Line to enhance the quality of their products, increase their production and income and ensure a better quality of life with the use of improved tools. This will also help reduce their migration to urban areas.

Salient features

Artisans from a variety of crafts, except weaving, tailoring, needle-workers and beedi-workers are to be supplied with suitable improved hand tools or a set of tools. The average cost of a toolkit is Rs.2,000 and in case of power driven tools the average-cost is Rs.4,500. 90% of the cost of the toolkit is a subsidy from the Government of India and 10% is to be contributed by the beneficiary and there is no State share.

The unit cost is to be fixed by tne District Rural Development Agency (DRDA) concerned. DRDA is the implementing agency. Prototypes of improved tools in pottery, carpentry, blacksmithy, leather work, woodcraft, metal craft and lacquerware have been developed by the National Small Industries Corporation, Regional Design and Technical Development Centres under the Development Commissioner (Handicrafts) and similar other organisations. The State Governments have been authorised to choose models/tools, which suit the needs of their artisans.

Target group

There is 50% reservation for SC and ST communities. Wherever SC/ST persons are not available, the DRDA Governing body can decide to allocate the percentage meant for SC/ST to other categories of artisans. There is no provision of reservation for women and physically handicapped persons. However, if eligible, preference will be given to such persons over other persons.

Monitoring and supervision

Regular monthly monitoring is done by the Ministry of Rural Areas and Employment. State and District Level Committees have been set up by the State Governments for implementation and monitoring of the scheme. Area officers nominated for various States by this Ministry also regularly inspect the implementation of the scheme in the field during their visits to the States.

Performance during eighth five year plan

During the Eighth Five Year Plan (1992-93 to 1996-97) a sum of Rs. 149.07 crores was released out of which Rs. 120.08 crores has been utilised which works out to be 80.55%. Against the target of covering 8.32 lakh beneficiaries, 6.52 lakh beneficiaries have been covered which works out to be 78.36%. Details are given below:

Performance during 1998-99

Allocation under the scheme during 1998-99 is Rs. 60 crores, which has been revised to Rs. 59.73 crores. An amount of Rs. 59 crores has been earmarked as subsidy for purchase of toolkits and Rs. 0.73 crore is earmarked for Research and Development of Toolkits and Evaluation of the scheme. An amount of Rs. 26.87 crores has been released as subsidy for purchase of toolkits to the States/UTs upto December 1998. Under the Research, Development and Evaluation head no funds have been released upto December. On the basis of the information available as per the reports last received, an expenditure of Rs.25.14 crores had been incurred upto November 1998. This accounts for an achievement of 52.78% in financial terms and 40% in physical terms. Details of achievement are given in the Annexure-XIV and XV.

Areas identified for further improvement

Based on the feedback gathered and with a view to further improving the implementation of the scheme and its efficacy, the following areas would receive attention in the Ninth Plan:

- The source of supply of toolkits would be wholly guided by the quality and cost parameters, the reputation and expertise of manufacturers, timely delivery and pre-delivery extension and post-delivery service facilities offered and suitability of the toolkits to the need of specific artisan groups.

- While it may be true that a majority of the rural artisans would be illiterate and therefore, cannot have access to documented literature, the need for such literature with plenty of graphics and illustrations cannot be discounted altogether. Efforts should therefore be made to prepare such literature and supply a copy to the artisans covered.
- Marketing linkages need to be established for more effective use of improved toolkits so that higher productivity and enhanced production can be absorbed leading to higher earnings for artisans. State Governments have been advised to make institutional arrangements for establishing such linkages.
- The State Governments have been requested to interact with the Department of Science and Technology, NSIC and IITs for the development of appropriate technology and designs for improved toolkits for various artisan groups.
- The Scheme would henceforth place due emphasis on the choice of the artisans. The designing and manufacture of tools should at least emerge from a wider level of consultations with groups of artisans. The process of consultation should be continued even after the supply of tools have been effected to find out whether these have fulfilled the objectives of the scheme and the needs of the artisans.
- There are pockets of rural technology, which have survived the onslaught of modern technological innovations by virtue of their sturdiness and locale specific utility. These need to be identified and replicated elsewhere.

- The scheme's objective also needs to include upgradation of skills through technological innovations resulting in additional income generation. The scheme would aim at capturing markets beyond the nearest rural areas, wherever feasible.
- Research and Development must be given due emphasis. States have been advised to take the initiative in developing toolkits at least in the case of one artisan trade to start with. Similar initiatives will have to be taken by the Small Industries Services Institutes.
- State Governments have been advised to sponsor evaluation of the scheme through institutions having an expertise in the field, experience of extension work and involvement in the field of technological and marketing promotion.
- For dissemination of technology, States have been advised to organise exhibitions in several locations on important occasions.

Ganga Kalyan Yojana

Ganga Kalyan Yojana (GKY) was launched as a sub-scheme of Integrated Rural Development Programme (IRDP) during 1996-97 with effect from 1.2.1997 and is being continued as an independent scheme with effect from 1.4.1997.

Objective

The objective of the scheme is to provide irrigation through exploitation of groundwater (borewells and tubewells) to individuals and groups of beneficiaries of small and marginal farmers belonging to the below poverty line.

Programme strategy

The individual/groups are assisted through subsidy by Government and term credit by financial institutions including SC/ST/BC Finance and Development Corporation.

Target group

The beneficiaries under the scheme are small and marginal farmers living below the poverty line, other than those who have already been assisted under any minor irrigation programme of State or Central Government.

Safeguards for SCs and STs

At least 50% of the funds have been earmarked for SCs and STs.

Funding pattern

The funding pattern is 80:20 Le 80% by Central Government and 20% by the State Government.

Allocation of funds to the states

The funds are allocated to the States according to the criteria fixed for IRDP allocation. The States are required to make district-wise allocations taking into consideration the potential for exploitation of groundwater resources, economic viability of exploiting such potential and other relevant considerations.

Subsidy

75% subsidy is allowed for SCs/STs and physically disabled groups and 50% for others. The monetary ceiling of subsidy per group (5 to 15 members) is Rs. 40,000 and for individual beneficiaries the subsidy is Rs. 5,000 per acre of land under the scheme subject to a ceiling of Rs. 12,500 per beneficiary.

5% of the project cost per annum is permissible as additional subsidy for SC/ST/Physically disabled groups as part of operation and maintenance cost for 3 years. For other groups and individual schemes, no subsidy on operation and maintenance is admissible.

Implementing agency

The scheme is being implemented by the DRDAs/ Zilla Parishads.

Financial progress

During the financial year 1997-98, a Central allocation of Rs. 20,000 lakhs was made which was scaled down to Rs. 10,000 lakhs in view of the lack of gearing up the scheme by the States and also the budgetary cuts imposed by Finance. The whole amount of Rs. 10,000 lakhs was released till 31st March, 1998. Against, this, the total utilisation of Rs. 566.65 lakhs has been incurred by the States as per the reports received.

During 1998-99, the Central allocation under the scheme is Rs. 94 lakhs which has been reduced to Rs. I lakh only at Revised Estimate stage. The reasons for such reduction is mainly on account of huge unspent balance available with the implementing agencies. The reasons for huge unspent balance is operational difficulties faced by the States in the implementation of the scheme.

Physical progress

The States/UTs were made responsible to fix the Suitable physical targets for the DRDAs/ZPs. During 1997-98, 1674 individual projects and 92 group projects under the scheme were implemented. During 1998-99, 2261 individual projects and 72 group projects have been taken up by the States.

Outlay for 1999-2000

The proposed Central Outlay of the scheme for the year 1999-2000 has not yet been finalised. Moreover, the scheme is proposed to be merged into IRDR.

7

Welfare of Persons with Disabilities

Estimates of the number of persons with disabilities vary, depending on the definitions, the methodology and the extent of use of scientific instruments in identifying and measuring the degree of disability, The National Sample Survey Organisation (NSSO) conducted in 1981 a country-wide survey covering 3 types of disabilities i.e.. visual, communication and locomotor disabilities. It identified 12 million persons as having at least one or the other disability-constituting about 1.8% of the estimated total population. In the year 1991, NSSO again conducted a country wide survey covering (i) visual (ii) hearing, (iii) speech and (iv) locomotor disabilities. About 16.15 million people were estimated to have one or the other of the types of disabilities mentioned above, This constitutes 1.9% of the total estimated population of the country. It has been observed that for the country as a whole, prevalence of physical disability was 20 per thousand persons in the rural area and 16 in the urban area, Between the two sexes, the prevalence is marginally more among males than among females.

Persons with mental retardation were excluded from both the surveys. However, a sample survey, conducted by NSSO in 1991, for persons with delayed mental development between 14 age group, estimates that about 3% of the estimated child population have delayed mental development. Certain studies conducted by some institution/NGOs suggest that about 2.5% of the estimated population suffer from mental retardation.

The number of leprosy-affected persons is estimated to be about 4 million, of whom about 1/5th are children. About 15 to 30% cam are with deformities. In 196 districts in the country, the prevalence rate is more than 5 per thousand. About 430 million persons live in these high endemic districts. Disability Division for the various schemes for the welfare of Disabled persons has the Budget provision of Rs. 165.35 crores for the year 1998-99.

The implementation of the provisions of the Act require a multi-sectoral collaborative approach of all concerned Ministries of the Central Government, the State/UT Governments and other appropriate authorities, While in the area of prevention, early detection. and intervention, Ministry of Health and Family Welfare and Department of Women and Child Development have to play a major role, in the area of education of children with disabilities, Department of Education has to integrate these programmes within their schemes/programmes. For the creation of barrier free environment, the Ministries of Urban Area and Employment, Surface Transport, Railways and Civil Aviation have to take various positive steps. In the area of employment and training, Ministry of Labour has an important role. Appropriate Government ensures the implementation of the Persons with Disabilities (Equal Opportunities, Protection of Rights and Full Participation) Act, 1995 by making necessary institutional arrangements and implementing various programmes for the people with disabilities within the limits of their economic capacity and development. In order to effectively implementing the provisions of the Act, the following measures have been taken by the Minis".

(i) The National Handicapped Finance & Development Corporation has been operationalised with effect from 24-10,97 to support entrepreneurial activity by the disabled.

(ii) Notification of Central Co-ordination Committee as per Section 3 of the Act, The Committee has undertaken two meetings so far.

(iii) Central Executive committee has been notified. The committee took two meetings so far.

(iv) The Chief commissioner for Persons with Disabilities has been appointed and he has assumed the office w.e.f. 1.9.98.

(v) Five Core Groups of experts and relevant Ministeries have been set up to make recommendations and formulate schemes to give effect to various provisions of the Act.

(vi) Rules under section 73(1) and (2) have been notified.

(vii) National Trust for Welfare of Parsons with Autism, Cerebral Palsy, Mental Retardation and Multiple Disability is proposed to be set up.

(viii) The Rehabilitation Council of India which is a statutory body for standardisation and training of rehabilitation professional recognition of training institutions and registration of professionals, has recently taken up a comprehensive plan for manpower in disability rehabilitation throughout the country. Sufficient Funds have been allocated to Rehabilitation Council of India (RCI) for this purpose.

(ix) Many State Governments have constituted State Coordination Committee and State Executive Committee to redress the grievances of the disabled persons.

(x) A Central Sponsored Scheme called National Programme for Rehabilitation of Persons with Disabilities has also been proposed for establishing necessary infrastructure to realise fully the objectives of the Act.

(xi) A conference of State Secretaries, in-charge of persons with disabilities was held on 12.2.97 at New Delhi to discuss the implementation of the Act. A Workshop of State Education Secretaries and State Labour Secretaries was also held at New Delhi to sensitise the State Officials.

(xii) An inter-ministerial Group has been constituted to monitor the progress made by the Central Ministries who have specific obligations under the Act.

(xiii) A two-day Conference on Social Economic Perspective for Development of the North Eastern States' was held in November, 1998 under the Chairmanship of MOS(SJ&E). It reviewed the effective implementation of the PWD Act and other schemes of the Disability Division in the North-Eastern States. It was attended by the Ministers for Welfare of these States and other important State Government functionaries.

National Institutes

In Consonance with the policy of providing a complete package of welfare services to the physically and mentally disabled individuals and groups and in order to effectively deal with the multi dimensional problems of the disabled population, the following national institutes have been set up in each major area of disability:-

(i) National Institute for the Visually Handicapped Dehradun.

(ii) National Institute for the Orthopaedically, Handicapped, Calcutta.

(iii) Ali Yavar Jung National Institute for the Hearing Handicapped, Mumbai.

(iv) National Institute for the Mental Handicapped, Secunderabad.

These Institutes are fore-runners as well as trend setters in their respective areas of specialisation. They have been staffed with talented professionals and equipped with modern and scientific equipment: They offer a variety of long-term training programme ranging from three year Degree courses Physiotherapy, Occupational Therapy, Mental retardation, Education of the deaf, Communication Disorders as well as degree and diploma courses for shorter periods in the above disciplines as well as prosthetic and orthotic engineering and audiology speech therapy and teachers training for the blind. These different courses are conducted either at the Institute's headquarters or in their regional centres located in different parts of the country. The role the Institutes is significant, firstly, because of the dearth of trained personnel and facilities for such training in the country to cater to the wide spectrum of needs of the disabled and secondly because the need for filling the gap which was essential owing to the commitment of the Government to provide comprehensive services to the disabled in I country. The clinical and rehabilitation units of the Institutes serve as an in-house laboratory for I trainers as well as the trainees and serve as sounding board for some of the research projects taken up by them, apart from providing model clinical and para medical services to the patients.

Besides the regular academic courses, institutes conduct a large number of short-term training courses, seminars, orientation courses camps their efforts have provided a forum creating awareness among the community at large for bringing the disabled population closet to organisations working for their welfare for exchange of information, knowledge and experience amongst the academicians, professionals, doctors, village/community level workers and all those associated with various aspects of disability.

Besides, two apex level institutions, namely, Institute for the Physically Handicapped, New Delhi and National Institute of Rehabilitation Training and Research, Cuttack, are also providing training and rehabilitation services and undertaking similar activities as the National Institutes.

It is proposed to set up a National Institute for Multiple Disabilities for providing rehabilitation services to people with multiple disabilities under one roof. The Institute will provide services like early detection and intervention, Medical rehabilitation educational, rehabilitation, psycho-social rehabilitation etc. It will also undertake manpower development and vocational training programmes. It will conduct a number of short-term and long-term training courses including orientation courses and develop material for creating awareness among the community at large. The Government of Tamil Nadu has donated 15.8 acres of land at Village Muttukadu near Chennai to the Ministry of Social Justice & Empowerment, for this purpose.

The Artificial Limbs Manufacturing Corporation of India (ALIMCO) was registered under Section 25 of the Companies Act. 1956 on 25th November, 1972 as a Government company, not for profit. The objectives of ALIMCO include (a) to establish facilities for manufacture of artificial limbs, accessories and constituents thereof, (b) To promote, encourage and develop the availability, supply and distribution, at reasonable cost of artificial limbs, accessories and constituents thereof to needy persons including disabled personnel, hospitals and other welfare institutions.

ALIMCO produces quality Aids and Appliances required for orthopaedically and visually handicapped persons. The products are ISI marked/conforming to standards approved by Bureau of Indian Standards. The product range includes Orthotic (Calipers) and Prosthetic (Artificial Limbs) appliances for both Upper and Lower Extremities, Spinal Braces, Cervical Collars, Traction kits, Rehabilitation Aids like Wheel Chairs, Crutches, Three-wheelers and Special Tools and Equipments required for fitment of Prosthetic; and Orthotic Assemblies by Limb Fitting Centres. ALIMCO will commence manufacture of quality hearing aids in collaboration with M/s Semi-Conductors Ltd., Chandigarh and Ali Yavar Jung National Institute for the Hearing Handicapped, Mumbai, shortly, ALIMCO is exporting its products to Afghanistan, Bangladesh, Nepal, UAE, Jordan, Iran, Angola, Cambodia and Uzbekistan.

The Corporation is in the process of manufacturing 1000 sets of below knee floor reaction orthosis kits of composite plastics. This is being done on collaboration with M/s C.P.D.C., Hyderabad.

In its endeavour to meet the growing needs of the physically handicapped population of the country, ALIMCO proposed to augment its manufacturing capacity of wheel chairs and tricycles by setting up Production Centres (APCs) in Eastern, Southern, Western and Northern regions. Capacity of wheel chair and tricyles at each of the APC has been envisaged on:

		Nos. per Annum	
		Phase-I	*Phase-II*
(a)	Wheel Chairs TD2 (51)	1200	3600
(b)	Tricycles TD2 (98)	2400	6000

ALIMCO has Regional Marketing Centres at Calcutta, Mumbai, Chennai, Bhubaneshwar and Delhi. Marketing of products is done through these Regional Marketing Centres with the help of extensive dealer network and direct sales to various National Institutes and voluntary organisations. ALIMCO is also an approved agency for implementing ADIP scheme through which Aids and Appliances are distributed to individual beneficiaries by conducting camps at various places with the assistance of the local administration and voluntary agencies. ALIMCO has provided aid and appliances. 1382 disabled persons under ADIP scheme of Government of India in 97-98.

ALIMCO had participated in the "Ability India" exhibition held in New Delhi between 14th and 20th September, 1998 and "2nd Pride of India Exhibition held at Hanoi (Vietnam) from October 23-26, 1998.

During 1997-98, against a budget provision of 3.00 crores, grant-in-aid of Rs. 2.85 crores was provided to ALIMCO. During 1998-99, against a budget provision Rs. 3.00 crores, grant-in-aid of Rs. 2.45 crores was provided to ALIMCO under plan, upto 31.12.98.

National handicapped finance and development corporation (NHFDC)

1. The National Handicapped Finance and Development Corporation (NHFDC) was incorporated on 24th January, 1997 under Section 25 of the Companies Act, 1956 as a Government Company not for profit. The registered office of the NHFDC is at Faridabad. NHFDC has an authorised share

capital of Rs. 400 crores, divided into 40 lakhs equity shares of Rs. 1000/- each and paid up capital of Rs. 200 crores. The entire equity is held by Government of India. The NHFDC is functioning as an apex Financial institution for routing funds through the channelising agencies authorised by the State Government/UT administrations. The outlay for the current financial year for the NHFDC is Rs. 28 crores.

2. The objectives of the NHFDC are to promote economic developmental activities for the benefit of handicapped persons. The Corporation will strive to promote self-employment and other ventures for persons/or groups of persons by way of loans and advances, subject to such income/economic criteria as may be prescribed by the Government, from time to time. It will also extend loans for pursuing general/professional technical education, besides assisting in the upgradation of technical entrepreneurial skills.

(i) Self employment in small business, e.g. service/ trading sector

(ii) Assistance to disabled entrepreneurs

(iii) Assistance to disabled for higher studies or professional training

(iv) Assistance to agricultural activities

(v) Scheme to promote manufacturing/production of assistive devices for disabled persons.

(vi) Assistance for skills and entrepreneurial development programmes.

(vii) Schemes to promote self-employment amongst persons with mental retardation, cerebral palsy and autism.

The corporation would provide loans to persons having disability of 40% or above and whose annual Income does not exceed Rs. 60,000/- per annum in urban areas and Rs. 55,000/- per annum in rural areas. Application for loans will be received and processed by the State Channelising Agency, nominated by respective State Government. They, in turn, will forward such applications with their recommendations to the NHFDC for approval and release of loan. Guidelines for funding of projects under various schemes has been sent by this Ministry to all State Governments/UT Administrations, Channelising Agencies, apex NGOs in the disability sector, National Institutes, DRCs and other concerned institutions and organisations.

(a) 1996-97 Rs. 1.00 crore

(b) 1997-98 Rs. 13.30 crores

(c) 1998-99 Rs. 28.00 crores

Project sanctioned by NHFDC:-(as on 31-12-98)

(i) Andhra Pradesh
Total No. 86
Total Amount: Rs. 67-08 Lakhs

(ii) Orissa
Total No. 182
Total Amount: Rs. 64.40 Lakhs

(iii) Assistance
Development

Rehabilitation council of India (RCI)

The Rehabilitation Council of India is a national level statutory body set up by the Govt. of India tinder the Rehabilitation Council of India Act, 1992 to enforce uniform standards in the training of Professionals/ Personnel in the field of rehabilitation of the disabled, maintenance of the Central Rehabilitation Register and other connected matters. The Council was reconstituted in June, 1998.

The following three major programmes have been approved for implementation by the Council:

National programme of bridge course is to give one time opportunity to all special educators/rehabilitation workers serving people with disabilities to become eligible to register themselves with the council as rehabilitation personnel by taking up just one month duration bridge course.

National programme for training of Medical Officers aims at giving 3 days orientation training to over 25,000 medical officers working in the PHCs to orient them towards disability and rehabilitation issues and enable them to make appropriate referrals.

Assistance to organisation for manpower

In order to promote training of teachers, vocational instructors, multi-rehabilitation workers and other professionals, grants are given to the training centres institutions/organisations for conducting Diploma/ Degree courses recognised by the Council, under the above programme.

The RCI Act covers the following categories of Rehabilitation Professionals/Personnel:-

i) Audiologists and Speech therapists

ii) Clinical Psychologists

iii) Hearing Aids and Earmould Technicians

iv) Rehabilitation Engineers and Technicians

v) Special Teachers for education and training the disabled

vi) Vocational Counsellors, Employment Officers and Placement Officers dealing with disabilities.

vii) Multipurpose Rehabilitation Therapists, Technicians

viii) Speech Pathologists

ix) Rehabilitation Psychologists

x) Rehabilitation Social Workers

xi) Rehabilitation Practitioners in Mental Retardation

xii) Orientation and Mobility Specialists

xiii) Community based Rehabilitation Professionals

xiv) Rehabilitation Counsellors/Administrators

xv) Prosthetists and Orthotists

xvi) Rehabilitation Workshop Managers

xvii) Physiotherapists

xviii) Occupational Therapists

xix) Ophthalmic Technicians

The Council has registered 1472 professionals/ personnel so far in the Central Rehabilitation Register and issued certificates to them. The Council has inspected/ recognized 35 institutions during the year to conduct various training programmes. The total number of institutions has increased to 114.

District rehabilitation centre schemes

The District Rehabilitation Centre Scheme (DRC) was initiated by the Ministry of welfare, Government of India, during 1985, to provide comprehensive rehabilitation services to the rural disabled right at their door step in 11 districts of the country. These Centres provide the following services:

(i) Prevention and early detection;

(ii) Medical intervention and surgical correction;

(iii) Fitment of artificial aids and appliances,

(iv) Therapeutical services such as Physiotherapy, Occupational therapy and Speech therapy;

(v) Provision of training for acquisition of skills through vocational training;

(vi) Job placement in local industries;

Four Regional Rehabilitation Training Centres (RRTCs) have also been set up at Chennai, Mumbai, Cuttack and Lucknow for training and manpower development in the field of rehabilitation, particularly for the DRCs.

National Trust for the Welfare of Persons with Autism, Cerebral Palsy, Mental Retardation and Multiple Disability is proposed to be set up. An amount of Rs. 1.25 crores has been earmarked for this purpose.

Earlier, the Government had introduced a National Trust for the Welfare of Persons with Mental Retardation and Cerebral Palsy Bill, 1995 in Lok Sabha on 6.2.1995 which could not be taken up for discussion. The Bill has since been modified after extensive consultations with professionals, parent bodies and voluntary organisations in the field of mental retardation and cerebral palsy.

The Trust will provide total care to persons with mental retardation with autism, cerebral palsy and multiple disability and also manage the properties bequeathed to the Turst.

The objectives of the Turst,

(i) To enable and empower persons with disability to live as independently and as fully as possible, within their own families.

(ii) To strengthen facilities to support persons with disability within their own families.

(iii) To extend support to organisations of persons with disability or parents and voluntary organisations for need based services during periods of family crisis.

(iv) To address to the concerns of persons with disability, who do not have family support.

(v) To promote measures for the care and protection of persons with disability after the death of their parents or guardians.

(vi) To facilities the realisation of equal opportunities protection of rights and full participation of persons with disabilities.

The Cabinet has approved the setting up of the National Turst for the Welfare of Persons with Autism, Cerebral Palsy, Mental Retardation and Multiple Disability. The Bill is likely to be introduced in the Budget Session in 1999.

The Indian Spinal Injury Centre (ISIC) has been set up in collaboration with the Italian Government, to provide comprehensive treatment, rehabilitation services and vocational training and guidance to patients with spinal injury. It is the first centre of its kind in Asia. The Centre would also conduct research in multi-dimensional aspects of rehabilitation of such patients. The machinery and technical expertise were made available to the Centre under Indo-Italian Cooperation from Italy. The Ministry of Social Justice and Empowerment has released one time grant of Rs. 2.50 crores to the ISIC in two instalments during 1989-90 and 1990-91. OPD and diagnostic services are already functional. Further support to ISIC to the extent of Rs. 5.8 crores has been approved for capital expenditure and Rs. 1.5 crores of this has been released. An amount of Rs. 1.67 crores with an escalation of 10%

per annum has also been approved for recurring expenditure from 1997-98 onwards in order to sponsor 30 free beds to the poor patients. During 1998-99, a provision of Rs. 3.00 crores (plan) has been made out of which an amount of Rs. 1.54 crores has been released upto 31.12.98 and a plan out lay of Rs. 7.00 crores has been proposed for the year 1999-2000.

Under the scheme of Assistance to Disabled Persons for Purchase/Fitting of Aids/appliances, assistance is provided to needy physically disabled persons in procuring durable, sophisticated and scientifically manufactured modern standard aids and appliances to facilitate their physical, social and psychological rehabilitation and integration in the mainstream. The scope of the scheme has been enlarged to include 'corrective surgery, use of mass media for information dissemination, etc., under its ambit.

Indian citizens, irrespective of age and sex, possessing a certificate from a Registered Medical Practitioner can avail benefits under the scheme. Aids/appliances costing from Rs. 50/- to Rs. 6,000/- are provided free of cost if the monthly income of the beneficiary is upto Rs. 5,000/- and at 50% of the cost, if the monthly income is between Rs. 5,001/- and Rs. 8,000/-. The scheme is implemented by registered Societies/ Trusts/Companies and any other Institutions recognised by the Ministry of Social Justice and Empowerment for the purpose. The DRDAs/RCSs, headed by the Collector/District Magistrates are also eligible to implement the scheme. Nehru Yuvak Kendra Sangathans have also been included in the list of agencies/institutions implementing the scheme.

Quantum of assistance

Aids/appliances which do not cost less than Rs. 50/- and not more than Rs. 6,0004 are covered under the Scheme.

These limits will apply to individual items of aid and where more than one aid is required, giving of the same will be permissible and the limits will be applied separately. There is no ceiling on amount of grant to be provided under the scheme. Branches of implementing agencies can be considered for separate grants on fulfilling procedural requirements.

During 1995-96, against a budget provision of Rs. 13.00 crores, grant-in-aid of Rs. 10.60 crores was provided to 77 implementing agencies. During 199697, the budget provision was Rs. 12.85 crores but grant-in-aid of Rs. 6.86 crores was given to 141 implementing agencies. The lower expenditure was due to the limit fixed on the quantum of grant-in-aid of Rs. 6 to 10 lakhs to an agency, even though the number of agencies assisted in 1996-97 increased appreciably. There was a budget provision of Rs. 8.00 crores (RE) for 1997-98 against which a total expenditure of Rs. 8.94 crores was sanctioned to 124 agencies. During 1998-99 Rs. 25.00 crores (plan) has been allocated, against, which an amount of Rs. 8.35 crores has been released to 94 agencies upto Dec. '98. Plan outlay of Rs. 26.00 crores has been proposed for the year 1999-2000.

Till 1995, World Day of the Disabled was observed on the 3rd Sunday of March every year. On this day, President of India gives National Awards to the achievers in the following categories:

(i) Best Employer of the People With Disabilities;

(ii) Best Disabled Employee and Self-Employed;

(iii) Best Individual working for the welfare of people with Disabilities:

(iv) Best Institution working for the welfare of people with Disabilities;

(v) Placement Officer;

(vi) Best Institution working ror the welfare of People with Disabilities.

From this year, (1998) two more categories of awards have been introduced which are as under:

(a) Outstanding Creative Individual with Disabilities

(b) Outstanding work in the creation of barrier-free environment for people with Disabilities.

In consonance with the Resolution of UN General Assembly, it was decided that 3rd December of every year would be observed as the International Day of Disabled Persons. Accordingly, in 1998, International Day of Disabled Persons was observed on 3rd December in Vigyan Bhavan, Prime Minister of India gave away 49 Awards under the various categories.

Disabled children from various pans of Me country are invited to witness Republic Day Parade. Boarding, lodging and travel expenses of the disabled children and their escorts is borne by the Ministry of Social Justice & Empowerment. In 1998, 64 disabled children witnessed the parade from PM's enclosure. As a new initiative, a group of mentally challenged children trained by CIMR, Thiruvananthapuram, participated in the Republic Day Parade giving the message that given the opportunity they are at pat with the other children. The group was also awarded the second prize by the Ministry of Defence.

National fund for people with disabilities

The National fund for People with Disabilities was created under the Charitable Endowment Act 1890 in the name of National Handicapped Welfare Fund to fulfil the following objectives:-

(i) to promote voluntary sector for creating services for

the persons with disability, including prevention, early detection of disabilities, education, training, physical and economic rehabilitation of disabled persons.

(ii) to undertake activities that are incidental and conducive to the above objectives.

The fund is managed by a Board of Management with Secretary (SJ&E) as Chairperson. The meeting of the Board are held at regular intervals to review the utilization and management of funds and the last meeting was held on 30.6.1998. Financial assistance has been sanctioned to 14 NGOs, 1 DRC, Bhiwani and 1 National Institute, NIVH, Dehradun (UP) for taking up projects under the scheme funded through the Fund.

Financial assistance for the welfare of persons with disabilities

The Scheme was started with a view to provide assistance to voluntary organisations working in the hold of handicapped welfare. It is a comprehensive scheme to cover different areas of rehabilitation physical, psychological, social and economic. Financial support is given upto a maximum limit of 90% of the total project cost, with built-in ceiling for certain items. Financial assistance is also given for projects such as vocational training centres, special schools, counselling centres, hostels, training centres for the personnel and placement services etc. Year-wise allocation, expenditure, number of NGOs assisted and number of beneficiaries are as under:-

Year	*Allocation (Rs. in crores)*	*Expenditure (Rs. in crores)*	*No. of NGOs*	*No. of Bene-ficiaries*
(1)	*(2)*	*(3)*	*(4)*	*(5)*
1992-93	4.00	77.90	302	42811

1993-94	6.00	8.55	240	60161
1994-95	7.00	14.36	409	141615
1995-96	16.70	16.70	350	118268
1996-97	16.70	16.70	357	118824
1997-98	18.00	17.86	334	119620
1998-99	26.70	14.30 Upto 31.12.98		

Note : From this year onwards, all the four schemes have been clubbed together under "Scheme to Promote Voluntary Action For Persons with Disabilities" to meet the objectives of the PWD Act.

Assistance to voluntary organisations for rehabilitation of leprosy cured persons

India has a large population of leprosy affected persons, the estimated figure being 4.50 lakhs. The scheme provides financial assistance to NGOs in phased manner for the rehabilitation of leprosy-cured persons both in rural and urban areas. Assistance is given upto 90% of the project cost. Programmes like awareness generation, early intervention, education and vocational training, economic rehabilitation, social integration, etc. are undertaken under the scheme.

Assistance to organisations for manpower development in the field of mental retardation and cerebral paisy

Under the scheme, assistance is given to NGOs, even to the extent of 100% in some cases, for running courses for teachers in the areas of cerebral palsy and mental retardation. Both recurring and non-recurring items are considered for sanction.

Employment of the disabled

The basic objective of the scheme is to help the disabled persons in getting gainful employment either through Special Cells in normal Employment Exchanges or Special Employment Exchanges for Physically

Handicapped located throughout the country. At present there are 39 Special Cells and 51 Special Employment Exchanges. The Scheme is implemented through the State Government/UT Administration. The financial assistance is 100 per cent in case of Special Cells and 80 per cent in the case of Special Employment Exchanges Lists of Special Cells and the Special Employment Exchanges for Physically Handicapped in States.

The Total number of disabled persons in the live register of these Employment Exchanges was 3,23,220 in 1992 , 3,37,602 in 1993, 3,40,304 in 1994 and 3,53,743 in 1995. The placements in the same period have been 4306, 4451, 4485 and 3706, respectively.

Establishment and development of special schools

The Scheme envisages assistance to the NGOs upto the extent of 90% for establishment and upgradation of special schools in the four major disabled areas-orthopaedic, speech & hearing, visual and mentally retarded. Priority under the scheme is given for setting up of schools in districts where there is no special school at present. There are about 240 districts in the country which are still uncovered. Both recurring and non-recurring expenditure are supported by the Ministry.

Yearwise allocation, expenditure, no. of NGOs assisted and number of beneficiaries are given below:

Year	*Allocation (Rs. in crores)*	*Expenditure (Rs. in crores)*	*No of NGOs*	*No. of Beneficiaries*
(1)	(2)	(3)	(4)	(5)
1993-94	1.50	0.10	7	295
1994-95	1.50	0.32	42	2731
1995-96	0.75	0.75	28	1675
1996-97	0.38	0.78	22	1427

1997-98	1.25	1.33	42	2216
1998-99 upto 31.12.98	10.00	1.84	-	

Technology development project in mission mode

For providing suitable and cost-effective aids and appliances and improving the mobility and enhancement of employment opportunities for the disabled, the scheme of Science and Technology Project in Mission Mode was launched in 1988. Under this project interdisciplinary S&T efforts are mobilised for generation of new technologies and guiding these to large scale use to meet social needs. The entire project cost is met by Government.

The objectives of the project are to coordinate, fund and direct application of technology for development and utilisation of -(a) suitable and cost effective aids and appliances, and (b) emphasis on education and skill development, leading to enhancement of opportunities for employment, easier living and integration in society. This was for the first time that Government of India launched a coordinated programme for developing aids and appliances for persons with disability. Financial assistance is provided on a 100% basis.

Relief assistance under bilateral agreements

Ministry of Social Justice and Empowerment operates bilateral agreements entered into by the Government of India with the Federal Republic of Germany, Sweden, Switzerland, United Kingdom and United State of America. These arrangements envisage duty free entry into India of donated supplies of relief and rehabilitation of the poor without discrimination of caste, creed or race. Under these agreements, commodities' like food grain, milk powder, cheese, processed food stuff, multi purpose stuff, medicines, multi vitamin tablets, hospital equipments, ambulance, mobile dispensaries, agricultural instruments are received by approved Indian organisations from approved donor organisations located in the above mentioned 5 countries.

National project to integrate mentally retarded in family and community

A National Pilot Project to integrate mentally retarded in Family and Community was launched in March, 1998, in 6 States namely Kerala, Karnataka, Tamil Nadu, Andhra Pradesh, Delhi and Madhya Pradesh, covering about 7,500 beneficiaries, The Pilot project was implemented by CIMR. Thiruvantanthapuram.

The objectives of the Project, are:

(1) Sensitise the families, and empower them to integrate the mentally retarded child in the family and community.

(2) Make early intervention in the lives of 7500 hitherto unreached mentally retarded, particularly from the economically weaker sections and provide them early developmental inputs.

(3) Introduce low cost, easy to follow teaching aids and training method relevant to rural and urban setting as a model for inclusion of all the mentally retarded in the family and community.

(4) Prepare the mentally retarded to receive further developmental and vocational education.

(5) Training of a large number of para-professionals within a short period to extend services in this field.

(6) Create awareness in society to focus on mentally retarded, their problems and rights

Ability India Fair-98

An international exhibition of Assitive Devices for people with Disabilities was held from 14th - to 20 September,

1998 at Pragati Maidan, New Delhi. It was Organised by the Ministry of Social Justice and Empowerment, Government of India.

It was the first Exhibition of its kind, which was held to display aids and appliances for the Disabled Persons. The basic objective of the exhibition was to disseminate information on aids and appliances available in India and in other countries. The Exhibition was inaugurated on 14.9.98 by the Hon'ble Minister of State for Social Justice & Empowerment, Smt. Maneka Gandhi, in the presence of Chief guest (Bharat Ratna), Dr. A.P.J. Abdul Kalam, Secretary (SJ&E), Addl. Secretary (SJ&E), Joint Secretary (DD) and Shri Lal Advani.

In the Exhibition, about 100 manufacturers from all over the country and 4 foreign countries, namely, USA, Sweden, Australia and Taiwan participated. The exhibitors displayed latest aids & appliances available and being developed. The 6 National Institutes and a Combined group of S&T Mission Mode also participated. A large number of visitors, including businessmen and people with disabilities visited the exhibition. A keen interest was shown by the visitors in the assistive devices being displayed.

8

TRIBAL DEVELOPMENT

India has people of diverse races and cultures living within it. The tribal communities belonging to various races are spread across the country, mainly in the forest and hilly regions. The word Tribe means a group of families bound together by kinship, usually descending from mythical or legendary ancestor, living in a common region, speaking a common dialect and having common historical past.

The essential characteristics of these communities are primitive traits, geographical isolation, distinctive culture, shyness of contact with outsiders and economic backwardness. According to Article 342 of the Constitution of India the Scheduled Tribes are the tribes or tribal communities or part of or group within tribes and tribal communities which have been declared as such by the President by the public notification. More than 70 per cent of the Scheduled Tribes population is concentrated in seven States of Madhya Pradesh, Maharashtra, Orissa, Bihar, Andhra Pradesh, West Bengal and Gujarat. No community has been specified as Scheduled Tribe in respect of States of Haryana and Punjab and UTs of Chandigarh, Delhi and Pondicherry.

According to 1991 Census the total population of the country was 846 million, out of which the population of Scheduled Tribe was 68 millions, constituting 8.08 percent of the country's total population 42.02% of the ST population were main workers of them, 54-50% were cultivators and 32.69% were agricultural labourers. Thus about 87% of the main workers, were engaged in primary sector activities. As against the national average of 52%, the literacy rate of Scheduled Tribes is around 29.60%. More than three quarters of Sch. Tribe women are illiterate. These disparities are compounded by higher drop-out rates in formal in their representation in higher education being disproportionately low. Not surprisingly, the cumulative effect has been, that the proportion of Scheduled Tribes below the poverty line is substantially higher than the national average. The estimate of poverty made by Planning Commission education resulting for the year 1993-94 shows that 51.92% rural and 41.14% urban ST population was still living below the poverty line.

The Constitution of India has laid responsibility on the shoulders of both the State Govt. as well as Central Govt. so far as development of STs is concerned. Article 46 states that the State shall promote with special care the educational and economic interests of the people and in particular of the Scheduled Castes and Scheduled Tribes and shall protect them from social injustice and all other forms of exploitation. Article 16(4) and 16(4A) empower the State to make provision for reservation in the appointment for posts in favour of Scheduled Tribes along with other categories both in direct recruitments and in promotions. Article 164(l) provides that in the States of Bihar, Madhya Pradesh and Orissa there shall be a Minister incharge of Tribal Affairs who may in addition be in charge of welfare of Scheduled Castes and Backward Classes or any other work. Article 244(1) provides that the provisions of Fifth Schedule shall apply to the Administration and control of Scheduled areas and Schedule Tribes. Article 275(1) provides that Grant in aid would be provided out of Consolidated fund of India to the States to meet the cost of such schemes of development as may be undertaken by them with the approval of Government of India for the purpose of promoting the welfare of schedule Tribes or raising the level of Schedule Areas. Articles 330 and 332 provide reservation for Schedule Tribes and Schedule Castes in Lok Sabha and State Legislative Assemblies respectively. Under Article 338 a National Commission for Scheduled Castes and Scheduled Tribes has been constituted which acts as a watch dog for safeguarding the interests of Scheduled Castes and Scheduled Tribes.

The Fifth Schedule to the Constitution empowers the Governor's of States having Schedule Areas therein to make regulations for good government and to modify the State and Central legislations regarding their applicability, Paragraph 4 of the Fifth Schedule provides for setting up of a Tribes advisory. Council which shall advise on such matters pertaining to welfare and advancement of Schedule Tribes which are referred to it by the Governor. Sixth Schedule to the Constitution which is applicable to the States of Assam, Meghalaya, Mizoram and Tripura, provides a mechanism of administering the local issues by the tribals themselves.

All the Central/Centrally Sponsored Schemes which are under implementation will continue during Ninth Plan. Revision of the schemes have been made after consultation with the Planning Commission and the Ministry of Finance. The Schemes are being implemented according to revised norms.

(i) A new central sector scheme for the development of Primitive Tribal Groups has been introduced during current financial year. Under this scheme cent percent assistance would be available to Integrated Tribal Development Projects (ITDPs), Tribal Research Institute (TRI) and Non-Governmental Organisations (NGOs) for undertaking activities such as awareness generation and confidence building, training for skill development of tribal youth organisations of self help groups and provision of services/inputs not covered by any existing scheme.

(ii) Scheduled Areas and Scheduled Tribes Commission It has been decided to set up 11 member Scheduled Areas and Scheduled Tribes Commission under Article 339(1) of the Constitution, The main objective of the Commission is to examine the existing TSP strategy and to suggest alternative arrangements, if necessary.

(iii) National Institute for Training and Research In Tribal Affairs It has been decided to set up a National Institute for Training and Research in Tribal Affairs at Delhi. The main purpose of setting up a National Institute is to coordinate research activities of 14 TRIs in various states and to assist the Ministry of Social Justice and Empowerment in formulating policies and programmes relating to protective laws, self-determination, socio-political movements, health, literacy, shifting cultivation, scheduling and descheduling, displacement and rehabilitation. There is also a need for training of different categories of public and service personnel in Tribal Development matters, which will also be coordinated by this Institute.

(iv) Revision of the Schemes have been initiated after consultation with the Planning Commission and the Ministry of Finance.

(v) Revision of Norms of the Scheme of Grant-in-Aid to Voluntary Organisation working for the Welfare of the Scheduled Tribes have been made raising the cost heads to a realistic and workable level.

In order to accelerate socio-economic development of the Scheduled Tribes and their protection against the exploitation, Government of India has adopted a separate strategy known at the TSP, since the Fifth Five Year Plan with the objective of (i) bringing them on par with other section of the Society and (ii) to protect them from exploitation by various vested interest groups. TSP strategy is in operation in 18 States, namely Andhra Pradesh, Assam, Bihar, Gujarat, Himachal Pradesh, Jammu and Kashmir, Karnataka, Kerala, Madhya Pradesh, Maharashtra, Manipur, Orissa, Rajasthan, Sikkim, Tamil Nadu, Tripura, Uttar Pradesh and West Bengal and two Union Territories, namely Andaman and Nicobar Islands and Daman & Diu.

In order to fulfil the above objective, 194 Integrated Tribal Development Projects (ITDPs) have been set up in blocks or groups of blocks where the ST population is more than 50% of the total population. Modified Area Development Approach (MADA) Pockets have been formed in groups of villages having population of 10,000 or more with, 50% or more tribal population, 252 MADA Pockets have been created. In addition, 79 Clusters have also been formed for groups of villages having population of 5,000 or more where STs constitute more than 50% of the population. 75 Primitive Tribal Groups (PTGs) have been identified in 15 States/ UTs on the basis of pre-agricultural level of technology and extremely low levels of literacy. The development of PTGs is undertaken through micro projects for these tribes.

The Special Central Assistance is given by the

Ministry of Welfare to !he Tribal Sub-Plan State Governments/UT Administrator to fill in the gaps in, their financial outlays. The SCA is to be utilised in conjunction with the TSP flow with a view to meet the gaps which are not otherwise taken care of by the State Plan. It is basically meant for family-oriented income generating schemes in sectors of agriculture, horticulture, minor irrigation, soil-conservation, animal husbandry, forest, education, cooperatives, fisheries, villages and small industries and Minimum Needs Programme.

The criteria for allocation of Special Central Assistance have been fixed on the basis of certain norms for ITDP, MADA Pockets, Clusters, Primitive Tribal Groups and Dispersed Tribal Groups. The allocation and expenditure for the years 1992-93 to 1997-98 is as follows.

(Rs. in Lakhs)

Year	*Allocation*	*Amount Released*
1	2	3
8th Plan (1992-97)	1,25,000	1,47,985
1992-93	25,000	25,000
1993-94	29,500	29,485
1994-95	27,500	27,500
1995-96	33,000	33,000
9th Plan		
(1997-2002)		
1996-97	33,000	33,000
1997-98	33,000	33,961,
1998-99	38,000	29,308 (as on 15.2.1999)

Tribal sub plan of central ministries

The Tribal sub Plan strategy seeks to ensure adequate

flow of funds not only from the State Plan funds, institutional finances and central sector/centrally sponsored schemes of the Ministry of Social Justice and Empowerment, but also from all the Central Ministries/Departments. The Planning Commission and the Ministry of Social Justice & Empowerment send letters to all the concerned Central Ministries/Departments every year on the need for quantification of funds from their annual plan in accordance with the population percentage of the Scheduled Tribes in the country.

The details of quantification of funds made by various Central Ministries during the year 199899 is given below:

Grants under first proviso to article 275(1) of the constitution

The Ministry of Social Justice and Empowerment gives grants to 18 Tribal Sub-Plan (TSP) and 4 Tribal majority States under First Proviso to Article 275(l) of the constitution to meet the cost of such projects for Tribal Development as may be undertaken by the State Government for raising the level of administration of the Scheduled Areas therein to that of the rest of the State.

The funds allocated and amount released since VIII Five Year Plan are as follows:

(Rs. In Lakhs)

Year	*Allocation*	*Amount released*
8th Plan (1992-97)	20,000.00	20,000.00
1992-93	4,000.00	4,000.00
1993-94	7,500.00	7,500.00
1994-95	7,500.00	7,500.00
1995-96	7,500.00	7,500.00
1996-97	7,500.00	7,500.00
9th Plan (1997-2002)		

1997-98	7,500.00	7,500.00
1998-99	7,500.00	5,385.22

In the case of the funds provided to the States/Union Territories under SCA and first provision to Article 275(l) the Ministry has devised a mechanism of monitoring under which quarterly reports are obtained from the States/UTs on utilisation of funds for various activities and the physical achievements in terms of beneficiaries assisted for their socioeconomic development.

Residential Schools: Since 1997-98, it has been decided to utilise a part of the funds under Article 275(l) of the Constitution for setting up 100 Residential Schools from Class 6 to 12 in States and U.Ts. for tribal students. For this purpose, it has been decided to provide Rs. 250.00 crores during the 9th Five Year Plan out of the funds available under Article 275(l) of the Constitution. The objective of setting up of the Residential Schools is to provide quality education to the Tribal Students. This will enable the tribal children to avail of the facility of reservation in higher and professional education courses as well as in higher levels of jobs in the government and Public Sector undertakings. The State Government have been requested to set up a Society on the pattern of Andhra Pradesh Tribal Welfare Residential and Ashram Educational Institutions Society (Regd.) Hyderabad. Each of the 100 schools would be provided non-recurring grant of Rs. 2.5 Crores. Out of the total allocation of Rs. 75.00 Crores during 1997-98, Rs. 50.00 Crores has been released to 22 States for opening 50 Schools, and it is proposed to release Rs. 25.00 Crores during 1998-99 to the States where the Societies have been registered and proposal for setting up of the Residential schools have been formulated.

Governors report

To provide an objective evaluation of the developments

in scheduled areas, the Governor of each State having scheduled area therein, is required to make a report to the President regarding administration of scheduled areas in that State. The scheduled areas have been declared in eight states namely Andhra Pradesh, Bihar, Gujarat, Himachal Pradesh, Maharashtra, Madhya Pradesh, Orissa and Rajasthan. The Governor's report has to give an unbiased assessment of the situation in scheduled areas highlighting, interalia, various measures taken for upgradation of administration of such areas, implementation of the protective laws, matters referred to the Tribes Advisory Council (TAC) and their recommendation etc. It has been generally observed that the Governor's report are normally a summary of achievements of State Governments in tribal development. Little efforts is made to qualitatively evaluate and critically analyse the problems of scheduled areas in these reports.

Tribes advisory council (TAC)

An important mechanism for tribal development and welfare, is the Tribes Advisory Council under Para 4 of the fifth Schedule of the Constitution. Eight States having Scheduled areas namely Andhra Pradesh, Bihar, Gujarat, Himachal Pradesh, Maharashtra, Madhya Pradesh, Orissa and Rajasthan and two non Scheduled Area States, namely Tamil Nadu and West Bengal, have constituted Tribes Advisory Councils.

The TACs consist of not more than twenty members of whom as many as three-fourths shall be the representatives of Scheduled Tribes in the Legislative assembly of the States.

As per the guidelines issued by the Ministry of Social Justice and Empowerment, the Tribes Advisory Council should meet atleast twice a year with adequate preparation to make them effective. It is only then that the TACs can become a meaningful and important forum representing tribal interest.

The states are required to send the Governor's report within six months of the closing of the financial year i.e. by the 30th September of each year. However, these reports are generally not received in time. The following table gives the position of reports which have not been received in the Ministry:

Under the Schemes of Research and Training, the Ministry provides financial assistance for three components, (i) Grants- to Tribal Research Institutes (TRls) of the State Governments on sharing basis of fifty-fifty of plan schemes, (ii) Award Of Research Fellowship in various aspects of Tribal Development (Doctoral/Post Doctoral Fellowship) to the students who are registered in Universities on 100% basis and (iii) Research Projects of All-India or Inter-State nature. The grant is provided on 100% basis to Governmental and Non-Governmental Institutes/ Organisation for conducting research and evaluation studies.

Position of governor's report upto January 1999

Sl.	*Name of States*	*Year for which the ReportNo. have not been received*
1.	Andhra Pradesh	1996-97 & 1997-98
2.	Bihar	1992-93 to 1997-98
3.	Gujarat	1997-98
4.	Madhya Pradesh	1997-98
5.	Maharashtra	1996-97 & 1997-98
6.	Orissa	1996-97 & 1997-98
7.	Rajasthan	1997-98
8.	Himachal Pradesh	1997-98

Tribal Research Institutes have been set up by State Governments to conduct Research and Evaluation, Seminars and Workshops on various subjects relevant to tribals, to provide training and orientation to State Government officials and to give support to State Governments for preparation of Tribal Sub Plan. Some institutes are also having Museums attached to them for exhibiting Tribal artifacts. Under the Scheme central grants are given on 50:50 basis to the Tribal Research Institutes. At present 14 Tribal Research Institutes in the states of Andhra Pradesh, Assam, Bihar, Gujarat, Kerala, Maharashtra, Madhya Pradesh, Orissa and Rajasthan, Tamil Nadu, Uttar Pradesh, West Bengal, Manipur and Tripura have been set up. This Ministry has also considered to establish a National Institute for Research and Training in Tribal Affairs at New Delhi. For 1998-99 a sum of Rs. 650.00 Lakhs have been allocated out of which Rs. 109.16 Lakhs have been released upto 17th February 1999.

The Ministry of Social Justice and Empowerment is giving grants for Research Fellowship on 100% basis to students/scholars, who are registered with a University for working on Tribal Development programmes/ problems. The rates of Fellowship for doctoral and Post doctoral courses were Rs. 1800 per month and Rs. 2200 per month respectively, which stands revised to Rs. 2800 and Rs. 3200 respectively. In Addition an annual contingency grant of Rs. 7000 is allowed.

The scheme relating to grant for Research and Evaluation project is being operated by the Ministry. Grants upto Rs. 1.50 lakhs per Project for a period of 8 months were given to Non-Government Organisation, which has been revised to Rs. 2.50 Lakhs per project for a period of 8 to 12 months (w.e.f. I st Dec. 1998)., During 1997-98 a -sum of Rs. 50.00 Lakhs has been budgeted but due to instruction of Finance Ministry, the Budget was revised to Rs. 15.00 Lakhs, the whole amount was released for new research proposals. During 1998-99 a sum of Rs. 50.00 Lakhs has been allocated out of which Rs. 25.00 Lakhs has been released upto 17th Feb. 1999.

Girls hostels for scheduled tribes

The scheme of girls hostel, which was started in the Third Plan, is a useful instrument for spreading education among ST girls, whose literacy still stands at 18.19% as per 1991 census against the general female literacy of 39.23%. Under the scheme, Central Assistance is given to the States/UTs for construction of now hostel buildings and/or extension of existing hostels. This is a Centrally sponsored Scheme where the cost of construction of the hostel building is equally shared between the Centre and the State in the ratio of 50:50. In case of UTs, the Central Government bears the entire cost of the building. The cost of construction is based on the State PWD schedule of rate or local CPWD schedule of rates, which ever is lower. Maintenance of the hostel is the responsibility of the concerned States/UTs. The number of seats in a hostel is limited generally to 100. The hostels are -for ST girls in middle and high schools, colleges and universities.

Out of Rs. 1405 lakhs provided in the Annual Budgets from 1994-95 to 1997-98, Rs. 1370.28 Lakhs was released to the States/UTs. for construction of 261 hostels. During the year 1998-99, the Budget provision for the scheme is Rs. 800 lakhs and an amount of Rs. 360.66 lakhs has been released for 46 hostels up to 15.2.99.

Boys hostels for scheduled tribes

This scheme was introduced in 1989-90 for construction of boys hostels. The norms followed are the same as those for the girls hostel.

Out of Rs. 1405 lakhs provided in the annual budgets from 1994-95 to 1997-98, an amount of Rs. 1250.69 lakhs was released to State/UTs For construction of 282 hostels. In the current year 1998-99, budget provision for the scheme is Rs. 800 lakhs and an amount of Rs. 531.44 lakhs has been released for construction of 15 hostels up to 15th February, 1999.

The scheme of Ashram School, a Centrally Sponsored Scheme, was launched in 1990-91 with an objective to extend educational facilities through residential schools for ST students. The funding for the scheme is done on matching (50:50) contribution basis with the States/UTs. Cent percent assistance is however, given to UTs. The scheme covers primary, secondary and senior secondary level of education.

Out of Rs. 1350 lakhs provided in the Annual Budgets during 1994-95 to 1998-99, an amount of Rs. 1386.98 lakhs was released to the State/UTs for construction of 297 schools. During the current year, Budget provision is Rs. 900 lakhs and an amount of Rs. 634.64 lakhs has been released for construction of 27 Ashram schools up to 15th February, 1999.

The main aim of this scheme is to develop the skills of the tribal youth in order to gain employment/self-employment opportunities. The scheme was introduced in 1992-93 as Central Sector Scheme and is implemented through the State Governments. The capacity of the vocational training centres is 50 with hostel facility for 25 of them. Each centre is to have a provision for training in 3 trades out of identified trades, the course of each trade being for a duration of 4 months, At the end of one years' training the trainee is to be attached to a master craftsman for a period of 3 months to sharpen his skills through practical experience. After this, the trainee is expected to emerge as a multi-skilled person capable of self employment. There is residential schools. The Budget provision for this scheme from 1994-95 to 1997-98 was Rs. 985 lakhs and an amount of Rs. 687 lakhs was released for setting up of educational complexes. During the current financial year, the Budget provision is Rs. 700 lakhs and amount of Rs. 215.43 lakhs has been released up to 15 February, 1999.

As part of Government's efforts to prevent deaths of children in remote and backward tribal areas, due to fall in nutrition standards, a scheme of Village Grain Banks has been launched during 199697. A one time grant towards purchase of grains, at the rate of one quintal per family of tribals in such areas, storage facilities for the grain and purchase of -weights and scales is provided by the Ministry of Social Justice and Empowerment, through TRIFED as the channelising agency. The banks will be managed by the Village Committees elected by the beneficiaries themselves, who as members of the bank can borrow grain from the Grain Banks at times of scarcity.

For 1996-97 Rs. 1.50 crores was released for setting up 234 Grain Banks while Rs. 1.80 crores for 281 Grain Banks was released for 1997-98. Allocation for 1998-99 is Rs. 3.00 crores.

Various important projects are being implemented by this Ministry through Voluntary Organisations which are working for the Welfare of the Scheduled Tribes. A wide spectrum of projects, which are of direct benefit to the tribals, are considered under this scheme. The projects include Residential Schools, Hostels, Medical Units, Computer Training Units, Shorthand and typing training units, Balwads/Creches (in areas not covered by ICDS Programmes) Libraries and Audio Visual units for dissemination of vital information relevant to the welfare of Scheduled Tribes. The grant is generally restricted to

90% of the approved total cost of project, the balance 10% is borne by the grantee organisations. There is a budget provision of Rs. 18.00 Crores during 1998-99. A summary of achievements during the last six years is as under:-

(Rs. In Crores)

Year	*Expenditure*	*No. of Vol. Orgn. Assisted*
1992-93	3.55	69
1993-94	4.03	66
1994-95	4.96	79
1995-96	5.30	86
1996-97	5.02	74
1997-98	7.00	113
1998-99	9.92*	161

* As on 15th February 1999.

Grant-in-aid to state tribal development cooperative corporations (TDCCs); and others for minor forest produce (MFP) operations

This is a Central sector Scheme with 100% grant, available to the State Tribal Development Cooperative Corporations; Forest Development Corporations; and Minor Forest Produce (Training and Development) Federation for taking up the minor forest produce operations. Under this Scheme grants can be utilised by the States for (i) strengthening the share capital base of TDCCs for increasing the volume of procurement of MFPs; (ii) construction of scientific warehouses; (iii) establishing process industries for value addition to MFP items; and (iv) research and Development activities by the Corporations. During the financial year 1997-98 the budget provision of Rs. 8.23 crores was disbursed to 8

State TDCCs. In the current financial year there is a budget provision of Rs. 6.25 crores.

The price of minor forest produce and surplus agricultural produce are subject to fluctuations. For meeting the unforeseen contingencies of losses because of such fluctuations in the prices and to ensure remunerative prices to the tribal farmers for their produce, the Ministry has been giving financial assistance to the TRIFED to set off part of such losses.

During the last financial year 1997-98, Rs. One crore was released to TRIFED. For the current financial year 1998-99, the budget provision under this scheme is Rs. 4.00 crores.

Investment in the share capital of TRIFED

TRIFED-Tribal Cooperative Marketing Development Federation of India Limited, was setup by the Government of India, under the administrative supervision of the Ministry of Social Justice & Empowerment, in the year 1987, with the prime objective of providing marketing assistance and remunerative prices to Scheduled Tribe Communities for their minor forest produce and surplus agricultural produce and to wean them away from exploitative private traders and middlemen. The Federation is a national level cooperative apex body functioning under the Multi-State Cooperative Societies Act, 1984.

The authorised share capital of TRIFED is Rs. 100.00 Crores and the paid up capital has gone upto Rs. 99.73 crore with the release of Rs. 6.00 crore provided in the budget of 1998-99. Out of Rs. 99.73 crore, the Government of India's contribution is Rs. 99.50 core and the balance Rs. 23.00 lakhs has been contributed by other shareholders.

The Scheduled Tribes, numbering 6.7 crores according to 1991 ensus, are the most disadvantaged section of the Indian Society and a large number of them are still below the poverty line. The main thrust of the point 11(b) of -20 point programme, economic assistance is provided to the Sch. Tribe families to enable them to rise above the poverty line. The Sch, Tribe families are assisted through various schemes like Agriculture, Rural Development, Horticulture, Animal Husbandry. Sericulture, Forestry, Small & Cottage Industries, Small business etc., funded from Central, Centrally sponsored and State Government.

The Ministry of Social Justice and Empowerment fixes the targets annually for the 20 TSP States/UTs and also monitors the progress of achievements on monthly basis. For 1998-99, a target of 11.01 lakhs ST families have been fixed for 20 TSP states/UTs. As against this target, till February, 1999. 5.96 lakhs ST families have bean economically assisted.

Based on the pre-agricultural level technology, low level of literacy and stagnant or diminishing population, 75 tribal communities in 1, States and 1 UT have been identified an categorised as primitive Tribal Groups (PTGs,) For their all round development new central sector scheme for the development in Primitive Tribal Groups has been introduced during current financial year.

9

INFRASTRUCTURE AND IMPLEMENTATION

The ministry has a common minister but each Department is separately headed by an independent Secretary. The Secretary is assisted by three Joint Secretaries and a Chief Director (Statistics) in the same grade. Out of the three joint Secretaries, one is Financial Adviser to the Ministry and looks after the work of other two departments of the Ministry-also. The other two joint Secretaries are Programme Officers, looking after various programmes relating to family welfare. The senior officers in the Department are taken from broadly three groups, firstly administrative services officers from All India Services and Central Secretariat Services, secondly medical officers from Central Health Services and thirdly statistical Officers.

The joint Secretary, Reproductive and Child Health is assisted by Programme Divisions for NGOs, IEC, Donor Coordination Division relating to International assistance, Infrastructure Division, Maternal Heath Division and Child Health Divisions. The other joint Secretary is assisted by programme divisions for Area

Projects, Policy Division, Training Division, Research & Studies Division and Supplies Division. The Chief Director (Statistics) is incharge of the large Division relating to data and Statistics. In the States there are Departments of Family Welfare supported by Directorates of Family Welfare. Generally, Principal Secretary (Health and Family Welfare) is incharge in the States of the whole of Health and Family Welfare and is assisted by one Secretary for Health matters and the other for Family Welfare matters.

All Family Welfare Programmes are implemented through the State Government set ups. For service delivery the set up for urban areas has 1562 Post Partum Centres which are either located in the medical colleges or in District Hospitals. These are supported by 1,291 Urban Family Welfare Centres and 871 Urban Health Posts. The latter two only have paramedics as its staff. For rural areas in addition to the Director/Sub-divisional Hospitals, there are 2,622 Community Health Centres. In addition there are 1,36,339 Rural Sub Centres.

The Rural Sub Centres have one Male Multipurpose Health Worker and Auxiliary Nurse Midwife and are provided for about 5,000 population. A Primary Health Centre is provided for about 30,000 population and a Community Health Centre is provided for 1.2 lakh population in a block. The Primary Health is headed by a Doctor and is assisted by 15 other persons. Community Health Centre has four Specialists in Gynaecology, Paediatrics, Medicines and Surgery and other staff. Rural Sub Centres are supported by the Government of India but only about 4,000 Primary Health Centres created in the beginning are supported by the Government of India. Rest of PHCs and CHCs have been set up by the State Governments. At District level, there is District Family Welfare Officer who along with his team is supported by the Government of India. At State level by the Directorate of Family Welfare is supported by the Government of India. Infrastructure division of the Department looks after programmes in respect of Urban and Rural Health Services in India.

Urban Health Services

The Post Partum Programme was started during the year 1969 in 59 District Level Hospitals. The Post Partum Programme is defined as a maternity centred hospital based approach to Family Welfare Programme to motivate women within the reproductive age group (15 - 44 years) or their husbands to adopt small family norms through education and motivation particularly during pre natal, natal and post natal period. Over the years, the concept of Post Partum has changed considerably and accordingly the functions of Post Partum Centres have also undergone a change.

The Post Partum Centres also function as referral centres for providing MCH and Family Welfare Service 550 Post Partum Centres are functioning at the District Level. The success of the Programme at District Level encouraged the Government of India to extend the Post Partum Programme to Subdivisional / Taluka Level Hospitals also. At present, 10-12 Sub-district Level Post Partum Centres are functioning under the programme. Under the Post Partum Programme, a set pattern of inputs in the form of staff, equipment, construction of a ward and operation theatre etc., is provided. The programme is 100% centrally assisted and is implemented through State Governments.

Table 1

The performance under Post Partum Programme at Sub-district Level during 1996-97 and 1997-98 is at Table 1.

Table 1

Percentage distribution of various acceptors of Family Welfare methods at Sub-District Level during 1996-97 and 1997-98 is as follows:

Family Welfare Method	*Sub-District Level 1996-97*		*1997-98*	
	Number of Acceptors	*Percentage Acceptors*	*Number of*	*per-centage*
Tubectomy	341694	53.0	353075	52.3
Vasectomy	6889	1.1	6007	0.9
IUD	229932	35.6	242213	35.9
Eq. OP Users	66749	10.3	73234	10.9
Total	645264	100.0	674529	100.0

PAP smear test facility programme

PAP Smear Test Facility Programme for early' detection of cervical cancer among women has been approved by Government of India in 105 Medical Colleges which are equipped with full fledged Department of Pathology and Services of a Senior Pathologist i.e. Professor of Pathology. Under the Programme a post of Cyto Technician for preparation/examination of slides and contingent expenditure for purchase of glassware and chemicals etc., have been provided by Government of India.

Contribution of post partum programme

The contribution in terms of performance of Post Partum Programme both at District and Sub-district Level is quite encouraging.

The performance under the programme for 1997-98 is as Table 2.

Sterilisation bed scheme

It was introduced during the year 1964 by reservation of

Sterilisation beds in Government/Voluntary Organisation and Local Body Institutions. The purpose of introduction of this scheme was to provide facility for tubectomy operations as the beds for such cases were not readily available in the hospitals. Under the Scheme, a total of 3170 bed are functioning at present (as on 1st April 1998).

Table 2

Performance of PAP smear Test Facility Programme

Item	*Number*
Number of Centres approved by Government of India	105
No.of slides prepared and examined	53684
No.of slides found normal	30625
Percentage found Normal	57.05
No.of slides found positive for carcinoma	1446
Percentage found positive for carcinoma	2.69

A recurring amount of Rs. 4500 per bed per annum is admissible for maintenance of the Sterilisation beds to Local Body/Voluntary Organisation on achievement of 60 tubecto-mies per bed per annum.

Urban revamping scheme urban health posts

The Urban Revamping Scheme has been introduced with a view to provide improved service / delivery out reach services of primary health care, family welfare and maternity services in urban areas particularly slum areas. The State Governments have established 871 Health Posts and 10 City Family Welfare Bureaux. The City Family Welfare Bureaux are entrusted with the responsibility of coordination, monitoring, supervision etc., of the Family Welfare Services provided by various institutions in the city.

Urban family welfare centres

Urban Family Welfare Centres are on ground since 1950

to provide Family Welfare Services in urban areas. There are three types of Urban Family Welfare Centres based on the population covered by them. In all there are 1083 Urban Family Welfare Centres functioning in the States/ Union Territories as on 1st April 1997 These Urban Family Welfare Centres; will be reorganised into Health Posts gradually as and when these cities will be considered for expansion under Urban Revamping Scheme.

Primary health care institutions in rural areas

The Primary Health Care infrastructure has been developed as a three tier system and is based on the following population norms:

Centre	*Population Norms*	
	Plain Area	*Hilly/Tribal Area*
Sub Centre	5000	3000
PHC	30000	20000
CHC	120000	80000

Sub Centres (SCs)

It is the most peripheral contact point between the Primary Health Care System and the Community. It is manned by one Multi-Purpose Worker (Male) and one Multi Purpose Worker (Female) /ANM. Only 97.757 Sub-Centres established after 1st April 1981 are funded by Ministry of Health and Family Welfare, out of a total number of 136818 Sub centres functioning in the country at the end of June, 98. The rest are being funded under the State Minimum Needs/ Basic Minimum Services (BMS) Programme.

Primary Health Centres (PHCs)

PHC is the first contact point between village community and the Medical Officer. These are established and maintained by the State Governments under the

Minimum Needs Programme (MNP)/BMS. A PHC is manned by a Medical Officer supported by 14 paramedical and other staff. It acts as a referral unit for 6 Sub Centres. It has 4 - 6 beds for patients. The activities of PHC involve curative, preventive, promotive and Family Welfare Services. Number of PHCs functioning in the country was 18,965 by 1st April 1990 which rose to 22991 by the end of-June, 1998.

Community Health Centres (CHCs)

CHCs are being established and maintained by the State Government under MNP/BMS. It is manned by four medical specialists i.e. Surgeon, Medicine, Gynaecologist and Paediatrician supported by 21 paramedical and other staff. It has 30 indoor beds with one O.T., X-Ray, Labour Room and Laboratory facilities. It serves as a referral centre for 4 PHCs. On 1st April 1990, the number of CHCs functioning was 1,910 which rose to 2712 by the end of June, 1998.

Rural family welfare centres

These are 5435 Rural Family Welfare Centres functioning in the country. These centres were established at all the block level PHCs sanctioned upto 1st April, 1980. The states have integrated the Rural Family Welfare Centres into their Primary Health Care System. There is therefore no separate identity for these RFWCs today. They are functioning as Primary Health Centres. The Government of India however, continues to provide financial support for maintaining these centres sanctioned before April, 1980. A provision of Rs. 265.00 crores has been made in B.E. 1998-99 for providing financial support to the states.

The details of staff sanctioned at each Centre is as under:

Assistant Surgeon	-	1
Block Ext. Educator	-	1

LHV	-	4
F.P. Health Assistant	-	1
Computer	-	1
ANM	-	1
Accountant	-	1
Driver	-	1
Vill. Worker		
(@ Rs. 50/- p.m.)		

Budget Allotted for Rural & Urban Health Schemes

(Rs in Lakhs)

Name of the Scheme	*Outlay for 1998-99*
Sub-Centres	34, 000
Health & Family Welfare Centres	700
Training of ANMs (M)	2,500
Training of MPWs (M)	600
Village Health Guide Schemes	1, 000
Rural Family Welfare Centres	26, 500
Post Partum Centres	4, 000
Sub Distt. Post Partum Centres	6, 000
Sterilization Beds	170
Urban Revamping Scheme	3, 400
Urban Family Welfare	3, 000

Gaps in infrastructure

As per the existing population norms, the existing infrastructure is not adequate in some states even if we take 1991 census population in to account. The number of sub centres, PHCs and CHCs required as per 1991 rural population. It may be seen that the present short-fall (as Funding for bridging the gaps.

The Department of Family Welfare is not directly providing financial assistance for setting up new Sub-centres and only maintenance grant is being given since 1st April 1981 for 97757 sub-centres out of a total number of 136815 sub centres. PHCs and CHCs are opened and maintained by the State Governments under the Minimum Needs Programme (MNP) which has since been reorganised into Basic Minimum Services (BMS) Programme. In view of the limited resources available, targets during the Ninth Plan period for establishing the subcentres, PHCs during and the CHCs have been kept at the level of shortfall as per 1991 population. While the progress of establishing SCs and PHCs may be viewed satisfactory, the gap in case of CHCs, the crucial First Referral Units (FRUs), is still wide. During the Ninth Plan the highest priority is to be given to bridge this gap through restructuring and strengthening of existing it infrastructure and redeployment of existing staff on 31st Dec. 1997) at the all India level is as in Table 3.

Table 3

Centre	*Shortfall as per 1991 Population*	*Shortfall as per Projected population for 2002*
Sub Centre	7686	22930
PHCs	1521	4182
CHCs	2903	3757

Each Sub-Centre is manned by one Male Health Worker and one Female Health Worker (Auxiliary Nurse Midwife). In order to train the required number of ANM in the rural areas, there are 480 ANMs Training Schools functioning in the country with an annual admission capacity of 16455 candidates (for 357 reporting schools). The duration of the training is 18 months. 10th pass girls preferably from the local villages where their services will be utilised later at the Sub-Centres and Primary Health Centres are admitted for the basic course.

Female health assistant training programme

One Female Health Assistant supervises the work of six

Sub-Centres in the rural areas. She provides technical guidance and supervision to the ANMs who are working in rural areas. The senior ANMs with a minimum of 5 years working experience are trained for 6 months to take up the post of LHV, which is a promotional post. 42 LHV training schools with an admission capacity of 2596 (for 38 reporting schools) are functioning in the country.

Village health guide scheme

The Village Health Guide Scheme was initially started as Community Health Workers' Scheme on 2nd October, 1977 in all the States except Arunachal Pradesh, J &K, Kerala and Tamil Nadu. The Scheme was renamed as Village Health Guide Scheme in 1981 when it was made 100% centrally, sponsored scheme under Family Welfare Programme. According to the scheme the village community selects a volunteer as Village Health Guide who after training acts as a link between the community and the governmental health system. He/She mainly provides health education and creates awareness on MCH and Family Welfare Services. He/She has to keep track of communicable diseases, treat minor ailments and provide first aid to the patients.

At present about 3.23 lakh VHGs are reported to be working. Each VHG is paid an honorarium of Rs. 50/- per month. The Scheme has recently been reviewed by a committee of expert which has looked into various aspects of the scheme such as the usefulness of the scheme, the work done by VHGs, capability of VHGs in the context of institutional arrangements available in the country, enhancement of honorarium and other facilities available to VHGs etc. The committee obtained feedback from the states and visited some of the states to get first hand information and it has submitted its final report / recommendations and the same is being examined in the Ministry.

Multi-Purpose worker (Male)

As per the norms, each sub-centre is required to be manned by a trained Female Health Worker (ANM) and a trained Male Health Worker known as Multi-purpose Worker (Male). The Government of India had initiated a scheme of training and thereby converting the uni-purpose workers under various programmes to multipurpose workers. The scheme of basic training for MPW (Male) was initiated during the 7th Plan period because of the shortage of MPWs (Male) at Sub-Centre level. Under this scheme, 10th pass candidates are selected and trained for one year before they are inducted into service. The basic training of MPW(M) was initiated in 47 Health and Family Welfare Training Centres throughout the country as 100% Centrally sponsored Scheme.

During 7th Plan (1985-90). It was observed that the training capacity was not enough to meet the requirement of MPW(M) in all the Sub-Centres, and hence the financial sanction to establish 50 new MPW(M) basic schools were given by the Government of India. At present, there are 28 HFWTCs and 23 New Basic MPW(M) Schools which are providing basic training to MPW(M).

Health and Family Welfare Training Centres (HFWTCs)

Health and Family Welfare Training Centres are established in the country with the objective of giving in-service training of health personnel in the rural health sector. These training centres are up with 100% financial assistance from the Central Government. There are 47 HFWTCs in the country at present.

The category of health personnel given in-service training at HFWTC and the period of training is as below:-

Medical Officer	2 weeks
Health Assistants (Male and Female)	2 weeks
Health Workers	2 weeks
Block Extension Educators	2 weeks
Key Trainers of ANM School and M.P.W. (M) basic schools	2 weeks

In addition to the above training, the HFWTCs take up in-service training under various vertical National Programme as well. From 1982, HFWTCs are giving basic training to MPWs(M) also the HFWTCs are funded under 100% Central Assistance from the Family Welfare Budget.

Regional health office

There are 17 Regional Offices of Health and Family Welfare functioning under Ministry of Health and Family Welfare located in the Capitals namely Hyderabad, Shillong, Lucknow, Ahmedabad, Imphal, Bhubaneswar, Patna, Chandigarh, Pune, Shimla, Jammu/Srinagar, Bangalore, Tiruvananthapuram, Bhopal, Jaipur, Calcutta and Chennai covering all the States/Union Territories. These offices have been established with the aim of liason and coordination of various National Health and Family Welfare Programmes with the States, monitoring of centrally sponsored Health and Family Welfare schemes, on the spot Technical guidance, test checking of records in the State, maintenance of Malaria clinic, review and analysis of monthly technical re ports, supervision of Health information and field units and association in various implementation and grant sanction committees. On the Family Welfare side there are 13 posts in every Regional Health Office headed by a Regional Director. Out of 17 Regional Directors, 11 are drawing salary from Family Welfare side and remaining 6 are from the Health side. However, the administrative control of all the 17 offices lies with Directorate General of Health Services of this Ministry. This department receives feedback in respect of all the National Health and Family Welfare Programmes by Monthly Progress and Tour Reports.

Family welfare training and research centre, Mumbai

Family Welfare Training and Research Centre, (FWTR & RC) Mumbai, is a Central Training Institute, responsible for the in-service training in Health and Family Welfare for the states in Western zone of the country, which includes the states of Gujarat, Madhya Pradesh, Andhra Pradesh, Goa, and the Union Territories of Daman, Diu and Dadra and Nagar Haveli. Training related to Primary Health Care, Family Welfare and other integrated National Health Programmes is imparted to various categories of health professionals of State and District levels, i.e. District Health Officers, District Extension and Media Officers, Key trainers from the Health and Family Welfare Training Centres of the above 1 states. This Centre is also conducting a one year Post-graduate academic course of Diploma in Health Education (D.H.E.) for candidates deputed from all over the country and also for candidates sponsored by the World Health Organisation (WHO)/UNICEF/ UNDP/DANIDA etc.

The first course of D.H.E. was started in the year 1987-88 and the XIIth course is in progress at present.

Apart from training and teaching, F.WT. and R.C., Mumbai is also involved in Health Services Research and Community-based Research in Health and F.W. and also delivering the comprehensive health services through Health Camps, organised at rural and urban areas.

Training programmes on Health and Family Welfare are also conducted for the W.H.O. Fellows, deputed through the Ministry of Health and F.W.

Regional Health Officers

Regional Director	*States under their Jurisdiction*	*Sources of Funds*
Hyderbad	Andhra Pradesh	Health
Shillong	Assam, Meghalaya and Arunachel Pradesh	Health
Lucknow	Uttar Pradesh	Health
Ahmedabad	Gujarat, Dadra and Nagar Haveli	Health
Imphal	Manipur, Nagaland and Mizoram	Health
Bhubaneswar	Orissa	Health
Patna	Bihar	F.W.
Chandigarh	Haryana, Punjab and Chandigarh	F.W.
Pune	Maharastra, Goa Daman and Diu	F.W.
Regional Director	States under their	
Shimla	Himachal Pradesh	F.W.
Jammu/Srinagar	Jammu and Kashmir	F.W.
Bangalore	Karnataka	F.W
Tiruvananthapuram	Kerala, Lakshwadeep	F.W.
Bhopal	Madhya Pradesh	F.W
Jaipur	Rajasthan	F.W.
Calcutta	West Bengal, Sikkim, Tripura and A and N Islands	F.W
Chennai	Tamil Nadu, Pondicherry	F.W

During the year 1998-99, training, education, research and clinic services of the Centre, were conducted as below:

Training activities

A training Programme on "Population and Sex Education" for the girl students of Regional Vocational Training Institute (R.V.T.I), Mumbai has been arranged by F.W.T. and R.C., Mumbai from 26th June 1998 to 27th June 1998. A total of 80 students were present for the above programme.

A workshop for launching the training programme for para-medical personnel working in F.W. programme has been arranged on 14th Oct. 1998, at F.WT and R.C., Mumbai.

Research activities

F.W.T and R.C., Mumbai, has been identified as a Regional Co-ordinating Centre to supervise the Annual Sentinel Surveillance activities, which has been already conducted for the states of Rajasthan and Himachal Pradesh. F.W.T and R.C., Mumbai, has undertaken the "Evaluation of Family Welfare Radio sponsored programmes" "Haseen Lamhe" and "Yeh Bhi Khoob Rahi" during the year. The research study "To develop a programme of preventive education on AIDS for the underprivileged adolescent boys and girls in urban slums" has been completed.

The dissemination workshop will be conducted during the month of December. The report has been finalised and dissemination workshop is to be conducted to disseminate the research findings to the researches and administrators working in the same field. A research proposal on "Study of sexual practices in relation to HIV/AIDS and STDs in selected tribal community of Maharashtra and Madhya Pradesh" has been submitted to NACO, New Delhi, for approval and funding.

Fellowships

Dr. (Mrs.) S.O. Verma, C.M.O. (NFSC) has been awarded a British Council Fellowship to attend a training course of Participatory and Rapid Appraisal for Evaluation in Health at Keel University, U.K., from 1st Sep. 1998 to 6th Sep. 1998 (A Collaborative Project of Nuffield Institute, Leeds, U.K. and NIHFW, New Delhi).

I.E.C. programme

F.W.T. and R.C., Mumbai has organised a health exhibition at Chhatrapati Shivaji Terminus (CST), Mumbai, on creating the awareness among the people regarding F.W, and AIDS from 12-13 Nov. 1998 (on the occasion of Nehru Jayanthi).

Clinical services

Service delivery to the mothers and children continued at the centre during the year 1998-99 through its Clinic and Laboratory. Medical and Health Care Services were delivered to the patients attending the clinic during the year. Along with M.C.H. services, counselling in Family Welfare is also imparted by the Centre.

International institute for population sciences, Mumbai

International Institute for Population Sciences, Mumbai is a "Deemed University" functioning under the administrative control of the Ministry of Health and Family Welfare, to confer training, conducting research and providing consultancy services in the field of Population Studies. The Institute has six specialised department viz. Department of Mathematical Demography and Statistics Department of Fertility Studies, Department of Public Health and Mortality Studies, Department of Migration and Urban Studies, Department of Population Policies and Programmes and Department of Development Studies. In addition, there is a Department of Development Studies. In addition, there is a Department of Extra Mural Studies functioning since 1993 on project basis.

Training: The Institute offers four regular courses viz. (a) The Diploma in Population Studies (DPS), (b) Master of Population Studies (MPS), (c) Master of Population Studies through correspondence and (d) Diploma in Health Education (DHE). In addition to the above courses, the Institute offers Ph.D. Programme. During the year 1997-98, 09 students (China - 05, Bhutan -02 and India -02) have attended DPS course. 23 students have attended MPS Course, 68 students were admitted to MPS Course. 16 students were admitted to DHE course. 72 students have been registered for Ph.D. Degree.

The Institute had also organised a Short-Term Training Programme on "Population Planning and Evaluation" for 10 officials from Sri Lanka during September 22-26, 1997 and on "Planning Management and Evaluation of Population Programme" during December 01, 1997 to January 01, 1998.

Research: The Institute has completed 15 Research Projects during 1997-98. There are 8 on-going research projects which were initiated during 1997-98 and are in different stages of completion. Also, 15 new research projects are being taken up during the year 1998-99, including two funded by other agencies. The new Research Projects are as under:

- Levels, Differentials and Determinants of Fertility: A District-wise Analysis of 1991 Census Data.
- Fertility, Mortality and Gender Inequality in India: A District Level Analysis of 1991 Census.
- Evaluation and Adjustment of 1991 Census Age Data and Estimation of Demographic Indicators for the Districts of Selected Indian States.
- Multi-region Demographic Analysis of India.
- Measuring Morbidity Diversity in India: A Spatio-Temporal Analysis.
- Reproductive Preferences and Achievement: An Investigation from Two Points Household Surveys.
- A Study of the knowledge, Attitude and Behaviour

of the Elected Members of Gram Panchayats on Population Issues and Health and Family Welfare Programme in Uttar Pradesh.

- A Study of Highway Communities Exposed to the Risk of HIV/AIDS.
- Causal Linkages Between Migration, Regional Disparities and Urbanization in
- India (Analysis of 1991 Data for Migration, Regional Development and Urban Economic Structure of Class I Cities).
- Survival Study of Tobacco and Food Related Cancers in Mumbai.
- Impact of Changes in vital Rates on Ageing Process in some Selected Stated of India over the Periods 1971-81 and 198191: An Analysis Based on Census Data.
- Proposal for Action Research Programme.
- Nirodh Use and Its Wastage in India: an Investigation from Field Study in Three States (Haryana, Maharashtra and U.P.)

Funded by other agencies

Social Assessment Survey (Beneficiaries) in Thane and Latur (Funded by Dept. of Health (Medical), Directorate of Health Services and Govt. of Maharashtra).

- Reproductive Behaviour of Women in Greater Mumbai: An Investigation from the Field Study (Funded by Public Health Deptt. Municipal Corporation of Greater Mumbai).
- In addition there are three research project viz. (i) Capacity Building in the area of Re productive Health, (ii) National Family Health Survey-II and (iii)

Rapid Household Survey under RCH Programme are under taken. These are funded by foreign agencies.

NFHS-II - Keeping in view the large utility of the valuable data for population management collected in the NFHS-I, the decision was taken to conduct the NFHS-II with the financial assistance of the USAID for total US $ 3.5 million for the local costs. The main purpose of NFHS-II is to measure changes over time and to gain a better grasp of the factors related to improvements in the population and health area. Under this survey, 25 States and I U.T. (Delhi) and about 94,000 ever married women in the age group of 15-49 years will be covered.

The three new and important feature of NFHS-II are (a) anaemia test for all respondent women and their children below 3 years of age, (b) Test of Iodine content in cooking salt and (c) Lead testing in the blood of children below 3 years in Delhi and Mumbai. UPS, Mumbai will function as Nodal Agency to make overall coordination and to disburse the funds to consulting Agencies, to finalise the questionnaires and sampling design and tabulation plan, under overall technical support of M/s. Micro International, Washington to prepare preliminary and final report at national level and to arrange dissemination of survey results through various forums and media.

Seminars/Conferences/ Workshops organised by the Institute

The following workshop/seminars were organised by the Institute during 1998-99:-

- State Institute of Health and Family Welfare (SIHFW) and IIPS jointly organised a seminar on Population and Development in Orissa from March 04-06, 19 98 SIHFW, Bhuvaneshwar.
- Questionnaire workshop on NFHS-II during March 19-20, 1998 at IIPS, Mumbai.

- Workshop on sampling design for NFHS-II during March 24-25, 1998.
- Workshop on Reproductive Health under the auspices of Ford Foundation Project on capacity building for PRC personnel 'and NGOs during April 6-8, 1998.
- Workshop on the use of Qualitative Research Methods on Health Research for the Research Staff of the Indian Institute of Health Management Research (IIHMR), Jaipur, September 29 to October 02, 1998.
- *Consultancy Services*: During the year 1997-98 the Institute provided consultancy services to various Institutions in India in the field of Population.
- *Publications*: The Institute brings out a quarterly Newsletter which furnishes details about various on-going activities of the Institute. During 1997-98 the Institute published four issues of IIPS Newsletter.
- *Library*: There are a total of 63100 books, 9945 bound periodicals and 13706 reprints in the Library. The Library receives 250 journals regularly, out of which 150 journals are by way of subscription and others are received as gifts or on exchange basis.
- *Data Centre*: Data Centre has been identified as "POPIN focal point" of the South Asian countries by Asia Pacific POPIN for three years period. Further it acts as "Supporting Centre" for "POPLINE" and getting the support from centre for population programmes, JHU, Baltimore, USA.
- *Notable Achievement of the Institute:* Institute is designated as a nodal agency to supervise and conduct the Rapid household survey (RCH Programme) with the help of 15 regional agencies in 50% of Districts of India.

- Institute is also entrusted with responsibility of being nodal agency for conducting NFHS-II covering above 1,00,000 household scattered all over the districts. Institute is also conducting projects funded by Ford Foundation to build capability of researchers in research on Reproductive Health. The Institute has been recognised on Popin Supporting Centre by UN ESCAP Bangkok for coming 3 years.
- The details of Rapid Household Survey and Facility Survey conducted by 15 Regional Institutions led by IIPS, Mumbai are given in under Management Information System.

National Institute of Health and Family Welfare, New Delhi

The National Institute of Health and Family Welfare, New Delhi is an autonomous body under the administrative control of the Department of Family Welfare. It is registered as a Society under the Societies Registration Act XXI of 1860 as extended to the 'Union Territory of Delhi. It was set up in 1977 as an apex technical Institute with the objective of promoting Health and Family Welfare Programme in the Country through education, training, advisory, consultancy and specialised services, research and evaluation.

The focus of these activities are the two major goals of Health for all by 2000 A.D. and Net Reproductive Rate-1 by 2011-16 A.D. The Institute has a faculty strength of 48 including its Director.

Education: In the area of basic education, the Institute continued to conduct (i) a three-year Post-Graduate Degree Course M.D. in Community Health Administration, (ii) a two year Post Graduate Diploma Course in Health Administration, (iii) a one-year Post-Graduate Certificate Course in Health & Family Welfare Management through Distance Learning; and (iv) a one-year Post- Graduate Certificate Course in Hospital Management through Distance Learning. During the year 18 students pursued the M.D. Course in Community Health Administration but discontinued later; 126 students were enrolled in the Certificate Course in Health and Family Welfare, and 133 students were enrolled in the Certificate Course in Health Management.

In-service Training: The in-service training programme of the Institute during this year included Integrated Skill Based Course in Health and Family Welfare, particularly in the area of Management, Communication, Training Methodology and Clinical Skills. The training highlight of the year included the Maternal and Child Health training course, which was previous conducted in collaboration with the Lverpool School of Tropical Medicine, UK, and which was conducted during the year exclusively in India by the NIHFW.

The Training Courses and workshops, numbering 33, covered a wide range of Health and Family Welfare personnel. The participants from all over the country are trained in the areas of Health and Family Welfare Communication, Management, Health Systems Research and Training methodology, clinical skills research methodology in biomedical research by participatory methods with hands on training in the field, hospital and laboratory.

Research: The research studies/ projects conducted by the Institute during the year were based upon crucial issues of the Health and Family Welfare Programmes and included monitoring and evaluation. The Institute has developed methodology for identifying research needs and conducting studies. NIHFW undertook different studies as a part of its regular activities. 14 studies were completed and 26 studies were in various stages of progress during the year. These are as under:-

Completed studies

- Policy Research on Private Practice by Government Doctors.
- Concurrent Evaluation of Pulse Polio Immunisation (PPI) Programme December 7, 1997 and January 18, 1998.
- Development of Low Cost Pregnancy Test Kit.
- Third Evaluation of the Strategies for health for All by the Year 2000 A.D.
- Evaluation and Standardisation of Health Management Training Courses in India (Under Health Management Consortium).
- Social Marketing of Contraceptives.
- Implementation Completion Report of India Population Project-VI.

Completed Studies under M.D. (CHA) Programme

- A Study of Health Care Services Provided to the Inmates of a Jail in Relation to their Health Problems.
- Assessment of IEC Activities in a District.
- A Study of the Existing Monitoring System for Select National Health Programmes and to Suggest Monitoring Indicators for these Programmes in a District.
- Evaluation of Quality of Maternal and Child Health Services at Maternal and Child Welfare Centre under the Municipal Corporation of Delhi.
- A Study on problem of Malaria and implementation of its Control Measures in Urban Slums of Delhi.
- Evaluation of National Child Survival and Safe Motherhood Programme in a District.

- A Study of Hospital Waste Management in a Tertiary Care Hospital.

On-Going Studies

- Assessment of Sperm Steriod Binding Proteins for the Regulation of Fertility in the Human.
- A Study on Willingness and Economic Capacity to pay for the Health Care Services.
- Integration of Health and Family Welfare Services in the States.
- Follow up Evaluation Study of Orientation Training Courses for District Extension and Media Officers in Communication Skills.
- Study on Selective Versus Comprehensive Features of Primary Health Care implementation in selected States in India.
- Development of Health Care Delivery Model for the Tribal Areas.
- An Evaluation Study of Bharat Gyan Vigyan Samiti's Literacy to Health project.
- An Epidemiological Study on Reproductive Health Problems among Males and Females in a District.
- A Study on Pre-marital Sexuality and Unmet Needs of Contraception among Sexually Active unmarried Youths in the Cities of India - Delhi and Lucknow.
- Development of Evaluation Tool Bank for Training.
- An evaluation study of Community Health Centres and Primary Health Centres in selected States.

  A Study on Involvement of Health, Care Providers in Delivery of Comprehensive Primary Health Care.
- A Study of Effectiveness of Integrated In-service

Training on, performance of Health Personnel in the Delivery of Health and Family Welfare Services in IPP-VII, States - a Three Phased Study.

- Partnership between Government and NGOs as an Alternative approach of Maximising Quality of PHC Services in North-East Hills.

  Study of organisation and Management of selected NGOs in four States of India (Under Health Management Consortium).

- Assessment of Training Needs of Primary Health Care Functionaries in Context of Reproductive and Child Health in a State.
- A Study on the Evaluation of National Malaria Eradication Programme in the States of Haryana and Rajasthan.
- Follow-up Evaluation Study of Hospital Administrations Courses conducted at NIHFW
- An Evaluation Study of Child Survival and Safe Motherhood Programme.
- HSP Gwalior Project - "Integrated Intervention Strategies".
- Evaluation of Obligatory Free Medical Care Services provided by Charitable Hospitals in Delhi.

On-going Studies under M.D. (CHA) Programme

- Study on Training Needs Assessment of Panchayat Raj Members in the Context of Local Decentralised Development Planning including Health.
- A Study of selected Health Problems of Elderly in a District.
- Assessment of Block Extension Educative Activities for Promoting Health and Family Welfare

programmes at Block level experience for trainers of all categories of health personnel, providing primary health care. In addition, management Institutes were also identified to conduct management training for health managers at district and State levels.

Specialised services: Specialised services of the Institute included services for MCH/infertility/endocrimological disorders provided at its clinic, the documentation and Library services provided through its National Documentation Centre and its research publications and course modules. The Institute also provided advisory and consultancy services to various national, international and voluntary organisations in various capacities during the year. Regarding Training Administrative Unit in NIHFW, the information has been detailed in the Chapter for Training.

Hindustan Latex Limited (HLL), Thiruvananthapuram

HLL, a public sector undertaking under the administrative control of the Department of Family Welfare, commenced its manufacturing operations on April 5, 1969 and is today one of the largest manufacturers of condoms in the country. It also manufactures Copper-Ts, Oral pills including 'Saheli'- the once-a-week non-steroidal contraceptive pill, Blood Bags, Hydrocephalus Shunts and is also marketing Surgical Sutures, an important Component for the hospital industry. HLL has three manufacturing plants two at Peroorkada and Akkulam in Thiruvananthapuram, Kerala and one at Belgaum, Karnataka.

Capital structure: The issued and paid up share capital of the Company is Rs. 1553.50 lakhs. The total capital employed is Rs. 49744.23 lakhs as on 31st March 1998.

Memorandum of understanding: Hindustan Latex has signed the Memorandum of Understanding with the

Department of Family Welfare, Government of India, for the financial years from 1991-92 onwards. HLL's performance has been rated 'Excellent' for its consistently achieving targets, on the basis of the performance criteria set by the Government of India during the year 1996-97

Performance: The sales turnover of the company was Rs. 66.06 crores for 1977-98 against Rs. 81.88 crores for 1996-97 The total sales achieved for its various products for 1997-98 were:-

a)	Condoms	568.74	Min.Pcs
b)	Latex Gloves	5.56	Min. Pcs
c)	Saheli Once a week Contraceptive Pill	9.41	Min. Tablets
d)	Mala D/N	11.62	Min.cycles
e)	Copper-T	0.87	Min.Pcs
f)	Hydrocephalus Shunt	2514	pcs
g)	Blood Bags	0.94	Min.Pcs
h)	Sutures (Trading)	0.053	Min.Dozen

Technological expertise: Over the past twenty-nine years, HLL has acquired technological expertise and are today leaders in the area of Latex Dipped Goods.

R&D department: The Company's R&D Department has made significant contribution for the improvement of the quality of the Company's range of condoms together with the indigenisation of raw materials and other equipments that were imported.

Quality assurance: The Company lays great emphasis on effective quality control at every manufacturing stage.

Hindustan Latex have been granted ISO 9002:1994 Certification, for the topmost quality management systems for its two Plants.

- At Peroorkada - Manufacturing Condoms
- At Akkulam - Manufacturing

  (i) Copper-T's

  (ii) Blood Bags and

  (iii) Hydrocephalus Shunt.

The ISO 9002:1994 certification signifies that the quality systems in force at its manufacturing units is a Model one, for quality assurance in - production, installation and servicing. This international acknowledgement for the Quality systems at HLL was awarded by the NQA Quality Systems Registrar Ltd., accredited by the Dutch Council for Certification; one of the topmost certification agencies of Europe. Earlier, in 1995 HLL was awarded the N F Mark - the official Quality Certification by the Premier French LNE after a detailed Quality Laboratory Audit. Again HLL is the only manufacturer from India to be awarded the prestigious CE Mark certification is a prerequisite for entry into the vast and competitive European Market.

HLL condoms today conform to the rigorous specifications prescribed by WHO, AFNOR (French Standards), ASTM (American Standards). Recently, HLL also received the SABS Mark from the South African Bureau Standards and the GMP Certificate from the Zimbabwe Regional Drug Control Laboratory.

Marketing and exports: The Company has regional marketing offices at Delhi, Madras, Bombay, Calcutta and Lucknow besides the headquarters at Thiruvanthapuram. Direct marketing operations of its own domestic brands includes:-

- Moods, a premium brand, is the first of such brands introduced in the market on a national scale, other brands introduced later were Share, Ustad, Rakshak Nymph and Moods Supreme.

- HLL introduced the world's first non-steriodal Once-a-week Oral Contraceptive Pill Saheli in 1992.
- Marketing of Mala-D Oral contraceptive Pill in the states of Rajasthan, Madhya Pradesh, Kerala, Tamil Nadu and Karnataka started in July, 1993.
- Other additions have been the high-tech medical aid for Neuro Surgeons-the Ceredrain Hydrocephalus Shunt; Surgical Sutures both - absorbable and nonabsorbable; and Blood Transfusion Bags, at its most modern facility at Thiruvananthapuram.
- During 1997-98 HLL achieved a sale of 169.83 Mln. Pcs. of condoms under the social marketing programme, 40 lakhs cycles of Mala-D and 94.03 lakhs tablets of Saheli oral pills.
- HLL has been retained by the Ministry of health and Family Welfare as a Procurement Consultant for their Reproductive and Child Health (RCH) programme. An agreement was signed between HLL and the Ministry to this effect on 30.4.98. As per the agreement, HLL has to procure 13 drug items and hospital rubber sheets. These items are to be assembled into Drug kit W and Drug kit 'B'. These kits are then to be delivered to 250 consignees located in various States/UTs. The Hospital rubber sheets are to be distributed in the States of Assam, Bihar, Rajasthan and Madhya Pradesh. The total value of procurement is estimated to Rs. 40.00 crores. HLL invited bids through advertisements and after evaluation of bids submitted the documentation to this Department of Family Welfare. After the approval of the competent authority in the Ministry, HLL placed orders on the firms. The total value of order of drug kits 'N and 'B' is Rs. 32.00 crores approximately. The total quantity to be procured is 1,33,600 no. each of Drug kit W and Drug kit 'B'.

- HILL has recently awarded a three year project by the State Innovation in Family Planning Service Agency (SIFPSA), Lucknow for marketing contraceptives in the rural areas of Uttar Pradesh. SIPFSA is a voluntary organisation set up with the Financial Assistance from U SAID. Under this project, HLL will set up a marketing network to market 89 million condoms, 70 million Oral contraceptive pills and 5.75 lakhs Copper-
- This project is to set up marketing infrastructure at an estimated cost of Rs. 4.22 crores over a period of 3 years. The Company has also been awarded a contract by AIDS Prevention and Control (APAC), Chennai, and envisage a market spending of Rs. 17 lakhs financed by the agency for a period of one year.
- Hindustan Latex Family Planning Trust (HLFPPT) promoted by HLL has been awarded a project for Social Marketing of Condoms, Contraceptive Pills, ORS and Sanitary Napkins, in around 2500 villages of Gwalior, Bhind, and Morana districts of Madhya Pradesh. The development objectives of the project include distribution of Social Marketing brands of contraceptives through unemployed, educated and mobile rural youth, supported by a comprehensive local media based IEC programme, thereby contribution to the reduction of total Fertility Rate (TFR) in the rural areas and also advancement of Family health through the promotion of sanitary napkins and Oral Rehydration Salts (ORS).

HLL's Branded Condoms and Examination Gloves received the 510 K certification from FDA (Food and Drugs Administration) USA, which is essentially a clearance for marketing these products in the US.

The International division of the company was set

up in 1993. HLL's exports during 1996-97 touched Rs. 11.92 crores. HLL exported its products during 1997-98 to 37 countries all over the world.

Population research centres

The Union Ministry of Health Welfare has established a network of 18 Population Research Centres (PCS) in various Universities (11), other Institutions (6) of national repute and one in Madhya Pradesh, scattered over 17 major States of India on the basis of facilities and other infrastructure available.

These Centres are responsible for carrying out research on various topics of Population Stabilisation, Demographic and Socio-Demographic Surveys and Communication aspects of Population and Family Welfare Programme. These Population Research Centres are autonomous in their functioning with 100% financial assistance, in the form of grants-in-aid on year to year basis towards salaries of staff, books and journals, stationery, vehicle for field for field surveys and the infrastructural equipments etc, from Government of India. At present there are two types of PRCs, one designated as 'Fully Developed' and others 'Not Fully Developed'. Staffing pattern varies according to the type of PRC. These grants-in-aid are released to the PRCs in three instalments in a year on receipt of essential prescribed documents/bonds and undertakings. The staff of these PRCs is also imparted training, both Nationally and Internationally, with a view to enhance the research capabilities and improve the quality of research.

These centres are monitored centrally to ensure that the research effort is not merely academic but also action oriented.

Strengthening of PRCs

The changes envisaged on the basis of the recommendations of the three committees

- *Permanent Status:* It is proposed to as sign permanent status of an Institute to the PRCs;
- *Pensionery Benefits:* Introduction of an element of flexibility is proposed. Staff can opt for Pension/CPF Scheme.
- *Ceiling on Non-salary Items:* The ceiling on non-salary items is proposed to be enhanced considerably to increase capability of PRCs.
- *Staff Strength:* A Fully Developed PRC will have a full time Director in the pay scale of a Professor assisted by two Readers and two Lecturers. A Non-fully Developed PRC will have full time director in the scale of Professor assisted by one Reader and two Lecturers. Approval of budget for these measures is being obtained for IX Plan.

Studies conducted by the PRCs Most of the studies conducted by these PRCs are on varying topics such as:-

- Population Growth;
- Socio-economic characteristics of rural/ urban population;
- Evaluation of Family Welfare Programme for non-acceptance of Family planning methods;
- Evaluation of Special School Health Check up Scheme; and
- Fertility and Socio-economic Indicators.

Some of the important topics of research covered by these Centres, in addition to the studies assigned by the Government of India are as under:-

- Integrated Nutrition and Health Programme: A Base-line survey Report of Andhra Pradesh;
- Multi-Indicator Cluster Survey in Urban Slums and Rural Areas;

- Status of Women and Reproductive Behaviour Among Urban Indian Women Understanding the linkages;
- Study to evaluate the Impact of TV Advertisement for Deluxe Nirodh and Mala-D in Madurai City;
- Population Growth and Quality of Life.

The ongoing process of regular monitoring and ensuring that the research effort is not merely academic but also action oriented has been further strengthened. A set of 15 studies on varying topics, has been assigned to the PRCs for completion during 1998-99 and 1999-2000. List of studies selected and assigned to t he Population Research Centres is as follows:-

- Verification of Authenticity of reported cases of Sterilisations (by each technique separately and IUD insertions by obtaining list of persons shown to have been sterilised or women shown to have been provided IUD insertions by the District Family Welfare set up and to verify from such persons whether actual sterilisation/ IUD insertion was made. In regard to IUD insertions also to verify the duration after which it has to be taken out and reason for taking out the IUD. To be taken up completely.
- Installation and utilisation of equipment supplied under CSSM. List of equipment should be obtained from the department of Family Welfare (Govt. of India) and from the Director, Family Welfare of the State Government. It should be verified through visits, when equipment was delivered at district level and when these have been shifted to the user hospitals and whether they are presently in use. To be taken up for a block of half the districts.

- Survey for functioning of RTI/STI Clinics. It should be ascertained from Chief Medical Officer of the District/ Director, Family Welfare of the State Government in which RTI/STI clinics are sanctioned and verification should be made by visits whether these clinics have distinct and visible identity, whether (and how many) doctors are posted exclusively for the clinic and how many men and women (separately) have availed these clinics in last three or six months. This study should be taken up for a block of roughly half the districts in the state chosen for study.

- Verification of last doses of vaccines for various vaccination programmes and verification of third pre-natal check up of pregnant women and third post natal checkup of women after delivery. This study should be taken up district as a unit but wherever it is taken up 100% verification should be ensured.

- Ascertaining and assessing the factors responsible for unwanted pregnancies-Study or selected areas. The study can be also for different religious groups of women.

- To ascertain availability of condoms and oral pills at village level. This study may take block sub-division or district as a unit and may ascertain for individual villages whether there is any out- let from where people of the village can obtain condom and oral pill when they require it.

- Assessment-of prevalence of Reproductive Tract Infections and Sexually Transmitted Infections in representative samples of population in selected areas.

- Assessment of Implementation status of Pre-natal

Diagnostic Techniques Act, 1994. To ascertain in identified Districts situation in regard to registration of clinics and situation in regard to prosecution under the Act.

- Assessing prevalence/incidence of Neo-Natal Tetanus in selected districts.
- Verification of utilisation of buildings constructed under IPP-V, IV & VII Projects. Whole state should be taken for such assessment. List of buildings constructed may be obtained from Director, Family Welfare of the state Government and utilisation should be ascertained by field visits.
- Study of the functioning of State Training Institutes of Health and Family Welfare. Position in regard to adequacy of building, training equipment, adequacy of faculty members and regularity/extent of training programmes may, be ascertained. If there are shortcomings, the reasons for that may be ascertained.
- Assessment of effectiveness of Mahila Swasthya Sanghs in selected districts and to assess what impact their functioning has had on population control/RCH objectives.
- Assessment of effectiveness of Nehru Yuvak Kendras in selected districts: assess what impact their functioning has had on population control/RCH objectives.
- Assessment of effectiveness of Village Health Guides in selected districts and to assess what impact their functioning has had on population control/RCH objectives.
- Abortions Needs Assessment
- An amount of Rs. 8.00 crore has been earmarked for the above PRCs during 1998-99.

The ongoing process of regular monitoring and ensuring that the research effort is not merely academic but also action oriented has been further strengthened.

(Rs. In lakh)

S.No.	*Name of State*	*Assistance Fund*	*Total* Amount
1st Phase			
1.	Kerala	248.80	
2.	Madhya Pradesh	248.80	
3.	Rajasthan	248.80	
4.	Tamil Nadu	224.00	970.40
IInd Phase			
Money released with IEFC sanctions dated 28.12.1998			
1.	Andhra Pradesh	256.00	
2.	Karnataka	256.00	
3.	Orissa	208.00	
4.	Punjab, D & N Haveli 227.20 Daman & Diu, Pondicherry, and Manipur		947.20
IIIrd Phase			
EFC sanction accorded on 05.01.1999			
1.	Andhra Pradesh	540.00	
2.	Gujarat	90.00	
3.	Haryana	72.00	
4.	Uttar Pradesh	360.00	
5.	West Bengal	234.00	1296.00
			3213.60

Transport

Mobility is a vital input for effective implementation of Family Welfare Programme.

The Government of India has provided 8089 vehicles to the States/UTs. Monitoring and evaluation of the existing fleet was done from 5th July 1998 to 15th Jan., 1999 during the year 1998-99 in the States of Kerala, Tamil Nadu, Andhra Pradesh, Himachal Pradesh, Punjab, Haryana, Rajasthan, Uttar Pradesh, Bihar, Madhya Pradesh and Maharashtra. POL and maintenance charges for the family welfare vehicles was made available to the States at the rate of Rs.15,000/- per vehicle per annum for diesel driven vehicles and Rs.20,000/- per vehicle per annum for petrol driven vehicles.

Mopeds to ANMs

Since 1996-97 with the assistance of UNFPA a project is being implemented under which ANMs are given interest free loans from a corpus fund for purchase of mopeds to enhance their mobility.

10

OTHER BACKWARD CLASSES

The Supreme Court in its judgement in Indira Sawhney and others vs. Won of India and others (Mandal Case), delivered on 16th November, 1992, upheld the reservation of 27 per cent of vacancies in the civil posts, and services under the Government of India in favour of Other Backward Classes (OBCs) subject to the exclusion of socially advanced persons/sections among them known as "Creamy Layer"

The Supreme Court had directed the Government of India to specify the socio-economic criteria for exclusion of the "Creamy Layer" from the OBCs. The Supreme Court had also directed the Government of India and each of the State Government/UT Administration to set-up a permanent body for recommending upon requests for inclusion and complaints of over-inclusion and under-inclusion in the lists of Other Backward Classes.

In the above judgement the Supreme Court, besides finally setting the legal position with regard to reservation made the following observations on various aspects of the reservation policy of the Government:

(i) Reservation of appointments or posts under Article 16(4) is confined to initial appointment only and can not be extended to provide reservation in the matter of promotion;

(ii) The reservation contemplated in Article 16(4) shall not exceed 50%; and

(iii) It is advisable to exclude from the purview of reservation certain services and posts where on account of the nature of duties attached to them or the level at which they obtain, merit alone counts.

Creamy layer

The Supreme Court directed the Central Government as well as the State Governments to specify the basis for applying the relevant and requisite socioeconomic criteria to exclude advanced persons/sections (Creamy Layer) from OBCs. Accordingly, an amended Government order dated 8th September, 1993 was issued indicating the category of persons/sections to whom the rule of exclusion will apply.

Creamy layer at a glance

As per the order of the Department of Personnel and Training No. 36012/22-93-Esft, dt. 08-09-1993 the rule of exclusion will apply to son(s) and daughter(s) of persons holding Constitutional positions like President of India, Vice-President of India, Judges of Supreme Court and High Court, Chairman and Members of Union Public service Commission and State Public service Commission, Chief Election Commissioner, Comptroller and Auditor General of India, Parent either of whom is a Class I Officer, Parents other or both of whom is or are in the rank of Colonel and above in the Army and equivalent posts in the Navy and Air Force and the para-military forces.

Families owning irrigated land which, is equal to

more than 85% of the ceiling limit in terms of irrigated land as per State land ceiling lam. Persons having gross annual income of Rs. 1.00 lakh or above or possessing wealth, above the exemption limits prescribed in the wealth Tax Act for a period of three consecutive years (income for salaries or agricultural land shall not lie clubbed).

Notifying the list of other backward classes

The common list of OBCs In respect of 14 States namely Andhra Pradesh, Assam, Bihar, Goa, Gujarat, Haryana, Himachal Pradesh, Karnataka, Kerala, Madhya Pradesh, Maharashtra, Punjab, Tamil Nadu & Uttar Pradesh was published in the Gazette of India extraordinary Part-I, Section 1 No.. 186, dated 13th September, 1993. The second common list of OBCs notified in the Gazette of India extraordinary Part 1, Section 1 No. 163, dated 20th October, 1994 related to States of Orissa, Rajasthan, Tripura & West Bengal. On 25th May, 1995 vide Gazette of India extraordinary Part I Section 1 No. 88, the common list of OBCs in respect of Jammu & Kashmir, Manipur, Sikkim, and NCT of Delhi has also been notified. The Central Government has included/amended/modified the names of some castes/communities in the Central List of OBCs in respect of Andhra Pradesh, Kerala, Madhya Pradesh, Maharashtra, Orissa, Tamil Nadu, Tripura, Uttar Pradesh and West Bengal vide Gazette of India, extraordinary Part I section 1 No. 60 dated 11th December, 1996. Besides, the common list of OBCs in respect of LIT of Chandigarh and amendment to OBC list of Uttar Pradesh have been issued on 11-12-1997 and 03-12-1997 respectively.

The Government has provided OBC candidates the benefit of relaxed standard in respect of written examination and interview as in the case of SC/ST candidates with effect from 13th October, 1994.

On 25th January, 1995 the Government of India has issued instructions relaxing the upper age limit for OBC candidates indirect recruitment by three years and the number of attempts for OBC candidates who are otherwise eligible has been increased to seven in respect of Civil services Examinations.

The National Commission for Backward Classes (NCBC) Act, 1993 was enacted on the direction of the Supreme Court to set up as permanent body for entertaining, examining and recommending upon requests for inclusion and complaints of over-inclusion and under-inclusion in the lists of Other Backward Classes of citizens. As per the provision of the Act, the advice tendered by such body shall ordinarily be binding upon the Government. I Commission was constituted on the 14 August, 1993 for a period of three years. The second National Commission has been constituted on 28th February 1997 for a period of three years.

National Backward Classes Finance & Development Corporation (NBCFDC) was set up by the Government of India under Ministry of Welfare on 13th January, 1992 as a company not for profit under Section 25 of the Company's Act with the objective of providing concessional finance to the members for backward classes living below double the poverty line for their socio-economic development by extending them loans for income generating schemes. The Corporation undertakes:-

(a) to provide additional channel of finance backward classes for economically a financially viable schemes and projects; and

(b) upgrade the technological and entrepreneur skills of individuals or groups belonging Backward Classes.

The authorised share capital of the Corporation was Rs. 200.00 crores and the same has been now raised to Rs.

700.00 crores. The issued and paid-up capital of the Corporation was Rs. 198.90 on 31.12.98, which has now been raised to Rs. 290.40 crores.

The Corporation has so far sanctioned loans amounting to Rs. 614.31 crores of which Rs. 330.94 crores were disbursed. The number of units covered persons benefited and the year-wise details of sanctions and disbursements are given below:-

Year	*Amount (Rs. in crores)*		*No. of units*	*No. of beneficiaries*	*Wages Employees*
	Sanctioned	*Disbursed*			
1992-93	33.80	6.90	25821	31939	21302
1993-94	105.07	50.07	71855	76139	47840
1994-95	122.28	68.09	39018	40798	25099
1995-96	29.35	23.35	8084	7794	4300
1996-97	123.33	49.42	61706	72376	30925
1997-98	125.02	70.82	48127	48277	33730
1998-99*	104.13	67.27	20709	28205	15944

NBCFDC can assist a wide range of income generating activities for employment generation to the members of Backward Classes in various sectors as, follows:

(a) Agricultural and Allied activities;

(b) Artisan and Traditional occupations;

(c) Technical Trades-Self- Employment;

(d) Small Scale and tiny Industry;

(e) Small Business; and

(f) Transport services;

These are illustrative and not exhaustive and each scheme may cover a number of identical units.

The Corporation has put great emphasis on training and education as the Corporation in furtherance of its objective spent about Rs. 119.40 lakh as grant-in-aid for 3198 beneficiaries out of which Rs. 30.15 lakh have been provided during 1998-99 upto 31-12-1998.

During the year 1998-99, Corporation continued its concerted efforts in identifying the systems deficiencies and taking corrective measures towards bringing about transparency in its operations.

Frequent field visits are being conducted by the Corporation to assist the SCAs in removing impediments in smooth implementation of Corporation's schemes. Corporation has been sending response cards to the beneficiaries submitted by the SCAs. Further one major scheme in each State is being evaluated through accredited institution, in order to get requisite feed back of the impact of Corporation schemes.

The Corporation has continued its thrust on recovery of loan from SCAs. The Corporation has recovered Rs. 11785.40 lakh as on date. The present repayment percentage is 80 per cent as compared to 74 per cent in 1997-98. Further due to continued efforts the utilisation of already disbursed funds is showing encouraging trends in as much as 76% of funds released have reportedly been utilised.

The Corporation has launched a special scheme for eligible women beneficiaries of backward classes under the name of 'SWARNIMA'. The women beneficiaries get financial assistance at concessional rate of interest upto Rs. 1.00 lakh under the scheme. The Corporation has directed the SCAs to ensure 30% coverage of women beneficiaries under NBCFDC schemes out of which 5% will be covered under 'SWARNIMA' scheme. Effective steps are being taken to achieve this coverage.

The following Schemes have been launched in the year 1998-99 for the welfare of OBCs by the Government of India:

Pre-examination coaching

The objective of the scheme is to coach/train candidates belonging to Other Backward Classes (OBCs) to enable them to compete on equal terms in various competitive/entrance examinations covering. Recruitment to various services under the Central and State Governments, Public and Private Sector Undertakings Banks, GIC, LIC etc. and Defence Forces, State and Central Police Forces and Para-Military Forces and admission to technical, vocational, engineering medical, agricultural management courses etc. The candidates whose parents' or guardians total income from all sources including the income of the candidates is below Rs. 1.00 lakh annually will be eligible for admission in the pre-examination coaching centre under the scheme. An outlay of Rs. 2.00 crores have been provided for the scheme in 1998-99.

Hostel for OBC boys and girls

The scheme aims at providing better education opportunities to students belonging to socially and educationally backward classes notified as such in the Central/State/UT admn. list of OBC, generally referred to as Other Backward Classes (OBCs). It would, however, not cover students belonging to the Creamy Layer as defined in the Government of India, Ministry of Personnel, Public Grievances and Pensions (Department of Personnel and Training) OM No. 36012/22/93-Estt. (SCT) dated 08-09-1993. The Hostels under the scheme will be constructed in States/UTs which have a large OBC population but inadequate hostel facilities. These hostels will be constructed for middle, secondary college and university level students. Out of the Hostels to be set up under this scheme at least one third will be exclusively for girls. Five percent of the total seats in these hostels shall be reserved for disabled students-

The organisations eligible for assistance shall be as follows:

(i) The State Governments and UTs concerned;

(ii) Institutions or organisations set up by the Government as autonomous body under statute or as a society under the Registration of Societies Act, 1860 or otherwise;

(iii) Educational and other institutions owned and controlled by either Central Government or State Government/UTs.

Under the scheme, 50% central assistance will be given for construction in such ewes. The remaining 50% of the construction cost will have to be borne by the concerned State Government. Under the scheme 100% Central assistance will be given to the Central Government institutions and UTs proposing to set up such hostels. The entire expenditure on procurement of land, staffing and other maintenance and day to day expenditure shall be borne by the State Govt./ UT concerned. An outlay of Rs. 2.00 crores has been provided for the scheme in 1998-99.

Pre-matric scholarship for OBCS

Under this scheme, scholarship award will be sanctioned in the case of students whose parents/guardians; income from all sources does not exceed Rs. 44,500 per annum. The scholarships are to be given to the students in class I or any subsequent class of pre-matric stage in the case of day scholars and class 11 or any subsequent class of pre-matric stage in the case of hostelers. The scholarship will terminate at the end of class X. The duration of scholarship in an academic year will be 10 months. The scholarship will be tenable in such institutions and for such pre-matriculation courses which have been duty recognised by the concerned State Government and Union territories Admn. 50% Central Assistance will be provided to the state Government under the scheme. An outlay of Rs. 2.00 crores; has been provided for the scheme in 1998-99.

Post-matric scholarships to the OBC students for studies In India

The objective of the scheme is to provide financial assistance to the OBC students studying at post-matriculation or post secondary stage to enable them to complete their education. These scholarship shall be available for' studies in India only and will be awarded by the Government of State/UT to which the applicant actually belongs, i.e. permanently settled 100% central assistance will be provided to State Governments/UT Admns for this purpose. The Central scholarships will be open to Indian nationals belonging to OBC as notified by the Central/State Government/UT Admn. These scholarships will be given for study in recognised institutions. Unemployed students whose parents/guardians' income from all sources does not exceed Rs. 44,500.00 per annum will be entitled for scholarship under the scheme. An outlay of Rs. 5.00 cores has been provided for the scheme in 1998-99.

Assistance to voluntary organizations for welfare of OBCs

The aim of the scheme is to involve the voluntary sector to improve educational and socio-economic conditions of the target group i.e.. OBCs through skill upgradation and enable , them to start income generating activities on their own or get gainfully employed. Assistance under the scheme will be admissible for establishing centres and developing services which may equip the OBCs by upgrading their skill to enable them to start income generating activities. The quantum of assistance is determined in each case on merit. The Government of India may, however, meet 90% of the approved expenditure on any or all of the specified items under the scheme. An outlay of Rs. 2.00 crores has been provided for the scheme in 1998-99.

11

PERSONNEL POLICIES

Publication of recruitment notice

Instructions have been issued providing that the requisitioning authority/Establishment while notifying vacancies to employment exchange, may, keeping in view administrative/budgetary convenience, arrange for publication of the recruitment notice in the "Employment News" published by the Ministry of Information and Broadcasting. Such recruitment notice should also be displayed on the office Notice Boards for wider publicity.

Time schedule

Time schedule has been prescribed for convening Departmental Promotion Committee meetings to ensure availability of panels for appointment sufficiently in advance. The time schedule has been prescribed in all cases including the cases requiring approval of the Appointment Committee of the Cabinet.

Enhancement of upper age limit

Upper age limit for direct recruitment through open competitive examinations to Central Civil Services and Civil Posts has been increased by two years.

Revision of orders

The following revised/consolidated instructions were issued during the year:

(a) Instructions on compassionate appointment under the Government.

(b) Guidelines for amending Recruitment Rules.

(c) Model recruitment rules for group 'A' and Group 'B' posts in the electronic data processing discipline incorporating computer engineering/service qualifications.

Recommendations of the Fifth Central pay Commission

In pursuance of the recommendations of the Fifth Central Pay Commission, the Government have issued the following orders:

Age of retirement

Age of retirement of Central Government employees was raised from 58 to 60 years. The decision came into force w.e.f. 13.5.98. Similarly, the age of retirement of the employees of Central Public Sector Undertaking, Banks and Insurance Companies was raised to 60 years. The age of retirement of Armed Forces and Central Para Military Forces personnel was also raised by two years.

Leave travel concession

The rules for grant of-Leave Travel Concession to Central Government servants were amended, as follows:

Entitlement to travel by Air/Train

The income limit for entitlement of Leave Travel Concession in respect of dependent family members has been increased from the existing Rs.500/- p.m. to Rs.1500/- p.m. Facility of Leave Travel Concession has been restricted to two surviving children only. This would, however, not apply to existing children of a government servant and a child born within one year reckoned from 20.10.97, and also in case of multiple births after one child.

	Pay range	*Entitlement*
(a)	Rs.18,400 and above	Air Economy (Y) Class by National Carriers or AC First Class by train, at their option.
(b)	Rs.16,400 and above but less than Rs.18,400	A.C. First Class.
(c)	Rs.8,000 and above but less than Rs.16,400	II AC II-Tier Sleeper
(d)	Rs.4,100 and above but less than Rs.8,000.	First Class/AC III-Tier Sleeper/AC Chair Car
(e)	Below Rs.4,100	Second Sleeper.

Revision of central secretariat allowance

The orders for revision of rate of Central Secretariat (Deputation on Tenure) Allowance based on revised pay scales to officers of Organised Group A services on their appointment as Under Secretary; Deputy Secretary and Director in the Central Secretariat under the Central Staffing Scheme were issued on 11.3.98.

Grant of headquarters allowance.

The orders revising the rates of Headquarters allowance to Group A service officers posted in Headquarters Organisations-were issued on 16.7.98.

Grant of duty allowance

The orders for revision of rates of deputation (duty) allowance on appointment on deputation to ex-cadre posts/foreign service were issued on 11.3.98.

Grant of special pay to cashiers

The orders revising the amount of special pay to Cashier were issued on 5.5.98.

Orders relating to quantum of special day

The orders relating to quantum of special pay (Special Allowance) in the revised scale of pay were issued on 22.4.98.

Grant of special pay to Group 'D' personnel assisting cashiers.

The orders revising the rate of special pay (Special Allowance) to Group 'D' personnel assisting cashiers were issued on 30.11.98.

Revision of rates of children educational assistance

The orders revising the rates of Children Educational Assistance (i.e. reimbursement of Tuition Fee and payment of Children Educational Allowance and Hostel Subsidy) were issued on 12.6.1998.

Fixation of pay of rates of duty allowance

The orders relating to revision of rates of deputation (duty) allowance to the personal staff of Ministers based on revised pay scales were issued on 11.3.98.

Recruitment Agencies

The Union Public Service Commission (UPSC) and the Staff Selection Commission (SSC) are the two designated recruitment agencies of the Central Government. The UPSC makes recruitment for Group 'A' and Group 'B' services/posts and the SSC makes recruitment for Group 'B' non-gazetted posts of Assistant and Stenographer Grade 'C' and other nontechnical Group 'C' posts. While the UPSC is a constitutional body set up under Article 315 of the Constitution, the SSC has been set up by a Resolution of the Government and has the status of an attached office of the Department of Personnel and Training.

Union Public Service Commission

The Union Public Service Commission comprises-a chairman and ten Members. As on 31st December, 1998, the Chairman and nine Members were in position and one post of Member was lying vacant w.e.f. 12,12,98.

Function and working of the commission

The functions of the Commission ate as specified in Article 320 of the Constitution. So far as the Working of the Commission is concerned, Article 323 of the Constitution provides for submission of annual report on its working by the commission and its laying before the Parliament.

Staff Selection Commission

The Staff Selection Commission (SSC) consists of a Chairman and two Members. As on 15th January, 1999, one post of member was lying vacant.

Regional/sub-regional offices

The Commission has its headquarters in New Delhi and seven Regional and two Sub-Regional offices located in different parts of the country. One more Sub-Regional office is proposed to be set up in, Patna shortly.

Recruitment

The Commission conducted three All India Level Open Competitive and three Limited Departmental Examinations during the period ist. April, 1998 to December, 1998. The Commission declared final results of five All India Open Examinations and three Departmental Examinations during the period from April, 98 to December, 98. Total number of 882 and 150 candidates were recommended in the Open and Departmental Examinations respectively.

Quarterly journal

The commission's quarterly journal Lodestar (English)/ Druvathara (Hindi) containing articles on different components of examinations conducted by the commission and also special features, current affairs and articles of topical interest, etc., was regularly published. The journal also published important information/instructions to candidates as well as results declared of different examinations and Selection Posts. The clientele of the journal included the prospective candidates throughout the country for various recruitment examinations held by the Commission.

Recruitment of SCs/STs

The Commission forwards every year schedule of examinations to the Directorate General of Employment and Training for imparting pre-recruitment training to Scheduled Castes and Scheduled Tribes candidates. The Commission forwards the list of candidates who qualify in the written test to the Coaching-cum Guidance Centres for SCs/STs on demand.

Optical mark reading system

Staff Selection Commission has introduced the Optical Mark Reading System (OMR) for evaluation of Answer Scripts of objective Type Question papers for most of its Recruitments.

During the year 1998-1999, the Recruitments of Sub-Inspectors in C.P.Os 1998, Sub-Inspectors in Delhi Police 1998, Clerks 1997, Junior Hindi Translator, 1997 and Inspector of Central Excise, Income Tax etc. 1996 (re-exam) have been/are to be evaluated on Optical Mark Reading system.

The processing speed of results has become much quicker in view of the fact that the salient details of information entered by the candidate in respect of his/her name, roll no., test booklet code, sex, category of caste etc. are also captured during the process of OMR evaluation/scoring.

The Commission has started processing the written result by working upon the database on electronic media containing score files and other relevant details. This has resulted in reduction of the time lag during the entire process.

Question bank project

The Commission organised four Question Bank Projects during the year 1997-98 two each, at Bangalore and Chennai respectively, It is proposed to hold series of five Question Bank/Projects/Workshop, one on each test component in General Intelligence and Reasoning, General Awareness Numerical/Arthmetical Abilities English Language and Comprehension and Hindi Language during the year 1999.

A large number of academicians, scholars, professors, readers experts on objective Testing Techniques will be invited from various universities and institutions to participate in these Projects. Eminent educationists and specialists in the respective fields will be nominated as Resource Faculty Members for these Projects.

Information facilitation counter

A fully computerised information facilitation counter is being set up at SSC (HQ) with technical support from NIC and it is expected to be made operational shortly.

The Staff Selection Commission have decided to hold Combined Preliminary. Examination of Graduate level, posts with a revised scheme of Preliminary Examination followed by main examination.

12

STAFF WELFARE

The Department is also the nodal agency for four registered societies get up for the welfare of the Government employees and their families. A brief account of the various welfare measures undertaken by this Department and the societies is as given in the subsequent paras.

Staff welfare measures

In order to foster spirit of mutual help and goodwill among Residents of Government colonies and to promote amongst them social, cultural and recreational activities, Residents Welfare Associations have been recognised in Delhi/New Delhi and in other parts of the country. At present, there are 168 such Associations.

The members of the Managing Committee of these Associations are elected by holding of elections every two years under the provisions of the Model constitution framed by the Department of Personnel and Training. This Department sanction's grants-in-aid to these Associations, subject to maximum of Rs.3000/- per annum. Area Welfare Officers (AWOs) are appointed in residential colonies having a large number of Central

Government employees. The AWOs serve as a link between the Government and residents in matters relating to the welfare of Government employees living in various colonies. They also work as field officers coordinating and maintaining liaison with the various agencies of Government such as CPWD, CGHS, Police etc., in matters relating to provision of various civic amenities to the residents.

The Central Government Employees Welfare Coordination Committees have been formed out side Delhi, at places where there are at least five Central Government offices and the total number of Central Government employees is not less than 1000. These Committees are responsible for coordinating the welfare activities of the Central Government employees serving within their jurisdiction. At present, there are 59 Coordination Committees located in different parts of the Country. Senior most officer in the station is the Chairman of the Committee.

These Committees receive grants-in-aid from this Department. To provide financial assistance to the Central Government employees in the event of their prolonged illness, death etc, Benevolent Funds have been in operation in the Central Government Departments. The employees who are members of this fund, have to contribute Rs.20/- each per annum.

The Government's contribution to this Fund is at the rate of Rs. 1/- per head per annum on the sanctioned staff strength of the concerned Ministry/Department. As a measure of Staff Welfare, Departmental Canteens/Tiffin Rooms have been set up in Central Government offices/establishments to make available beverages, snacks and meals prepared in hygienic conditions, to the employees during the working hours at reasonable rates. At present, 1332 recognised Canteens/Tiffin Rooms are functioning in various offices of the Central Government.

These Canteens are run in accordance with administrative instructions and guidelines issuer' by the Department of Personnel and Training, from time to time. Some of the important measures taken during the year are as given below:

(a) The ban on recruitment of staff in the Departmental Canteen imposed in January, 1992 has been lifted to facilitate the filling up the vacancies so that the Canteens are able to render proper service.

(b) With a view to bringing about uniformity in the accounting procedures followed by Canteens, the possibility of issuing detailed instructions in the matter is under consideration. It is expected that the standardisation of such procedure will significantly improve both the methodology and performance of Canteens.

(c) The Canteen employees, who are being treated as Government employees w.e.f. 1.10.91, have come to enjoy all the benefits that are -available to other sections of Government Staff at comparable levels. Accordingly, the revised scales of pay recommended by the Vth Pay Commission and other benefits have been extended to the Canteen employees.

(d) As a measure of welfare for the Canteen Staff of the non-statutory Canteens in Central Government offices, a Scholarship Scheme in favour of children of Canteen Staff showing merit in their academic studies has been introduced. The expenditure on the Scholarship Scheme will be met from the money available in the discretionary fund with Director, which was created out of small subscription recovered from the Canteens before 1991 i.e. before the Canteen employees were declared as Government servants.

Functioning of the societies

The Central Civil Services Cultural and Sports Board, a Society registered under the Societies Registration Act, 1860, is the Central Agency for promotion of sports and cultural activities amongst civil servants in the country. The Board was set up in 1964 as Central Secretariat Club in the Ministry of Home Affairs. Initially the objective of the Board was to promote cultural and sports activities amongst the Central Government employees located in Delhi only. In course of time, the activities of the Board increased manifold. It now caters to the needs of the Central Government employees located even outside Delhi.

Regional Sports Boards for Culture and Sports have therefore, been set up, where the number of Central Government employees is more than one thousand. At present, there are 18 such Regional Boards. The senior most Central Government officer in station is the Chairman of Regional Board. These Regional Boards are responsible for promotion of cultural and sports activities amongst the Central Government employees in their respective areas.

Inter-ministry tournaments

The Board has already conducted 10 Inter-Ministry tournaments in sports disciplines and 9 more tournaments and 2 cultural disciplines are expected to be completed during the year.

All India civil services tournaments

The All India civil Services (AICS) Tournaments in sports and cultural events are jointly organised by the Board and State/Union Territory Governments. The allocation of responsibility for holding these tournaments is coordinated by the Board after ascertaining the convenience and choice of the States/UT Governments. A part of the expenditure for conducting the AICS

Tournaments is met by the Board in the form of financial assistance to the State/UT Governments who come forward to host these tournaments. The tournaments are open to civilian Central/State Government employees. The uniformed personnel from the police, and other paramilitary organisations are not eligible for participation in these tournaments. The Board has conducted All India Civil Services Tournaments in 12 sports disciplines so far in collaboration with State Governments.

Board's affiliation to national federations

The Board is affiliated to a number of sports Associations/Federations at the National level. The Board's teams participate in the National Tournaments organised by these Associations/Federations. Three Central Secretariat employees participated in the International events. Shri Sukhminder Singh was selected to represent India in the Master World Powerlifting Championship held in Argentina. Shri Jai Kanwar and Shri Dinesh Singh Rawat were selected to represent India in the XIIIth Asian Games held at Bangkok. Shri Dinesh Kumar Singh Rawat was the member of the team that won Silver Medal in 4 × 400 meters relay race in the 13th Asian Games.

Trekking programmes

The Board sponsors trekking programmes for Central Government employees in collaboration with the Youth Hostel Association of India. The Board also encourages Central Government employees to undertake trekking programmes on their own.

Playing facilities

The Board provides playing facilities in Delhi for the Central Government employees and has a sports complex at Vinay Marg, Delhi which has facilities for Football,

Hockey, Cricket, Athletics, Volleyball and Tennis. The Board also maintains Tennis Courts at Bharti Nagar, R.K. Puram and Brassey Avenue and Floodlit Tennis Courts at Vinay Marg. There are cricket practice pitches at Brassey Avenue and two volleyball Courts at the North Block ground. Facilities are also available for Carrom and Table Tennis at Nirman Bhavan. These facilities are extensively used by the Central Government employees and their dependents.

Grih Kalyan Kendra (GKK)

The Grih Kalyan Kendra, a Society registered under the Societies Registration Act, 1860, was set up with the following objectives:—

(i) To promote social, cultural and educational activities for the benefit of the Central Government employees and their dependents.

(ii) To impart technical and vocational training in home crafts and other household arts for fruitful utilisation of leisure time of these people.

(iii) To organise and promote economic activities that may provide opportunities for gainful employment to the members of the families of the employees for supplementing the family income.

During the year, GKK has been:—

(a) Running training classes in cutting, tailoring and embroidery for the housewives and other members of the families; at welfare centre in residential colonies of Central Government employees. At present, there are 25 such centres.

(b) Providing nursery education for children in the age groups of 3 to 5 year.. At present, 22 nursery Schools are being run in Govt. colonies.

(c) Running Creches or Day Care Centres for children between the age group of 90 days and 7 years for a male child, and 10 years for a girl child. At present, GKK is running 22 Creches.

(d) Stitching liveries for Group 'C' Group I'D' employees of Government Departments and Public Sector Undertakings with a view to provide gainful employment to women;

(e) Helping the needy dependents of the deceased, retired or serving Government employees to enable them to earn through part-time work for supplementing their family income. This provides them an opportunity for acquiring new skills and experience in order to improve their career prospects elsewhere.

Craft classes

The Craft Centres situated in the residential colonies of Central Government Employees provide training in tailoring, cutting knitting, embroidery etc., to the dependents of Central Government employees and others irrespective of their educational qualifications and age.

The period of training for courses in tailoring and embroidery is one year while for machine embroidery, it is six months only. Successful candidates are awarded certificates after the completion of training.

Nursery centres

The Nursery schools run by the Grih Kalyan Kendra are intended for pre-schooling of children of Central Government Employees and others.

Creches

Creches render valuable service to the working parents and their children. There are a total of 22 creches run by the Grih Kalyan Kendra, out of which 21 are located in Delhi and one at Jaipur.

Samaj Sadans

Grih Kalyan Kendra runs 37 Samaj Sadans, out of which 23 are in Delhi and 14 outside Delhi. In these Sadans facilities like Indoor Games, Sports, Health Club, Multi-Gyms, Karate, Yoga, Dance and painting Classes are also provided. These Samaj Sadans are also made available on hire for organising various social functions, both to Central Government Employees and wherever available to others. Hiring out of these Sadans is the main revenue-earning source of the GKK.

Production centres

Grih Kalyan Kendra has its main Production Centre located at Chennai and a small one at Delhi. These Production Centres undertake stitiching work at liveries.

Civil Services Officers Institute

With a view to providing facilities to senior and middle level Government servants and their families in Delhi for social interaction as well as recreation and sports, a Civil Services- Officers Institutes (CSOI) has been set up as a registered society under the Societies Registration Act, 1860. The Institute started functioning from the February 28, 1998. It is presently operating from the Grih Kalyan Kendra's premises situated in MS Apartment, Kasturba Gandhi Marg, New Delhi.

The Government has paid grants-in-aid amounting to Rs.11,42,800 for renovation of the Institute premises through GKK during 1998-99. The Institute has also received a sum of Rs.25 lakhs as grants-in-aid from the Delhi Government during 1998-99.

Kendriya Bhandar

Kendriya Bhandar (Central Government Employees Consumer Cooperative Society), a registered Cooperative Society, was established in 1963 as a welfare project for the benefit of Central Government Employees and the public at large with the main objectives to provide essential commodities of daily needs at reasonable prices. The Society operates a network of 110 stores out of which 100 are Self Service Stores and 42 Fair Price Shops located in Delhi, Mumbai, Chennai, Hyderabad, Bangalore, Trichi, Cochin, Tirupati, Daman, Gwalior, Lucknow, Faridabad, Ghaziabad, Kapurthala and Chandigarh, including a fleet of 4 Mobile Shops in Delhi, which provide service to the customers in such colonies where stores of Kendriya Bhandar do not exist. Stationery is sold to the Central Government offices at P-Block, Raisina Road. The society achieved a record sales turnover of Rs.205.89 crores (including agency sales) in 1997-98 as compared to Rs.186.60 crores in 1996-97 and will exceeded the target of Rs.200 crores. Its target for 1998-99 is tentatively placed at Rs.220. crores. Kendriya Bhandar has been registering profits (net) continuously since 1982-83.

The net profit earned during 1997-98 was Rs.4.07 crores as compared to Rs.3.05 crores during the year 1996-97. The gross profits increased from Rs.7.15 Crores to Rs.9.26 Crores over this period. The Society paid a significant role in ensuring availability of Onions and Palmoleen and its contribution in this regard was highly appreciated. During the year 1998, the Society paid dividend @ 10% to the shareholders and bonus to the employees at the maximum permissible rate of 20%. Its contribution to exchequer during the year 1997-98 by way of income tax, sales tax and dividend on the Government equity was more than Rs.5.00 crores. Kendriya Bhandar ranks as the Top consumer Cooperative Society of the Nation with the sales turn over of Rs.205.89 crores during the Cooperative year 1997-99 being the highest amongst all Consumer Cooperative Societies/Stores.

Kendriya Bhandar also occupies first rank amongst

all Consumer Stores in the Country in regard to the net profit, dividend declared and income Tax paid during 1997-98.

Redeployment of surplus staff

A scheme for redeployment of surplus staff has been in operation since 1966. The work relating to redeployment and readjustment of surplus employees belonging to Group 'A', 'B' and 'C' are handled by the Central Cell located in the Department of Personnel and Training, while the work relating to redeployment and readjustment of Group 'D' surplus staff is handled by the Directorate General of Employment and Training, Ministry of Labour.

From 1.1.1998 to 30-11-1998, 52 new cases of surplus employees belonging to Groups 'A' 'B' and 'C' were reported to the Surplus Cell in the Department of Personnel and Training for redeployment. Besides, 43 employees declared surplus earlier, were awaiting redeployment at the beginning of January, 1998, thus making a total of 95. Of these, 32 were redeployed till 30-11-1998. The Department is in the process of redeployment of the remaining 63 surplus employees. The overall position of deployment of the surplus staff, since the inception of the scheme is as given in the next page.

Categry of sur-plus staff in the annuation	*No of persons accepted*	*No of persons redeplo-yed*	*No. of persons resigned on super ment*	*No.of persons retired*	*No. of person awaiting redeploy*
Group 'A'	85	59	4	14	8
Group 'B'	372	340	3	20	09
Group 'C'	8499	8188	65	200	46
Total	8956	8587	72	234	63

Redeployment of surplus staff

A scheme for redeployment of surplus staff has been in operation since 1966. The work relating to redeployment and readjustment of surplus employees belonging to Group 'A', 'B' and 'C' are handled by the Central Cell located in the Department of Personnel and Training, while the work relating to redeployment and readjustment of Group 'D' surplus staff is handled by the Directorate General of Employment and Training, Ministry of Labour. From 1.1.1998 to 30-11-1998, 52 new cases of surplus employees belonging to Groups 'A' 'B' and 'C' were reported to the Surplus Cell in the Department of Personnel and Training for redeployment.

Besides, 43 employees declared surplus earlier, were awaiting redeployment at the beginning of January, 1998, thus making a total of 95. Of these, 32 were redeployed till 30-11-1998.

Pension and Pensioners' Welfare

Department of Pension and Pensioners, Welfare is the nodal agency of the Government of India for formulation of policy on pension and other retirement benefits, as also for redressal of grievances on retirement benefits. The Department was set up in 1985 as a part of the Ministry of Personnel, Public Grievances and Pensions and has been rendering service for the benefit of pensioners. Since then, a number of steps have been taken for streamlining the pension administration system, for greater convenience and welfare of the pensioners. Some of the more important decisions taken during the year are explained in subsequent paras.

Dearness relief to pensioners/family pensioners

Two instalments of Dearness Relief (DR) were sanctioned to pensioners/family pensioners payable from 01.01.1998 and 01.07.1998. The rates of DR were also published in the leading newspapers. Banks were authorised to credit the amount of DR to pensioner' account on the basis of press advertisement.

Consolidation of family pension

Family pension in respect of those retired/died between 01.01.86 to 31.12.95 has been consolidated at the uniform rate of 30% of the pay notionally fixed in the pay scale recommended by Fourth Central Pay Commission. Detailed orders in this regard were issued on 08.05.1998.

Enhancement of rate of pension and family pension

It has been decided to step up the pension/family pension of all pre 1996 pensioners/family pensioners with effect from ist January, 1996 as given below:-

Pension: 50% of the minimum of revised scale of pay as on 1.1.96 of the post last held by the pensioners subject to the existing provision in the rules relating to qualifying service.

Family pension: 30% of the minimum of the revised scale of pay as on 1.1.96 of the post last held by the deceased employee.

General provident fund (CS) rules

The limit of maximum amount payable under the Deposit-Linked Insurance Scheme has been enhanced to Rs.60,000/- from the existing Rs.30,000/ special benefit in case of death and disability while in service. Orders have been issued for grant of ex-gratia lump-sum compensation to the families of Civilian Government employees who die in the performance of their bonafide official duties under various circumstances as under:

		Rupees in lakhs
(a)	Death occurring due to accidents in the course of performance of duties.	5.00
(b)	Death occurring in the course	5.00

	of performance of duties attributable to acts of violence by terrorists antisocial elements etc.	
(c)	Death occurring during (i) enemy action in International war or Border Skirmishes and (ii) action against militants, terrorists, extremists, etc.	7.50

Scheme for payment of pension to Kashmir migrants

As a measure of providing relief to the Central Government pensioners' who have moved out of Kashmir Valley on account of disturbances there, a temporary scheme for disbursement of pension is being implemented.

Meeting of the Standing Committee on Voluntary Agencies (SCOVA)

The 15th meeting of the SCOVA was held on 21.11.1998 under the Chairmanship of Secretary (P). Matters relating to implementation of recommendations of Vth Central Pay Commission were discussed in the meeting.

13

AREA DEVELOPMENT PROGRAMMES

Introduction

Drought Prone Areas Programme (DPAP) is one of the area development programmes launched by the Government in 1973-74 to tackle the special problems faced by those fragile areas which are constantly affected by severe drought conditions. These areas are characterized by large human and cattle populations which are continuously putting heavy pressure on the already fragile natural resource base for food, fodder and fuel. This continuous biotic pressure is leading to fast and continuous depletion of vegetative cover, less and less rainfall, increasing soil erosion and fast receding ground water levels due to continuous exploitation without any effort to recharge the under ground acquifers.

Though the Programme created some positive impact in terms of creating durable 'public assets in the programme areas, the overall impact of the programme in effectively containing the adverse effects of drought was found to be not very encouraging. In addition, many of the programme States had also been demanding inclusion of additional areas under the programme. Keeping this in view a High Level Technical Committee under the Chairmanship of Prof. C.H. Hanumantha Rao, Ex-Member, Planning Commission critically reviewed the contents, methodology and implementation processes of all area development programmes and suggested suitable measures for improvement. Based on the recommendations of the Hanumantha Rao Committee, comprehensive Guidelines for Watershed Development commonly applicable to the DPAP, DDP IWDP, EAS (50% allocation in DPAP and DDP areas) were issued in October, 1994 which came into effect from 1995-96.

Objectives

The basic objective of the programme is to minimise the adverse effects of drought on production of crops and livestock and productivity of land, water and human resources ultimately leading to the drought proofing of the affected areas. The programme also aims to promote overall economic development and improving the socioeconomic conditions of the resource poor and disadvantaged sections inhabiting the programme areas.

Strategy

The common Guidelines for Watershed Development provide for a uniform strategy in the implementation of all area development programmes viz. DPAP, DDP, IWDP and EAS. The main features of this strategy are:

- Area development programmes to be implemented exclusively on watershed basis.
- Programme activities to be confined to the identified watershed of about 500 hectares and are to be executed on a project basis spanning over a period of four years.
- Watershed project to cover a village, as far as possible.

- Elaborate institutional mechanisms at various levels clearly defined for effective participation of the local people and the Panchayati Raj institutions in all stages of project management.
- DRDA/ZP to be the nodal Government agency at the district level to act as a facilitator and provider of finances and technical assistance to the people's organizations executing the watershed projects.

Coverage

At present, DPAP is in operation in 947 blocks of 155 districts in 13 States. The corresponding physical area for treatment under the programme works out to approximately 7.45 lakh square kilometers. The States where DPAP is under implementation along with number of districts and blocks may be seen in the Table.

S.No.	Name of State	Districts	Blocks
1.	Andhra Pradesh	11	94
2.	Bihar	16	121
3.	Gujarat	10	52
4.	Himachal Pradesh	3	9
5.	Jammu & Kashmir	2	22
6.	Karnataka	11	81
7.	Madhya Pradesh	25	134
8.	Maharashtra	22	148
9.	Orissa	8	47
	10. Rajasthan	10	32
11.	Tamil Nadu	15	80
12.	Uttar Pradesh	18	91
13.	West Bengal	4	36
	Total	155	947

Funding pattern

The programme allocation is shared on 50:50 basis between the Centre and the State Governments. The cost norms adopted under DPAP for various ecosystems depending on the severity of the problem are as below :

S. No.	*Ecosystem type*	*Per Ha. cost Average (Rs.)*	*Watershed project cost (Rs. In lakhs)*
1.	Semi-Arid Region	4,000	20.00
2.	Dry-Sub-Humid Region	3,000	15.00
3.	Dry Sub-Humid (Hill) Region	4,000	20.00

Physical and financial performance

Under DPAP, 6454 Watershed Projects have been sanctioned in four different batches - two batches in 1995-96 and one batch in 1996-97 and 1997-98. Against this, 5956 Watershed Projects have so far been taken-up by the programme States and were under various stages of implementation during 1998-99. Table - 4.2 shows the number of Watershed Projects sanctioned and taken up during the last four years since the introduction of the new Guidelines.

In addition, financial assistance of Rs.10 crores was provided to CAPART during 1997-98 for execution of 400 watershed projects through the voluntary sector. Against this provision, CAPART had so far sanctioned 41 watershed projects at a total cost of Rs. 183.50 lakhs and released Rs. 69.59 lakhs to the implementing agencies.

There are two districts, Doda and Udhampur, in Jammu and Kashmir where DPAP is being implemented. But the State does not figure in the above table as the Government of Jammu and Kashmir continues to follow the old Guidelines in the implementation of DPAP during 1998-99 also due to the disturbed conditions prevailing in these districts. The State is expected to operationalise the new watershed guidelines from the next financial year.

The Statement at Annexure-XVIII provides State-wise physical and financial performance under DPAP during 1998-99.

Desert development programme

Introduction

Over the years, the increase in human and livestock population in desert areas has placed the natural resources of the region under great stress. The major problems are continuous depletion of vegetative cover, increase in soil erosion and fall in ground water table. All these factors account for diminishing productivity of land and loss of natural resources.

The problems would have been worse but for the introduction of some specific highly focused area development programmes in these areas. On the recommendations of the National Commission on Agriculture in it's Interim Report (1974) and Final Report (1976), the Desert Development Programme (DDP) was started in the year 1977-78. The programme was started both in the hot desert areas of Rajasthan, Gujarat and Haryana, and the cold desert areas of Jammu & Kashmir and Himachal Pradesh.

The objective of the programme has been to mitigate adverse effects of desertification and adverse climatic conditions on crops, human and livestock population, combating desertification and restoring ecological balance of the area. In hot sandy desert areas, sand dune stabilization and shelter belt plantations were given greater weightage.

On the other hand, in cold desert areas, since rainfall is negligible, crop cultivation and afforestation could be taken up only through assured irrigation. In these areas, the main activity was water resources development by construction of channels for diversion of water flow from the glacier and springs to the fields and lift irrigation works in the valleys.

Though the Programme created good impact in the

areas treated, overall impact in the identified areas in the country was not very encouraging. Some State Governments had also been requesting this Ministry for inclusion of additional areas under the programme. With a view to identifying the infirmities in the programme and also to consider the cases for inclusion of additional areas, a Technical Committee on the DPAP and the DDP was constituted in 1993-94 under the Chairmanship of Prof. C.H. Hanumantha Rao, Ex-Member, Planning Commission. The Committee submitted its Report in April, 1994.

The main reasons identified by the Committee for the far from satisfactory results under the programme was that area development was not taken up on watershed basis and the involvement of the local people both in planning and execution of the programme was virtually nonexistent. Besides inadequacy of funds, non-availability of trained personnel and taking up of too many activities, which were neither properly integrated nor necessarily related to the objectives of the programme, were also identified as contributory factors towards reducing the impact of the programme.

Based on the recommendations of the Committee, new districts/blocks were included under DDP and a fresh set of Guidelines for Watershed Development applicable to DPAP, DDP, IWDP and EAS (50%) were issued in October, 1994. These Guidelines were made applicable from the year 1995-96.

Objectives

In a broad sense, the objectives of the programme are to promote the economic development of village community, restore ecological balance and improve the economic conditions of resource poor and disadvantaged section of society through creation, widening and equitable distribution of resources and increased employment opportunities. DDP has been envisaged as an essentially land-based activity and conceived as a long-term measure for restoration of ecological balance by conserving, developing and harnessing land, water, livestock and human resources. Objectives of the programme have been recast as under :-

- Combating drought and desertification.
- Encouraging restoration of ecological balance.
- Mitigating the adverse effects of drought and adverse edapho-climatic conditions on crops and livestock, and productivity of land, water and human resources.
- Promoting economic development of village community.
- Improving socioeconomic conditions of the resource poor and disadvantaged sections of village community viz. assetless and women.

Strategy

Although the DDP has been under implementation in several areas, its impact had been felt only in the areas actually treated by core activities. Growing population and poverty compounded the problem by increasing pressure on fragile ecosystems. On the basis of lessons learnt, the major elements of new strategy are :-

- Area development under the programme will be on watershed basis only and a watershed project of about 500 hectares would be the field unit for implementation and it will be developed in four years.
- The strategy adopted to achieve these objectives involved development of the programme area on watershed basis. However, in some sandy areas where it is not physically feasible to demarcate a watershed, programme is to be implemented by

adopting either a cluster of village or an Index Catchment as the unit of planning.

- There would be direct participation of the local people in planning and development of watersheds and maintenance of assets after the project is completed through Watershed Association (WA) comprising of all adults residing within watershed project area and its executive body named as Watershed Committee (WC).
- The Zilla Parishads, Panchayat Samitis and Gram Panchayats have the right to monitor and review the programme at district, blocks and village levels. The Panchayati Raj Institutions can also function as Project Implementation Agencies (PIA) if they so desire.
- Similarly, in the new system of programme implementation a voluntary agency can be selected as a Project Implementation Agency by the DRDA/ Zilla Parishad. The voluntary agencies have an effective role particularly in motivating people, community organizations and training.
- Keeping in view the problem of sand dune stabilization in 10 districts of Rajasthan, 50% of funds under DDP for implementation of watershed projects allocated to each concerned district, has been permitted for three activities namely; sand dune stabilization, shelter belt creation and afforestation.

Coverage

Under DDP 227 blocks of 36 districts having an area of 457,432 sq.kms. in 7 States are covered. The States where DDP is under implementation are Andhra Pradesh, Gujarat, Haryana, Himachal Pradesh, Jammu and Kashmir, Karnataka and Rajasthan.

Number of districts and blocks covered under DDP

S.N.	*Name of the State*	*District*	*Blocks*
1.	Andhra Pradesh	1	16
2.	Gujarat	6	47
3.	Haryana	6	44
4.	Himachal Pradesh	2	3
5.	Jammu & Kashmir	2	10,
6.	Karnataka	3	22
7.	Rajasthan	16	85
	Total	36	227

Guidelines for watershed development

Main features of new Guidelines for Watershed Development are :-

- At the district level the District Rural Development Agency/Zilla Parishad will be in overall charge of implementation of the programme. The DRDA/ZP will be advised in regard to selection of Project Implementation Agencies (PIAs), approval of Watershed Plans, training, publicity etc., by a district level Watershed Development Advisory Committee under the chairmanship of Project Director, DRDA/CEO, ZP.
- The DRDA/ZP will select the PIAs which could be besides DRDA/ZP itself, other line departments, autonomous organizations, public sector undertakings, voluntary organizations, cooperatives, banks, etc. The PIA will remain in-charge of implementation of the Watershed Projects (WPs). A multi-disciplinary team designated as Watershed Development Team (WDT) shall assist each PIA in the implementation of these WPs.
- Planning and implementation of the Watershed Project will be done with the technical support of multi-disciplinary Watershed Development Team by

the WA comprising all adult members of the village(s) in the watershed area. 75% of the project fund will be spent directly by the Watershed Association on the development works of each project.

- The Watershed Committee comprising of 10- 2 nominated members by the Watershed Association from amongst the user groups, self-help groups, with representation from Gram Panchayat, Watershed Development Team, women, Scheduled Castes, and Scheduled Tribes will be the executive body of the Watershed Association.
- As per Guidelines for Watershed Development issued by this Ministry, 10% of the total project cost is earmarked for administrative expenditure, 5% for community organization works, another 5% for training to people associated with the implementation of Watershed Projects and 80% for works.
- As regards the Panchayati Raj Institutions (PRIs), the Zilla Parishad at the district level may remain overall in-charge of implementation. The Panchayat Samiti and Gram Panchayat will have the right to monitor and review the implementation of programme and can take the responsibility of implementing the projects as PlAs.

The Guidelines also provide for an elaborate institutional arrangement at the, Centre for monitoring, review and policy making, at the State level for monitoring and review of programmes and at the district level for selecting Watershed Projects and Project Implementation Agencies, monitoring and review of the implementation of the programme. Problem of inadequacy of funds has been tackled by allowing utilization of 50% of the Employment Assurance Scheme (EAS) funds for the development of watersheds. Training has been made a continuous process and 5% of the funds of each project has been earmarked for training of the WDT members, field functionaries and the local people. There is an inbuilt provision in the guidelines for maintenance of assets created under the watershed development projects.

People's participation

The guidelines for Watershed Development issued by this Ministry is an instrument, which provides an opportunity to local people to not only involve themselves in the implementation of the programme but is a tool for capacity building and empowerment of participating village community. The critical key factor in the implementation is people's participation in all aspects of the programme. It has been envisaged under the Guidelines that the local people through User Groups and Self-help Groups formed by the Watershed Association shall execute the whole work of Watershed Development Projects.

Under the new Guidelines, area development on watershed basis has been made mandatory. To ensure people's participation, an elaborate institutional mechanism at various levels has been prescribed which include the formation of Watershed Association and a Watershed Committee for each watershed project. Watershed Association comprises of all adults residing within a watershed project area. Watershed Committee is the executive body of the Watershed Association constituted by it by nominating 10- 12 members from amongst the Self-help Groups (3-4), User Groups (45), Gram Panchayat (2-3) and a member of the Watershed Development Team (WDT). This Committee has been made responsible for planning and development of Watershed Projects with the technical assistance from the Project Implementation Agency. PIA provides technical input through a Watershed Development Team having four experts in the disciplines of Animal Sciences, Plant Sciences, Civil/ Agricultural Engineering and Social Sciences.

Role of Panchayati Raj institutions

Panchayati Raj Institution have been assigned very active role at the district, block and village levels in the programme. The State Governments have been authorized to empower the Zilla Parishads to discharge all functions of the District Rural Development Agencies (DRDAs) for planning and development of the watershed projects. In that capacity, the Zilla Parishad will select the Watershed Projects and the Project Implementation Agencies, approve Watershed Plans, release funds to the PlAs and the Watershed Committees and monitor and review the implementation of the programme.

The Panchayat Samitis have been given the right to monitor the implementation of the programme at the block level and give guidance for integration of other area development programmes. At the village level, the Gram Panchayat is to be fully involved in mobilizing the community, training, dovetailing of other programmes and maintenance of common property resources such as pasture lands, fisheries tanks, plantation etc. The Gram Panchayat has been entrusted with the task of monitoring the implementation of the programme. In addition to the above mentioned functions, the Panchayati Raj Institutions are also entitled to take on the responsibility of planning and development of a cluster of watershed projects. In the capacity of a Project Implementation Agency, the Zilla Parishad/ Panchayat Samiti/Gram Panchayat concerned shall be subjected to the complete discipline and control of DRDA as any other PIA. They will have to constitute Watershed Development Team on the same lines as any other PIA and shall accordingly be entitled to demand and receive the prescribed administrative cost for each project.

Finding pattern

The DDP is a Centrally Sponsored Programme and funds are released to DRDAs/ZPs for implementation of the programme. The Central share under each type of project area based on the ecosystem type is as under :-

S.No.	*Type of ecosystem*	*Central share*
1.	Hot arid (non-aandy) areas	75%
2.	Hot arid (sandy) areas	100%
3.	Cold arid areas	100%

The State-wise number of Watershed Projects to be taken up has been arrived at on the basis of the following criteria fixed at block level.

Area of block (Sq.kms.)	*No. of WPs to be taken up*	*Block allocation (Rs. in lakhs)*
Upto 400	3	16.86
401-800	5	28.10
Above 800	6	22.72

In different ecosystems, project cost has been fixed according to the severity of the problems. At present the following rates are applicable in different areas:-

S. No.	*Ecosystem Type*	*Per ha. cost (Rs.) Average*	*Watershed project cost (Rs. in lakhs)*
1.	Hot sandy aricl region	5,000	25.00
2.	Hot arid region	4,500	22.50
3.	Cold arid region	5,000	25.00

Achievements

Under DDP, a number of projects have been targeted and sanctioned for implementation in identified areas. All these projects are envisaged to be completed in a 4-year period and are at different stages of implementation.

The year 1995 - 96 was the first year of implementation under the new Guidelines for Watershed

Development. A considerable amount of time was therefore, spent on preparatory works, making institutional arrangement viz. selection of watersheds and PIAs, imparting training, community organizations and planning before commencement of actual works. This led to slow down in expenditure. The details of budgetary provision and expenditure incurred during in the last three years are given below:

(Rs. in lakhs)

Year	*Budget*	*Release*
1994-95	8,400.00	8,459.55
1995-96	10,000.00	10,100.00
1996-97	65,00.00	6,536.38
1997-98	7,000.00	7,000.00

Since inception till 1994-95 as core sector activities, 1.85 lakh ha. under land resource development, 0.83 lakh ha. under water resource development and 2.85 lakh ha. under afforestation and pasture development have been developed. Since inception till 31 st March' 1998, a total sum of Rs.845 crores has been spent on the programme. In 1997-98, a sum of Rs.70 crores was released to different DRDAs/ZPs. During 1998-99, a provision of Rs. 90 crores has been made. In the Ninth Five Year Plan (1997-2002), a sum of Rs. 1,430 crores has been proposed.

INDEX